NF

AUTHOR
Burke, John
TITLE
Buffalo Bill

DATE DUE	BORROWER'S NAME
3/24/2010	983
0102 6 2	858
5/29/10	
DEC 0 8 2010	#1013
DEC 2 0 2010	#1013

Buffalo Bill

THE NOBLEST WHITESKIN

Books by John Burke

WINGED LEGEND

DUET IN DIAMONDS

BUFFALO BILL

Buffalo Bill

THE NOBLEST WHITESKIN

by John Burke

G. P. Putnam's Sons
New York

Contents

------◆------

8   CONTENTS

Illustrations appear after page 160

Introduction

———◆———

TODAY, when the only good Indian is not only alive but well nourished, well educated, and well motivated, William F. Cody would not be regarded as a national hero. In a time when the buffalo is cherished, protected, and carefully conserved, Buffalo Bill would be regarded as an ecological villain, a menace to wildlife, a bloodthirsty villain who helped all but wipe out the great bison herds of the West. Quite a different view once prevailed. Less than a century ago the only good Indian, according to Lieutenant General Philip H. Sheridan, one of their chief exterminators, was a dead Indian. As for the buffalo, providing a ton of meat on the hoof for the Indians, he was deliberately wiped out as a matter of high military policy, to force the warlike tribes of the Great Plains to quit their old way of life, learn how to plow a straight furrow, and stop shooting at the white men who were stealing their land. Within the memory of any middle-aged American is the old silent-screen title triumphantly following a minor exercise in genocide: AND ANOTHER REDSKIN BIT THE DUST!

Today's youth could hardly be expected to comprehend the once glittering legend of Buffalo Bill Cody. Here was a man whose fame was derived, somewhat meretriciously, from the claim that he had waded knee-deep in Indian blood; that he was the most ferocious of the Indian fighters, the buck-skinned knight of the old frontier, the preserver of white womanhood and the protector of white children. Never mind that his legend was largely and unconscionably inflated by a pioneering essay in press agentry that made piddling in comparison the process by which John D. Rockefeller, Sr., was transformed into a Baptist saint. So magnificent were the efforts of Buffalo Bill's press agents that the persona they concocted is still with us today.

The Buffalo Bill Wild West Show was revived twelve years ago and every year tours the country with successful results at the box office. A Cody grandson, who bills himself likewise as Buffalo Bill Cody, ranges the West opening supermarkets. A graduate of Harvard Law School who fought valiantly in the Battle of the Bulge during World War II, he has served as city attorney of Cody, Wyoming—his grandfather's pros-pering and enduring monument to himself—and founded the local rodeo and radio station, as well as developing var-ious projects connected with what is widely advertised as "Bill Cody Land." And every summer that Wyoming town founded by the original Buffalo Bill attracts thousands of tourists with its various monuments and memorabilia, all dedicated to the proposition that its founder was the epitome of whatever was noble and valiant about the winning of the West. The artifacts of his career are boldly valued at $10,000,000 by the Cody Chamber of Commerce. No town in America so assiduously cultivates the memory of its founding father as Cody, Wyoming.

Indubitably an afterglow of the legend lingers on, hardly dimmed by currently fashionable concerns for the Indian. Buffalo Bill, to several generations of Americans, was the no-blest whiteskin of them all.

What other man had 1,700 books—granted, they were mostly dime novels—written about him?

What other American of his time hobnobbed with so

much of European royalty, bedded so many duchesses (by whispered account), or had six former mistresses confronting his widow across his catafalque?

Who but Buffalo Bill could have made a film about the now shameful battle of Wounded Knee and persuaded 100 of the Sioux survivors, or victims, to portray themselves as bloodthirsty savages?

What other American, not excluding Presidents and military heroes, was so worshiped in his lifetime?

Who but the handsome and courtly Buffalo Bill could have made himself the living symbol of the winning of the West, what with so many rivals for the honor dead, mad, alcoholic, or retired to more peaceful pursuits?

For forty years William F. Cody was the apotheosis of all that was chivalrous about conquering the West. Three generations of Americans—and of Western Europeans, for that matter—would carry with them the indelible memory of the tall, stalwart, noble-featured Buffalo Bill riding through the swirling dust of an arena, waving his white sombrero, breaking targets with his rifle or pistol, daunting hordes of howling (though hired) redskins as his Wild West Show presented its capsule of living history. Who cared about documentation, about nit-picking accuracy of minor details, when confronted with this living legend of whom it was written in pulp-magazine prose:

"Face to face, knee to knee, and hand to hand, Raven Feather and Buffalo Bill met. [Never mind that Raven Feather existed only in the writer's imagination.] Twice the borderman parried the deadly thrusts of the wily chief— twice again the steel of the savage drank his blood, but weak from twenty wounds, the Indian's eyes were not sure, and soon the knife of the brave borderman reached his body with a fearful thrust. . . . Buffalo Bill, anxious as he was to hurry back to his loved ones, had to delay to have the blood staunched which poured from many a sad gash in his noble frame. . . ."

A continuous publicity campaign, conducted by as many

as a dozen press agents, reinforced by scores of volunteer workers in the dime novel and Western-fiction fields, kept his legend well stoked and burning bright until a few years before his death. Even newspapers ordinarily a little more careful with the facts breathlessly reported that Cody's body was scarred by 137 bullet, arrow, lance, and tomahawk wounds; hardly a Western prairie, it seemed, was not drenched with his blood. His wife, however, said he had been wounded only once, in a skirmish with the Sioux in which his scalp was creased by a bullet possibly fired by a comrade.

The Buffalo Bill myth was not only accepted but propagated by some of the most eminent of his contemporaries, possibly because the pre-World War I establishment profited so greatly from the exploitation of the West and the gallant figure of Buffalo Bill Cody served so perfectly as the metaphor for that endeavor; it was best for the public's peace of mind that it believe the Indians were all bloodthirsty savages straight out of the Stone Age and all whites were law-abiding, home-loving folk who only wanted to work their little farms and raise their families. There was vast profit in the destruction of the Indian race, in the acquisition and exploitation of tribal lands; that and other realities were best concealed by legend and myth. Thus the buildup for Cody. General Sheridan, who certainly knew better, proclaimed that Buffalo Bill had killed more Indians than any white man who ever lived. Governor Curtis Guild of Massachusetts also succumbed to hyperbole when he described Cody as a home-grown superman: "Tall beyond the lot of ordinary mortals, straight as an arrow, not an ounce of useless flesh upon his limbs, but every muscle firm and hard as the sinews of a stag . . . the frank kindly eye of a devoted friend . . . a natural courtly grace of manner which would become a Marshal of France . . . from spur to sombrero one of the finest types of manhood this continent has ever produced. . . ." And so on. Theodore Roosevelt regarded Cody as the exemplar of Anglo-Saxon manhood and also sounded the superman theme: "Buffalo Bill was one of those men, steel-thewed and iron nerved, whose daring progress opened the great West to settlement and civilization. His name, like that of Kit Carson, will always be associated with old adventure and pioneer days of hazard and hardship when the great plains and the Rocky Mountains were won for our race. . . . He embodied those traits of courage, strength and self-reliant hardihood which are vital to the well-being of our nation."

It may seem from the foregoing that this will be a demolition project, a determined effort to cut William F. Cody down to size. That would be a misapprehension. Cody himself was a lovable man, generous enough to have allowed millions to slip between his fingers, attractive in his loyalty and modesty. The legend created around the real facts of his life was not of his making, but of course he acquiesced in it. He was a showman and understood the close relationship between publicity and the number of tickets sold at the box office. "Gosh," he would sigh over the tales told by his platoon of press agents, "the things they write!" He always avoided, if possible, any close questioning on just how many hostiles he slew. When pinned down by a merciless inquisitor, he would reply with a certain archness, "If you want a definite answer, you can say simply that I never killed an Indian in my life except when my life was in danger."

As with most legends, there was a residue of fact in Buffalo Bill's. He had scouted for the cavalry, he had faced danger and risked his life, he had undertaken missions through hostile country and performed more than creditably. So had many other cavalry scouts under contract to the government. If his several years in that service were glorified beyond their due, it was not because of his vanity, it was not a symptom of egomania, it was all done in the cause of showmanship. If there is evidence of a cantankerous insistence on verifiable fact on these pages, it should not be taken as denigratory of Cody the man but Buffalo Bill the legend and, more particularly, the ways in which that legend was put to use.

Book I: Hunter

1

The Descendant of Irish Royalty

ON a late summer day in 1869 a stumpy little man with a seamed face and deeply pouched eyes, rather seedily dressed, yet carrying himself with the air of a man who had seen everything and survived much, stepped off the coach of a Union Pacific train at North Platte, Nebraska. He looked like a confidence man down in his luck. His face was the sort you saw on "wanted" posters. Yet there was nothing spurious about his air of distinction. He was one of the most remarkable men on the continent.

His real name was Edward Zane Carroll Judson, but he was renowned, though not among professors of English literature, as Ned Buntline, the author of hundreds of paperbacked novels of adventure at sea and in the Seminole, Mexican, and Civil wars. They sold for only a dime, but Mr. Buntline was able to boast of the highest literary income in the United States. Much of what he wrote was derived from a highly adventurous and picaresque career, which included naval and military episodes, many of them discreditable, and a matrimonial record which was even less conventional. He had also survived a Tennessee lynching, which left him with a permanent crick in his neck.

A Connecticut Yankee, Buntline had enlisted in the Navy and attained midshipman's rank before his undisciplined conduct forced his superiors to demand his resignation. In the mid-1840's he had served as a sort of freebooting soldier and marine in the Seminole War. Later in that decade he showed up in New York and began publication of *Ned Buntline's Own*, a blood-and-thunder periodical, meanwhile turning out paperback books on adventure themes that sold for a dime. Subsequently he became a leading organizer and conspirator in the Native American (Know-Nothing) Party. As the nativists' chief propagandist, he flooded the country with editorials, cartoons, and faked "news" stories pointing out the danger to American culture in the millions of German and Irish immigrants then pouring into the United States under the prod of a potato famine in Ireland and political turmoil in Germany. And Buntline did more than talk. He spent a year in a New York jail for his leading role in the Astor Place riot, in which he mustered a Bowery mob to protest the appearance of the great English actor William C. Macready, an affray which left twenty-three persons dead or dying in the streets. In 1852 he showed up in St. Louis to support the candidacy of Know-Nothing candidates in a city election; again there was a riot in which a number of persons were killed and much property destroyed. He was indicted for fomenting the disturbances. Several of his supporters were persuaded to put up bail, which Buntline promptly skipped. He was always a nimble fellow. When the Know-Nothing Party collapsed in 1856, he resumed his production of dime novels.

Buntline had come West on a twofold mission. His profitable avocation was delivering temperance lectures, which supplemented his literary income and offered an outlet for his exhibitionistic tendencies. The fact that Buntline often launched his jeremiads against the evils of alcohol with a quart of whiskey seething around his insides did not detract from their dramatic quality, and in those days the temperance lecture was a form of folk theater. He delivered his lectures without advance billing wherever he could hire a hall and gather an audience.

His second purpose was to scrounge for fresh material for his dime novels. The Western frontier was just then beginning to catch on as a subject for popular literature, and Buntline, if anything, was a keen opportunist. So he had come to North Platte after reading in the newspapers an account of a cavalry engagement at Summit Springs on July 11. Chief Tall Bull's band of "renegade" Sioux and Cheyenne warriors had been pursued by General Eugene A. Carr, his Fifth Cavalry, and Major Frank North's battalion of Pawnee scouts. Trailing the hostiles, they had come across the print of a woman's shoe . . . what a beginning for the story already taking shape in Ned Buntline's mind. Led by the Pawnee scout battalion, the Fifth Cavalry located Chief Tall Bull's fugitive band out on the prairie, charged in, and killed men, women, and children. After the dust and smoke had settled, the cavalrymen found two white women in the tepees. One had just been killed with a tomahawk. The other was a German immigrant woman who could speak no English. Meanwhile Major Frank North and his brother Lute had followed the Indians who escaped from the cavalry charge. Tall Bull was trailed to a gully where he had concealed himself. Major North dismounted and told his brother to ride away with both horses in hope of tricking Tall Bull into peering over the lip of the arroyo. The major knelt and raised his rifle to the firing position. Tall Bull's head appeared, North fired once, and that was the end of Chief Tall Bull.

Immediately after reading the official accounts of that engagement, Ned Buntline had proceeded to Fort Sedgwick in Colorado Territory, where he learned that Major North was up the Union Pacific line at Fort McPherson in Nebraska Territory. Buntline was determined to track him down, hear his story, and create a new Buntline hero on the grayish pulp of a Street & Smith magazine serial. Since he had just been given a new contract by Street & Smith to produce a fresh

crop of serials and dime novels, there was some urgency to
his mission.

On journeying out to Fort McPherson in a hired carriage,
Buntline looked up Major North immediately. The major, a
lean, reticent fellow with faded blue eyes, did not take to
Buntline or his proposition. He couldn't see himself as the
hero of a pulp series. Real men didn't boast about their exploits; already the stereotype of the strong, silent Westerner
had been formed, and Major Frank North was one of its
exemplars. Furthermore, this shifty-eyed Easterner was a
braggart himself, who claimed to have been the chief of
scouts of a Union cavalry regiment, whose breast shimmered
with a score of medals and decorations, none of them recog-
nizable to Major North, and who bragged all the harder as
the level sank in the whiskey bottle between them at the post
sutler's.

They strolled outside in the heat-stricken barrack square.
A number of men, seeking shelter from the blazing prairie
sun, were sleeping under the supply wagons drawn up
nearby.

"No, I'm not your man," Major North was saying. Then
he grinned and pointed to the figure of a young man covered
with straw and sleeping in spite of a swarm of flies under one
of the wagons. "If you want a man to fill that bill," North
somewhat sardonically remarked, "he's over there under the
wagon."

The man whom North so casually nominated for eternal
fame was one William Frederick Cody, twenty-three years
old. At the moment he was suffering from a severe hangover
induced by a long, wet night at the sutler's establishment.
Flies crawled around his mouth and eyes, and an alcoholic
sweat beaded his face. At first glance he didn't look much
like a hero, but Buntline crawled under the wagon and woke
him up. Once he had brushed away the flies and straw, young
Cody was a much more prepossessing specimen: handsome,
broad-shouldered, with brown eyes, long brown hair, and a

brown goatee. There was a dauntless look in his eye. Above
all, he was eager to talk about himself and his experiences
and not at all reluctant to have them publicized. If Buntline
was a writer in search of a hero, Cody was a hero in search of
a role.

It may have seemed to anyone watching that it was an in-
auspicious meeting which would probably lead to nothing
more than a long boozing session at the sutler's that night,
the middle-aged hack writer and the frontier roustabout just
half his age. Yet it was truly a historic moment. By the time
Buntline and Cody crawled out of the shade of the wagon
box they had agreed upon a collaboration—prose by Buntline, heroics by Cody.

Young Cody was equally impressed by the man who would
make him famous. Eyeing "perhaps twenty badges of secret
societies and gold medals" pinned to Buntline's breast, as he
recalled in his autobiography, he decided that Buntline had
"a good mark to shoot at on his left breast but he looks like
a soldier." He also remembered telling Buntline that he was
going out on a scout to hunt down a war party that had
raided the Union Pacific line and killed several section
hands and that Buntline was welcome to accompany them
the next day, and that Buntline promptly replied, "I was to
deliver a temperance lecture tonight, but no lecture for me
when there is a prospect of a fight."

They hit it off splendidly during the next week or ten
days. Buntline accompanied Cody and a troop of the Fifth
Cavalry on its search for the Sioux war party. The cavalry
sweep failed to round up any miscreants, but Cody and his
squinty-eyed Boswell spent the nights profitably. Under the
stars, with the two men bunked down on their saddle rolls,
Cody elaborated enthusiastically, perhaps at some expense to
the truth, on the details of his brief career. And Buntline
needed only a few facts on which to build the foundation of
a legend; the reading public was eager to swallow anything
written about the glorious West so long as it did not dimin-

ish the cherished concept of Anglo-Saxon manhood, impelled by an ill-defined but manifest destiny, conquering an empire in the wilderness west of the Mississippi.

Ned Buntline went back East, wrote furiously for weeks at a stretch, and before the year 1869 ended, Street & Smith's *New York Weekly* was advertising a serial titled *Buffalo Bill: The King of the Border Men* and subtitled *The Wildest and Truest Story I Ever Wrote*. No one was more astounded by the apotheosis, achieved by fiat on pulp paper, than young Cody himself. There were many "Buffalo Bills" on the frontier, but no one until now had attached the sobriquet to Will Cody. Perhaps he was even more surprised to learn that he was a fiery temperance advocate. At any rate, he gracefully submitted to the ministrations of fame.

There may have been a prenatal influence guiding his easy acceptance of the centerpiece role in the Buffalo Bill myth. His father's side of the house asserted, on the wispiest evidence, that it was directly descended from the first high kings of Ireland. Many an Irishman under alcoholic influence has proclaimed that he stemmed from Brian Boru, but few have the temerity to trace their genealogy even farther into the prehistoric mists. The Codys did apparently migrate to the United States from the province of Connaught, from County Galway; as members of the Norman conquest they may, as they claimed, have descended from one of the kings of Connaught.

In a genealogy compiled long after Will Cody became famous, however, the family boast that it was descended from King Milesius was also included. Milesius was the Celtic King of Spain whose sons invaded Ireland and established the first Irish kingdom. This was long before the island was Christianized and English monks arrived to teach the natives how to record their history in writing. Just how any record of Milesius' sons' descendants could have been kept or their lineage traced in prehistorical times was a mystery which the Cody genealogists did not bother to explain. Enough that "genuine royal blood courses in Colonel Cody's veins," as the genealogy of the clan firmly stated, and that the family crest featured a lion rampant, just as the Spanish royal coat of arms did.

Aside from such royal fantasies, the Codys could claim a century of respectable history in this country. The first ones came over in 1747 and were said to have distinguished themselves in the American Revolution. They drifted westward, like so many of the early colonists. A restless impulse drove them across the Alleghenies; they settled in Ohio for a while, then pushed on to Indiana and Illinois. Isaac Cody, Will's father, married Mary Ann Leacock, who came of English stock but did not boast of any Plantagenet blood lines. Isaac was one of those restless Irishmen always looking for something over the horizon, while his wife was a sensible woman who wished that her husband concerned himself more with raising corn and breeding hogs, less with his royal lineage and his visions of a fairer land.

They were settled on a small farm near Leclair, in Scott County, Iowa, when Will was born on February 26, 1846. (This is the date inscribed in the family Bible, though his tombstone gives 1845 as the year of his birth.) He was one of eight children, not all of whom survived childhood. One of his earliest memories was of Indians slouching along the main street of Leclair, frightening in appearance, "but they bore no hostility toward anything save work and soap and water."

Three years after Will's birth there was a great stirring along the frontier when the news of the California gold strikes spread. Isaac Cody was eager to join the rush; he was not successful at farming, but his family then included four small children, and gold prospecting was for bachelors or men willing to desert their families. In 1853, just after Will's older brother Samuel was killed in a farm accident, the Codys finally sold out, packed up, and joined the westward movement. The urge to move West, in search of something indefinable, ran like a fever in the blood of the frontier people. For the Codys the impulse turned out to be disastrous, for they settled in Kansas just as that territory was being turned into a battleground by Abolitionists and pro-slavery Southerners.

At least they traveled in comparative style and comfort. Improvident as any royal sprig he claimed descent from, Isaac Cody used the money obtained from selling his farm to outfit the family for the journey, with nothing left over for building a new home, buying seed, or acquiring stock. "Father had very extravagant ideas regarding horses and vehicles," his daughter Helen wrote in her memoir, "and such a passion for equestrian display that we often found ourselves with a stable full of thoroughbreds and an empty cupboard. For our western migration we had, in addition to three prairie schooners, a large family carriage, drawn by a span of fine horses in silver-mounted harness. This carriage was made to order in the East, upholstered in the finest leather, polished and varnished as though for a royal progress. . . ."

As young Will remembered that journey of thirty days over the rolling plains of Iowa and Missouri, his father converted one of the Conestogas into a trading wagon and "stocked it with red blankets, beads, and other goods with which to tempt the Indians." It was still widely believed along the middle border that the Indians would give up their ancestral hunting lands for a few blankets and a handful of beads. But it wasn't the Indians so much as other white men whom the Codys should have been worrying about. Free Staters were determined to keep slavery out of the Territory of Kansas, while newcomers from the Southern states were campaigning to extend slavery to the new territories of the Great Plains. There were only 800 white citizens of Kansas, but most of them were at each other's throats.

At the moment it looked peaceful enough in the undulating grasslands of the Salt Creek Valley, about twenty miles from Leavenworth, where Isaac Cody and his young son began building the homestead. It was a log cabin, located on the claim along the Salt Lake Trail, up which came caravans of prairie schooners, trading wagons, and pack trains winding through the valley on their way to Utah and the gold-fields of California. There was a trading post three miles away, and the reservation of the friendly Kickapoos even closer, where the seven-year-old Will learned their tongue from the Kickapoo children. Forested hills bounded the valley in which wild game could be shot for the family larder.

What particularly fascinated young Will were the trains of freight wagons, twenty-five of them, which the Leavenworth firm of Russell, Majors & Waddell sent out with supplies for all the Army's posts on the Great Plains. The heavy wagons, each with six yoke of oxen, attended by wagon masters and bullwhackers, rolled up the trail only a short distance from the Cody homestead. He was also enthralled by his first glimpse of military life, when his father took him to Fort Leavenworth and they watched a squadron of dragoons, with flashing sabers, maneuvering on the parade ground.

It could have been the bountiful life for the Codys, they might have prospered on the virgin soil of their section in the Salt Creek Valley, if only the violence of pre-Civil War politics had not erupted—or if Isaac Cody had been less of a contentious Irishman. He was an Abolitionist, a member of what was called the Free Soil Party, while most of the settlers flooding into that part of Kansas were pro-slavery Missourians. The year following the Codys' arrival in Kansas Congress passed the Kansas-Nebraska Act, which repealed the Missouri Compromise and allowed the citizens in the new territories to decide for themselves whether they would permit slavery.

Both factions were being armed and reinforced from the outside. The Free Soil advocates were receiving shipments of Sharps rifles, jocularly called Beecher's Bibles in honor of the Abolitionist Reverend Henry Ward Beecher, and the New England Emigrant Aid Society was encouraging the migration to Kansas of men of their persuasion. At the same time the towns of Leavenworth, Kickapoo, and Atchison were being converted into pro-slavery strongholds, with their leading journal advising its followers: "Stake out your claims and woe be to the Abolitionists who shall intrude upon it or come within range of your long rifles, or within pointblank range of your revolvers. . . . Vote at the point of Bowie knife and revolver. . . . I tell you to mark every scoundrel among you that is the least tainted with free-soilism, or Abolition-ism, and exterminate him. . . ." Not only journalistic rheto-ric helped to form the climate of violence. It was also encour-aged by the producers of what was called "double-rectified, copper-distilled, trigger-lightning, sod-corn juice," later known as forty-rod, red-eye, rotgut, and other highly descrip-tive terms for the whiskey produced by local unlicensed distilleries.

Politics, the more passionate the better, are irresistible to an Irishman. Isaac Cody was no exception. Furthermore, he had a Celtic taste for oratory. Probably at the pleading of Mrs. Cody, he held his tongue for the time being and tried to keep out of disputes with his neighbors, who were almost en-tirely Southerners, and to stay away from the Saturday night rallies at the Salt Creek trading post, where the pro-slavery men got liquored up and listened to speeches urging them to wipe out the Abolitionists.

One June night in 1855 Isaac Cody, accompanied by his ten-year-old son, rode over to Fort Leavenworth to collect for hay and wood he had supplied to the garrison. On their way back home they halted at Rively's trading post, which was thronged by Salt Creek settlers who had done their trading and then passed around the demijohns of whiskey. They were ripe for trouble when Isaac Cody and his son arrived on the torchlit scene. "There were many men in the crowd and they were all drunk," as the boy would recall years later, "yelling and shooting their pistols in the air. They caught sight of us immediately and a few of them advanced toward us as we rode up. Father expected trouble, but he was not a man to turn back."

Somebody in the crowd shouted for Isaac Cody to get off

his horse and mount the dry-goods box, which served as a speaker's platform, to "declare himself."

Possibly he thought that his neighbors wanted a debate on the subject, or that they could be swayed by a display of logic, or at least that they would respect him for frankly stating his opinions. More likely he was unable to resist the temptation of speechmaking, which he had kept under control for so long.

He clambered up on the wooden box and began to "declare himself" to the hostile crowd. As his son later recalled the sense of his argument, if not the exact words, it went like this:

"I was one of the pioneers of the state of Iowa, aided its settlement, helped to organize it as a state. I voted that it should be a white state, that Negroes whether free or slave should never be permitted to locate within its limits. I say to you now, and I say it boldly, I propose to exert all my power in making Kansas the same kind of state. And I shall always oppose the further extension of slavery—"

His speech was interrupted by wild yelling from the crowd. "Men began crowding around him, cursing and shaking their fists," as his son later described the scene. "One of them, whom I recognized as Charlie Dunn, an employe of my Uncle Elijah [Isaac Cody's brother, who operated a trading post at nearby Weston, Kansas], worked his way through the crowd, and jumped up on the box directly behind my father. I saw the gleam of a knife. The next instant, without a groan, Father fell forward stabbed in the back. Somehow I got off my pony and ran to his assistance, catching him as he fell. His weight overbore me but I eased him as he came to the ground. Dunn was still standing, knife in hand, seeking a chance for another thrust. . . . Another man, with a vestige of decency, restrained the murderer." Someone helped the boy carry Isaac Cody to a wagon after the crowd dispersed. "I held his head in my lap during the ride home. I believed he was mortally wounded. He had been stabbed down through the kidneys, leaving an ugly wound. But he did not die of it —then. Mother nursed him carefully and had he been spared further persecution he might have survived."

The slavery faction, it seemed, would not rest until Isaac Cody was eliminated. Several times while he was convalescing bands of armed men raided the Cody homestead, and Isaac escaped only by hiding in a cornfield. Finally he was spirited away to the home of an Abolitionist at Fort Leavenworth to complete his recovery.

Even while convalescing from that near-fatal wound, Isaac Cody could not stay out of trouble. It only convinced him that, whatever the cost to himself and his family, the pro-slavery faction had to be driven out. When his wound had more or less healed, he joined the Free State forces led by the flamboyant Jim Lane in their advance on the town of Lawrence, which the Free Staters then made their stronghold in the territory. Later, to the neglect of his responsibilities as head of a growing family, he joined the Free State colony at Grasshopper Falls and built a sawmill. It wasn't safe for him to return to the Salt Creek homestead, but the family never found any explanation for his not sending for his wife and children to join him at Grasshopper Falls.

Certainly Mrs. Cody was enduring more than her share of privations at Salt Creek, surrounded as she was by hostile neighbors. They drove off her cattle, killed her chickens and pigs, and generally terrorized the family. So much for the vaunted Southern chivalry, considering that in addition to her other troubles Mrs. Cody was pregnant. Yet she was determined not to be driven off the homestead and would not yield to the urging of her relatives to move in with them. "We had now been reduced to utter destitution," as her son would recall. "Our only food was what rabbits and birds I could trap and catch with the help of our faithful old dog Turk, and the sod corn we grated into flour."

Isaac Cody returned to the Salt Creek homestead in the spring of 1857. He was desperately ill, never having recovered from the knife wound, and one morning in April he died in the log cabin he had built only three years before. Will Cody was eleven years old, big for his age and determined to be the family's breadwinner; he could ride and shoot, herd cattle, drive a wagon, and he was already weary of being educated in the one-room Salt Creek schoolhouse.

His advance into man's estate was aided by his family's acquaintance with the partners in the freighting firm of Russell, Majors & Waddell, which was rapidly expanding. It not only handled most of the freight headed West but operated the Overland stage line and the Pony Express mail routes; until the transcontinental railroads were built, it supplied and reinforced the advancing frontier. The moral tone of the company was considerably higher than the prevailing ethos of the frontier; each employee was required to sign an oath —most of them with the X's of the illiterate—that he would "not use profane language, not get drunk, not gamble, not treat animals cruelly, and not do anything else that is incompatible with the conduct of a gentleman." But they were not hiring Christian gentlemen, who were in short supply west of the Mississippi, and the oath was fractured on all possible occasions.

In 1898, at a celebration in honor of the man who became Buffalo Bill, an ancient Alexander Majors recalled with tremulous feeling, "Forty-three years ago this day, this fine-looking physical specimen of manhood was brought to me by his mother—a little boy nine years old, and little did I think that the boy standing before me was going to be a boy of such destiny as he has turned out to be." Two years later the boy applied for a job, as Majors recalled, and was accepted despite his tender years. "When the boy Cody came to me, standing straight as an arrow, and looked me in the face, I said to my partner, Mr. Russell, who was standing by my side, 'We will take this little boy, and we will pay him a man's wages, because he can ride a pony just as well as any man can.'"

So eleven-year-old Will Cody was signed on at a man's wage, his job designated as "driving cavayard"—that is, herding the cattle that followed the company's wagon trains. The $40 a month he earned was paid to his mother and was sufficient to support the fatherless family.

His first assignment was with a small wagon train and a large herd of cattle, led by Bill and Frank McCarthy, which were consigned to Colonel Albert Sidney Johnston, later a Confederate general killed at Shiloh, and a cavalry force charged with subduing the rebellious Mormons in Utah. The Mormons then were trying to establish an independent "empire" around Salt Lake City, and Washington was determined to quell such separatist ambitions.

The first wagon train the boy accompanied as a drover on muleback reached Plum Creek, near the banks of the Platte River, without incident. During a noon halt near Fort Kearney the outfit was attacked by a band of Indians who stampeded the cattle and killed three of Will's fellow drovers. A skirmish along the sloughs of the Platte followed, with young Cody banging away at the marauders with his Yaeger rifle, a muzzle-loader that fired a ball and two buckshot.

Then occurred, supposedly, the first episode in Will Cody's progress toward legendary status. At age eleven, he always maintained afterward, he shot and killed his first Indian.

Will and his comrades were returning to camp along the riverbank. As he told the story in *The Great Salt Lake Trail,* a volume dealing somewhat garishly with his wagon-train experiences, "I, being the youngest and smallest of the party, became somewhat tired, and without noticing it I had fallen behind the others for some little distance. It was about ten o'clock and we were keeping very quiet and hugging close to the bank, when I happened to look up at the moonlight sky and saw the plumed head of an Indian peeping over the bank. Instead of hurrying ahead and alarming the men in a quiet way, I instantly aimed my gun at his head and fired. The report rang out sharp and loud in the night air, and was immediately followed by an Indian whoop; the next moment about six feet of dead Indian came tumbling into the river. . . ." He admitted to being badly scared, fearing other Indians would be attracted by the shot, but was overcome by pride a few minutes later when Frank McCarthy announced, "Little Billy has killed an Indian stone-dead—too dead to skin."

This was the foundation stone of a mighty legend, but it was something less than granitic. It tended to crumble, in fact, on closer examination.

The McCarthy wagon train had to return to Fort Leavenworth, having lost the cattle herd, and by the Cody accounting, "The news of my exploit was noised about and made me the envy of all the boys in the neighborhood." He also claimed that he was interviewed by the Leavenworth *Times* and "my name was printed for the first time as the youngest Indian slayer of the Plains."

Like so much of the Cody canon, this "exploit" is impossible to verify, or even to refute. Supposedly the Leavenworth *Times* story appeared in July, 1857, but the paper was not founded until the following year. There is no record of the killing in the Russell, Majors & Waddell records—not too damaging to the story, because such trifling incidents as the erasing of an Indian were not often regarded as worthy of mention. Nor is it mentioned in that pioneer's archive the *Annals of Kansas*, though the deaths of three white drovers should have attracted a certain amount of historical attention. In later years Cody would chuckle over his first human kill and remark, "That Indian has been hitched to my name like a tin kettle to a dog's tail." He did not add that the "hitching" was largely his own doing. Nor did he like to be questioned closely on details of the affair or be asked to supply any sort of supporting evidence.

Will was next assigned to a larger caravan of which the hard-bitten Lew Simpson was wagon master. A train of twenty-five wagons, followed by cattle, was taking the trail westward to supply Colonel Johnston's column in its Utah operations. The outfit hardly got rolling, according to Cody's

legend makers, when he met up with one James Butler
Hickok, later better known as Wild Bill, whose fame would
come close to equaling Cody's. Young Will was being bullied
by a couple of teamsters during a halt, so the story went,
when Hickok crawled out from under a wagon where he had
been resting and told the bullies, "Let that boy alone." It
never happened. Hickok did not join Russell, Majors & Waddell until 1860, and that was far away in the Raton Pass, on
the Colorado border.

The Simpson train survived a buffalo stampede but came
to disaster on a ridge overlooking the Green River, which is
about 115 miles east of Salt Lake City and well within the
limits of what the Mormons regarded as their theocratic empire. Atop the ridge Simpson and his thirty men found themselves surrounded by one Lot Smith and about 200 armed
followers who constituted the Danites, or Destroying Angels,
charged with defending the Mormon country and cutting off
supplies to the federal column. They had no chance to de-
fend themselves and were forced to surrender their weapons
and hope they would not be slaughtered. Not long before a
Mormon militia company had perpetrated the Mountain
Meadow massacre, in which 120 non-Mormons crossing their
territory in a wagon train were killed. Lot Smith, however,
was disposed toward mercy. He seized the supplies and the
cattle, proposing to turn Simpson and his men loose without
weapons or supplies for the long walk back to Fort Leavenworth.

As Cody later quoted him, Simpson sounded a bit petulant
in appealing to the angelic rather than the destructive side of
the Destroying Angels. "You're a *brute* if you don't let us
have one wagon and provisions enough for the march. . . . I
think you're a mean coward to set us afloat in a hostile country without giving us our arms." Surely a hard-case wagon
master like Simpson would have expressed himself more
pungently. At any rate, Lot Smith allowed Simpson and his
men to depart with one wagon, a load of supplies, and their

firearms. After thirty days of plodding, they arrived back at Fort Leavenworth.

His mother took Cody in hand and insisted that he return to school the winter of 1857–58. A swaggering twelve-year-old, Will resisted the educational process to the best of his ability, and "the master of the frontier school wore out several armfuls of hazel switches in a vain effort to interest me in the 'three R's.' "

Apparently he was also a handful for his mother. His sister Helen in her memoir recollected Will returning home one night singing, reeking of hard cider, and shouting that he was going to be President of the United States. "Will," she added, "never touched hard cider again." Perhaps not, but there was plenty of other ardent spirits available, and her brother became one of the really heroic topers of his time. For years he required a daily minimum of ten tumblers of whiskey, as he explained, to keep his kidneys functioning properly. On special occasions, which were plentiful, his consumption was the pride and joy of distillers everywhere from San Francisco to Budapest.

In the spring of 1858, Will again escaped from the schoolmaster, his mother and sisters, and their joint ambition to turn him into a proper little gentleman and back into the world of the bullwhackers and cattle drovers beating up the trail west. He accompanied a train again captained by Lew Simpson, this one bound for Fort Laramie, the base for the Army's operations against the Mormons. Young Cody was completely enthralled by life on the trail: the endless sea of grass, the blue mountains in the far distance, the nights under the stars, the presence of danger, the rhythmic routine of driving the prairie schooners and caring for the stock.

Fort Laramie was the great bastion of Western settlement before the Civil War. It had seen the passage of the first trappers and settlers, the gold rushers to California, Fremont's expedition, the Mormons on their way to Utah. It was surrounded by the villages of several thousand Sioux, Cheyenne, and Arapaho who came to trade their furs at the post, and it could then be said to be the capital of Indian country. Simpson's wagon train was kept at Fort Laramie to haul supplies to various outlying forts, and between such assignments young Will Cody was privileged to hang around and listen to such famous scouts and Indian fighters as Kit Carson and Jim Bridger and others who had been trading, trapping, and scrounging around the Rockies since the pristine days before their fellow whites began coming out in larger numbers.

Bridger, a tall, rough-mannered man who had come West forty years earlier, was acting as a scout for Colonel Johnston's forces. But it was the small, dapper Kit Carson, who had served as guide for General John C. Frémont and won him his reputation as the "great pathfinder," who most fascinated young Cody. From these and other veterans Will got his real schooling and learned how you found your way through wilderness without maps, how you got along with the Indians, how you could survive in rough country with nothing but a knife and gun. He admired the quiet and fastidious Carson so much that he named his only son Kit Carson Cody. "I used to sit for hours and watch him and the others talk to the Indians in sign language. Without a sound they would carry on long and interesting conversations, tell stories, inquire about game and trails, and discuss pretty much everything that men found worth discussing. I was naturally desirous of mastering this mysterious medium of speech, and began my education in it with far more interest than I had given to the 'three R's' back at Salt Creek." He played with the children of the Sioux villages and began picking up a working knowledge of their language.

Will escaped school that year because the Simpson train spent most of the winter around Fort Laramie. On its return to Fort Leavenworth it was attacked by a Sioux war party. Simpson and his men "forted up" with their wagons and withstood the daylight attack. That night the Sioux started a prairie fire to burn out Simpson and his men, but the buffalo grass was too short at that time of year. The next morning they were rescued by the approach of another wagon train.

When he returned to the Cody homestead at Salt Creek, Will and his mother went to the Russell, Majors & Waddell office in Leavenworth to draw his accumulated pay. Mrs. Cody was grateful for the money but she wept when he had to make an X instead of signing his name on the payroll. Young Will was twelve years old, could communicate in sign language and talk Sioux, could do a man's job at a man's wages, but he hadn't learned to read or write properly. "To think," Mrs. Cody sobbed, "my boy cannot so much as write his name!"

So Will was shamed into going back to school and studying hard enough for three months to learn reading and writing, although his grasp of arithmetic was always a source of joy to those with whom he had business dealings. "From that day," as his patron Alexander Majors noted, "he began to study hard and learn to write; in fact his acquiring the art of penmanship got him into heaps of trouble, as 'Will Cody,' 'Little Billy,' 'Billy the boy messenger,' and 'William Frederick Cody' were written with the burnt end of a stick upon tents, wagon-covers and all tempting places, while he carved upon wagon-body, ox-yoke and where he could find suitable wood for his pen-knife to cut into, the name he would one day make famous."

Now at least semiliterate, Will continued the career of juvenile adventure which one day would be the envy of every red-blooded boy in America. During the next several years he trapped, prospected for gold, rode for the Pony Express, and was a general roustabout on the far frontier.

His first venture as an independent was with a boy a little older than himself named Dave Harrington. They set out with a wagon and a yoke of oxen and set up a trappers' camp on Prairie Creek about 200 miles west of Salt Creek, where they found fur-bearing animals plentiful. Even in that remote spot the cry of "Pike's Peak or Bust"—the slogan of

Colorado gold-rushers—reached them. He and his companion decided that trapping was a dull existence compared to
the lure of the gold rush, and they joined the stampede to
Denver and beyond. Denver was then a tent city. Young Will
hardly gave it a passing glance as he hurried on to the gold-
fields. He and Harrington poked around the mountains for
a few weeks but failed to find even a nugget of gold. They returned to the Cody homestead and Harrington helped Will
work the farm for a few months until he caught a cold, rapidly declined, and died of pneumonia.

There was a bitter lesson in the older boy's death for the
fourteen-year-old Will. You could survive Indians, blizzards,
wild animals, mining camps, and all the other hazards of the
frontier and yet die of something so prosaic as a cold. You
might just as well live dangerously. Will, accordingly, found
himself just about the most perilous occupation available:
riding for the Pony Express. This was a subsidiary of the
Russell, Majors & Waddell firm, which had established a
mail-carrying route over the 2,000 miles from St. Joseph,
Missouri, to Sacramento, California. Each rider was mounted
on the best ponies money could buy and covered about 45
miles a day, stopping to change horses at relay stations built
about 15 miles apart. Through hard riding, and with luck, a
letter could be carried from St. Joseph to Sacramento in
eight days—a record, as some cynics have observed, which
the modern postal system would do well to equal.

Will Cody's route lay between Red Buttes and Rocky
Ridge. The headquarters of that division of the Pony Express was at Rocky Ridge. Its superintendent, and Cody's direct superior, was the notorious Alf Slade. "Killer" fitted
Slade's disposition and career like a mustard poultice. Fortunately Slade took a liking to his youngest rider and did not
add him to the lengthy list of men who fell before his pistols.
"Slade, though always a dangerous man, and extremely
rough in his manner, never failed to treat me with kindness,"
Cody would write. "Sober, he was cool and self-possessed, but
never a man to be trifled with. Drunk, he was a living fury."

Will loved the life of a rider for the Pony Express, galloping over the prairie with his pouch full of messages written on the thinnest paper available and always staying on the alert for hostiles on the horizon. So many riders were picked off by the Indians that Cody's route was lengthened from Red Buttes to Sweetwater, a distance of 76 miles. Will himself came under attack one day just as he was leaving the Horse Creek relay station. Fifteen warriors, by his account, pursued him for 11 miles. Mounted on a fresh pony, he managed to outrun them.

It was apparent in 1860 that big trouble with the Indians was brewing. Generally the Indians, despite the onrush of white settlers, had been peaceful for five years. Whatever fighting occurred between whites and Indians was usually, by impartial account, started by the former. Kit Carson himself said "the difficulties arose from aggressions on the part of the whites." A President's commission in 1869 investigating the pre-Civil War period put it in even stronger terms: "The history of the border white man's connection with the Indians is a sickening record of murder, outrage, robbery and wrongs committed by the former, as the rule, and occasional savage outbreaks and unspeakably barbarous deeds of retaliation by the latter, as the exception."

Will Cody himself was indoctrinated in the border whites' belief that killing an Indian was no more reprehensible than shooting a rattlesnake. A curious dichotomy arose. He could learn their language, share their food, play with their children, and even accept help from them, yet he could see them as only soulless subhumans who deserved to be slaughtered the moment they got in the way of a white man's ambition of the moment.

Naturally he experienced no qualms, engaged in no Hamlet-like self-questioning, when Alf Slade organized a punitive expedition of stage drivers, express riders, and stock tenders to go after the Indians who had been harassing that division of the Russell, Majors & Waddell route. Will eagerly accompanied it. Another member of the Indian-killing crew was James Butler Hickok, who a year later would be renowned as Wild Bill, the tall, yellow-haired pistoleer who supposedly wiped out a whole band of evildoers. Wherever the Cody and Hickok legends coincide—as they do at several junctures—the truth seeker must pick his way over a quagmire created by ghost-writers, pulp-magazine operators, and the two men themselves, who were touchingly proud of their expertise in the Western sport of telling tall tales. Historical documentation of any of their deeds is necessarily scant. The main source of information is the accounting given by Hickok and Cody themselves, filtered through the hyperactive imaginations of those who transcribed those experiences. Thus any map of their joint exploits must be bounded on all sides by the cautionary "Beyond this point there be monsters of untruth."

Cody accompanied Hickok and a number of other bloodthirsty bravos on an expedition up the Powder River. Hickok, Cody said, was in command. When they reached Clear Creek they sighted a large Indian encampment. Naturally they did not bother to determine whether this camp contained any of the hostiles who had been raiding the stage and Pony Express line; nor were they bothered by the fact that they were outnumbered four to one. They followed the sacred tactical doctrine that held that one white man was equal to any number of Indians, the same kind of reasoning to which the Indians eventually applied a stern corrective at the battle of the Little Big Horn.

Hickok, Cody, and their companions simply waited until nightfall and then, whooping like madmen, rode into the Indian village shooting anything that moved. The Indians fled into the night, with Hickok and company in hot pursuit. How many were killed, including women and children, was not included in their report of the incident; that was immaterial. The main thing was that they rounded up 100 ponies, some of them allegedly stolen from the Russell, Majors & Waddell relay stations.

The victory was celebrated with a drunken orgy when the cavalcade returned to the town of Sweetwater Bridge. Cody later described it as a "grand spree," a subject on which he became a qualified expert. On the third day of the celebration, Superintendent Alf Slade himself rode into Sweetwater Bridge to congratulate his men and join in the fun-making. Given his tendency toward mixing gunplay with boozing, Slade was the life—and death—of the party. On the fourth day of nonstop merriment he quarreled with a stage driver and shot him dead. The celebration was halted only long enough to bury the victim. Cody and his friends were so overstimulated by the cheap but plentiful whiskey, as he later recorded, that most of them "were in favor of going back and cleaning out the whole Indian race."

Once Sweetwater Bridge was depleted of its liquid stores, everyone went back to work. Cody rode the mail route for a while, then Slade, as a mark of favor, made him "supernumerary" at Horseshoe Station, which meant he drew full pay merely for doing a few chores around the place. He was lounging around the relay station in April, 1861, when news arrived that the Union had gone to war with the newly proclaimed Confederate States of America. To the people of the Kansas border that event seemed less important than their own private war with Missouri. For years, in fact, the Free State partisans and the Missourians had been fighting an undeclared war over the fate of Kansas. Young Cody was more interested in that sideshow of bushwhacking, night-raiding, and barn-burning than the main event, his hatred of the "southrons" naturally inflamed by his father's death at their hands.

Which is not to say that he was quite as bloodthirsty as Ned Buntline made him out to be in *Buffalo Bill: King of the Border Men*. In that free-form biography he was quoted as telling Wild Bill Hickok of his determination—so long and strangely delayed—to track down the man who killed his father: "I want to take him back to the spot where he mur-

dered my father and roast him there over a slow fire. Death
—a mere man's death—is too good for him. He wants, and
shall have, a taste of what he'll get when he is dead!''

Nevertheless Will Cody, with laggard steps, did finally join
in the battle to save the Union.

2

"Under the Influence of Bad Whiskey . . ."

NOT even the most imaginative of his press agents or the most idolatrous of his early biographers could make much of William F. Cody's war record. About the most that could be claimed for his military career was that he achieved promotion from recruit to full private.

War on a massive scale was not something to attract a thoroughgoing individualist. The metronomic routine of drilling, marching, and maneuvering—not to mention the necessity of being bullied by sergeants and looked down upon by beardless lieutenants—was monotonous and unappealing and life in a barracks or camp as confining as a prison. And all the glory, as well as most of the comforts, were the province of generals and colonels pompously tracing fingers over their maps a safe distance from the fighting.

It was not the sort of life he chose for himself. The voice of John Barleycorn spoke for him and enlisted him in the ranks of the Union Army while he was under its treacherous influence. It was almost enough to make a man quit drinking.

He had returned home to his mother and sisters shortly after war was declared. By then Mrs. Cody was desperately ill with tuberculosis, the fate of so many frontier women worn by overwork and constant worry. She exacted from her son a promise that he would not run away and join the Army, at least not until after she died. He did keep the letter if not the spirit of the promise and worked for a time as a teamster and dispatch rider out of Fort Leavenworth. Then a hankering for action overcame him and he joined up with the Jayhawkers, as they were called—Free State partisans who were conducting a guerrilla war against such Confederate sympathizers as Quantrill's Raiders and the Missourians settled in Kansas. It was a dirty little war on both sides. Will enlisted with the Red Legs, who in the name of God and Country raided the Missourians' farms and settlements, often crossing the river into Missouri to make a lightning attack and then returning to Kansas soil before sunup. He did not gloss over his career as a night rider: "Few of us ever returned empty-handed. . . . We were the biggest gang of thieves on record. . . . I thought I had a right to hound the Missourians, drive off their horses and cattle, and make life miserable for them."

In between Red Leg operations he continued to work as a teamster and was in Denver the fall of 1863 with an Army wagon train when he received a letter from his sisters summoning him home because his mother was dying. Mary Cody died on December 23, more an unsung heroine, in her quiet way, than her son was ever a hero, in his more clamorous way.

Her death did not free him of all obligations. There were still his younger sisters to be cared for, and young Will manfully met his responsibilities. His older sister Julia was married to a man named Al Goodman and kept the family together under one roof, but by himself Al Goodman could not earn enough to support them all.

Will was employed as a scout for the Ninth Kansas Cavalry, which was assigned to keep the Kiowas and Comanches from raiding the white settlements of western Kansas, when he received a letter from his sisters Helen and May complaining that Julia and her husband weren't providing them with pretty dresses. Will promptly and cheerily replied, "I am sorry that I cannot help you and furnish you with such clothes as you wish. At this writing I am so short of funds myself that if an entire Mississippi steamer could be bought for ten cents, I couldn't purchase the smokestack. I will soon draw my pay and I will send it, every cent, to you. So brave it out, girls, a little longer."

His scout's pay was $150 a month and—family loyalty being then and always one of his more attractive and durable qualities—he sent it all to his sisters. And no matter how harum-scarum, how improvident and dissipated his later career, he always remembered to send money home for his orphaned sisters.

Soon after that Will abandoned his scouting job, though it paid $150 a month, and returned to Fort Leavenworth. Later he confessed that at eighteen "I was becoming a very hard case" and "leading a dissolute and reckless life with gamblers, drunkards and bad characters generally." The Seventh Kansas Volunteers returned to Leavenworth on a thirty-day furlough after service against the Confederate forces in the West, and there was an uproarious celebration. Young Cody, of course, flung himself into the festivities with a willing heart and flexible elbow. He knew many of the Seventh Kansas' soldiers; they urged him to enlist, and Will was always an amiable fellow. With drink in him, he could just as easily have been persuaded to join the French Foreign Legion, then engaged in propping Emperor Maximilian on his shaky throne down in Mexico.

One morning he woke up with a hangover and a funny feeling that he had done something stupid in the last twelve hours. His bed was an Army cot, his costuming had been provided by the Union Army. It seemed that overnight he had rushed to the colors—or, as he candidly put it years later, "under the influence of bad whiskey, I awoke to find myself a soldier in the 7th Kansas. I did not remember how or when I had enlisted, but I saw I was in for it, and that it would not do for me to endeavor to back out."

For the first time the name William F. Cody was placed on the public record. The War Department's files described the new recruit as follows: "Age, 18; born in Scott County, Iowa; occupation, teamster; eyes and hair, brown; complexion, fair; height, five feet, ten inches."

Unfortunately, the War Department's laconic archivists provided little information on his military career beyond the fact that he served for fifteen months, was honorably discharged as a hospital orderly, and had earned no decorations or citations.

Across this gap his early biographers, with the willing assistance of their subject, leaped with great intrepidity. They concocted a military career of some distinction, since it was unthinkable that Buffalo Bill could have been anything but a gallant soldier. If he had performed one-tenth as nobly as they contended, however, he would certainly have risen above the rank of private and his deeds would have been garnished with at least a medal or two; even the Congressional Medal of Honor, in that war, was passed out by the thousands.

The war record claimed for him was worthy of a paladin. It was asserted that he was appointed a scout for the Union forces then trying to pin down the Confederate General Nathan Bedford Forrest's cavalry division in southern Tennessee; that he disguised himself as a Tennessee farm boy, risking the possibility of being shot as a spy, and gathered intelligence vital to the Union cause; that he served valiantly in the battle of Pilot's Knob, an affray which even the most obsessed Civil War scholar would find it difficult to recall. The fifty volumes of the *Official Records of the War of the Rebellion* simply ignore all this. The Seventh Kansas as a whole, in fact, saw little action during eight months on active service, taking part in eight minor engagements and suffering only five casualties; it was about as safe a shelter as anyone could have found in wartime.

One certain thing about Will Cody's nineteenth year is that late in 1864 the Seventh Kansas was withdrawn to the rear area, with headquarters in St. Louis. Cody himself was detached for service as a hospital orderly. In later years, he may often have wished that his regiment had been flung into the Battle of the Wilderness, for in St. Louis he met the combative young woman—whose temper he would find more daunting than a massed charge by Stuart's cavalry—whom he hastily and unwisely married.

The girl was Louisa Frederici, a rather spoiled only daughter who lived with her family on Chateau Avenue in what was then called Frenchtown. Her father, John Frederici, was a French immigrant (actually an Alsatian).

There are several versions of how they met. In the Buntline account Will rescued her from the unsought attentions of a crowd of drunken Union soldiers on a St. Louis street. "With one blow of his clenched hand he dashed the bulky miscreant to the earth, with his other arm he encircled the waist of the lovely girl, and lifting her to his saddle-bow, gave the word 'on' to his noble horse, and dashed through and over the crowd before a hand could be raised to check him. . . ." Another account—this one with a Horatio Alger flavor—described how he rescued her when her horse ran away. The most reliable was Louisa's own, as transcribed by a collaborator for *Memories of Buffalo Bill.*

As she told it, her cousin William MacDonald asked permission to bring over a young Union soldier and introduce him. Louisa was then twenty-two years of age. She was sitting in the parlor dozing over the pages of *Family Fireside* when someone pulled the chair out from under her. She struggled to her feet and confronted a strange young man, whom she promptly slapped hard across the cheek. She flounced out of the parlor and would not return until Cousin William apologized profusely for the prank. Will Cody, she later wrote, was "about the most handsome man I had ever seen! I never knew until that evening how wonderful the blue uniform of the common soldier could be. Clean-shaven, the ruddiness of health glowing in his cheeks; graceful, lithe, smooth in his movements and in the modulations of his speech, he was quite the most wonderful man I had ever known, and I almost bit my tongue to keep from telling him so."

Private Cody was soon a fixed feature of the Frederici parlor. Although he was only nineteen to Louisa's twenty-two years, he played to the hilt the role of the melancholy hero suffused with *Weltschmerz*. "I killed my first Indian when I was eleven years old," she quoted him as saying. "Sometimes I think I've been fighting my way through life ever since the day I was born."

Will ran through his repertoire of tall tales, and the girl was impressed. "It all seemed inconceivable," as she rightly noted. "And yet there was something about the quiet, modest seriousness of the tone that told me that every word he was speaking was the truth. . . . I felt a shiver run through me. I had always been romantic, dreaming of adventures and of weird happenings—just like many another convent-bred girl—but I never had imagined that I would ever meet a man who had killed an Indian."

No doubt Will Cody was smitten. This was the first respectable girl, outside of his sisters, whom he had gotten to know. He was flattered by her wide-eyed admiration of his exploits. And in her youth, Louisa, though she would come to resemble an angry bulldog, was attractive enough, with dark hair and jet-black eyes and squarish but symmetrical features.

The trouble was, though they did not realize it until too late, they were diametrically opposed in personality and temperament. In her father's cozy parlor, she believed herself to be a "romantic," but actually she was a very practical young woman with the overriding ambition to have a comfortable home and an orderly domestic life. Emotional and financial security were more important to her than anything else; as her father's darling, she had been taught to expect them. She was a properly reared French girl, very conventional, with a strong instinct for privacy. She was also vain, jealous, and possessive and became almost hysterical if Cody's eyes strayed toward another woman—and only a few years after their marriage there would be a female multitude sashaying around, fluttering their eyes, and trying to attract his attention.

Then and always Will Cody would have opposite ambitions. Quiet domesticity drove him up the wall. He clamored for public attention and sought lively companionship. He was openhanded with money and could not conceive of saving for any purpose. To her love of privacy he opposed a tendency toward exhibitionism. And he would always be haring off on some venture with only the most dubious connection with providing a comfortable home for Louisa.

More or less engaged, they parted in the spring of 1865 when Cody had to return to Fort Leavenworth to be discharged. The understanding was that he would earn enough money in the next year to set himself up in business and support a wife—Louisa was not so madly in love that she forgot a husband's first duty was to be a good provider. Back in Kansas he got a job driving a Concord stagecoach between Kearney and Plum Creek, saved his pay, bought an old boardinghouse at Salt Creek, near the Cody homestead, and renamed it the Golden Rule Hotel. Early in March, 1866, doggedly following a trail that could only lead to matrimonial disaster, he returned to St. Louis and took up his option on Louisa Frederici. They were married in the Frederici parlor where he had introduced himself, ominously enough, by pulling the chair out from under his future bride.

Late that afternoon, accompanied by the wedding party and Father Frederici, who was laden with misgivings about handing his daughter over to a "wild-looking groom" (as Cody described himself), bride and groom were conveyed in a carriage to the dock of the river steamer *Morning Star*, which would take them upriver to Kansas.

The honeymoon got off to a bad start. A ruffianly crowd on the dock, old enemies from the border fighting, began shouting, "Where's that Jayhawker? Tell him to come out and show himself!" As a Southern sympathizer, Frederici was disturbed by this designation of his new son-in-law. He was

even more upset when other passengers on the *Morning Star*
took him aside and told him, "That son-in-law of yours is the
most desperate outlaw, bandit and house-burner on the
frontier."

The distraught father marched down to the stateroom occupied by his daughter and son-in-law and announced, "I'm
going to take my daughter off this boat and bring her back
home."

Cody pleaded his cause with eloquence, Louisa less enthusiastically "said gamely that she had taken me for better
or worse and intended to stick to me," and Mr. Frederici
finally agreed to let her go.

The bridal night was memorable less for sexual transports
than the bride's incessant weeping. Every turn of the *Morning Star*'s paddle deepened the realization that she was going
out into the wilderness with a very youthful bridegroom
whom she hardly knew. "Now," as she later recalled, "I
began to realize that I had said goodbye to civilization, that
the old comforts and safety of St. Louis might be a thing of
the past forever. I knew I was going to this vague thing
called the West . . . this place where Indians still regarded
the white man as an interloper and where death traveled
swift and sure. . . . I wanted to cry to him that home was
calling, that I cringed at the thought of what was before me."

There was much more "cringing" in store for Louisa when
she viewed Will in his role of Mine Host of the Golden Rule
Hotel. The first and only rule of that short-lived establishment, it appeared, was Will's genial shout, "It's on the
house!" First two of his sisters moved in, then more distant
Cody relatives, then a whole tribe of "pards," old pals, drinking companions, and freeloaders. Will could rarely bring
himself to present anyone with a bill, which seemed a breach
of hospitality. The Golden Rule rarely had an empty bed,
and its barroom, with Will in charge of the bottles and bung
starter, was thronged night and day. Little of this activity was
reflected in the ledger. "Socially," as his sister Helen remarked, "he was an irreproachable landlord, but financially

his shortcomings were deplorable." Bankruptcy loomed within six months, until Will announced that he was sick of civilization and wanted to go to work on the railroad, both the Union Pacific and the Kansas Pacific then being extended westward from the Kansas border. This sounded reasonable enough to Louisa, so she agreed that he should sell the Golden Rule Hotel and leave her at Salt Creek to await the birth of their first child.

Carefree as a kid playing hooky from school, Will hightailed it to Junction City, where he immediately found his old friend Wild Bill Hickok, similarly at loose ends, and forgot all about working on the railroad. Their reunion was celebrated in the usual robust manner, and Hickok persuaded him to join in scouting for the Army. Cody was signed on at Fort Harker, then the advance post of the vigorous campaigning against the dissident tribes.

Just then, in fact, the combative Plains Indians were bitterly resisting the encroachments renewed by the white men after the end of the Civil War, an invasion signalized by the railroads being built through what had been regarded as Indian country, by the columns of settlers' wagons and the fresh cavalry regiments flooding the frontier forts. The elders of such self-respecting tribes as the Kiowa, the Cheyenne, the Arapaho, and the Comanche had signed the Medicine Lodge Treaty providing that reservations would be established for them in Indian Territory (later the state of Oklahoma) and that white settlement would not be allowed between the Arkansas and Platte rivers. A generation gap appeared between the older chiefs and the younger warriors, who justifiably had little faith in treaties with the whites. By early 1867 the prairies were alive with the war parties of the Southern Plains tribes. Up in the Sioux country, north of Fort Laramie, Chief Red Cloud was placing Forts Kearney and Fetterman under siege.

The Army shook up its frontier command and brought the runty but extremely aggressive Major General Philip H. Sheridan, who had been the Union Army's most successful cavalry commander, up from the Mexican border to take charge of operations. Sheridan was a seasoned campaigner against the Indians, but many of his officers and most of his troops—the latter largely Irish and German immigrants fresh from Ellis Island—were innocent of any knowledge of what they were up against. They could ride and shoot, after a fashion, but knew nothing of tracking, smelling out the terrain, avoiding ambush, or dealing with the mentality of the Indian enemy. To fill this gap in expertise, civilian scouts were as necessary as bullets and beans. And first-class scouts, as opposed to braggarts lounging around the frontier saloons (a type beautifully limned by the late W. C. Fields sonorously declaiming on how he had "slashed my way through a wall of Indian flesh"), were in desperately short supply.

A good scout might be an old slammerkin like Bridger, an eccentric like Carson, a gunslinger like Hickok, or a roisterer like young Cody, but he was worth a brace of brevet major generals or a whole covey of staff officers who could discourse on Jomini's works but didn't know a Teton Sioux from a Pawnee squaw. "There were plenty of so-called 'Indian scouts,' whose common boast was of having slain scores of redskins," as General Sheridan remarked in his *Memoirs*, "but the real scout—that is, a guide and trailer knowing the habits of the Indians—was very scarce and it was hard to find anybody familiar with the country south of Arkansas, where the campaign was to be made. Still we managed to employ several men, who, from their experience on the plains in various capacities, or from natural instinct and aptitude, soon became excellent guides and courageous and valuable scouts, some of them, indeed, gaining much distinction." He singled out Cody for his "endurance and courage."

Cody served as a scout for various detachments of Colonel George Armstrong Custer's Seventh Cavalry and the Tenth Cavalry, which was a black regiment with white officers. A letter from home informed him that Louisa had given birth to a daughter, Arta, but he did not go back to Salt Creek. Instead, after guiding a detachment of the Tenth Cavalry into and out of a near-disastrous skirmish with hostiles on the Saline, he went into the town-promoting business with a contractor named William Rose. They surveyed a site on Big Creek, a mile from Fort Hays, and staked it out into town lots. The name they chose for their projected town was, in keeping with Cody's taste for the grandiose, Rome. Cody and Rose gave lots to anyone who would build a house or store on them, reserving the corner lots for themselves, and waited to get rich quick. "I have the world by the tail," Will wrote his wife, "and will soon be worth $250,000." That dream was punctured shortly after Louisa and her baby came out to join him in Rome. A land agent for the Kansas Pacific decided to establish Hays City a mile away, where repair shops for the K.P. would be built and employment would be plentiful.

One day Cody returned from a hunt on the prairie to find Rome, Kansas, literally vanishing before his eyes. "The town was being torn down and carted away," he subsequently reported. "The balloon-frame buildings were coming apart section by section. I could see at least a hundred teams and wagons carting lumber, furniture, and everything that made up the town over the prairies to the eastward." He found Mrs. Cody sitting on a dry-goods box in front of their house, one of the few left standing. There was a brief and bitter exchange with the infuriated Louisa, as he later recalled:

Will: "What has become of our town?"

Louisa: "You wrote me you were worth $250,000!"

Will: "We've got no time to talk about that now."

The upshot was that Louisa took their daughter and moved in with her parents in St. Louis while Will went to work as a buffalo hunter, or butcher, and incidentally earned the sobriquet conferred upon him by Ned Buntline.

The Kansas Pacific line had been extended to Hays City, most of whose buildings had formerly constituted the town of Rome, and its army of graders, track-layers, section hands, and gandy dancers had to be fed as cheaply as possible. The buffalo herds, soon to be driven away by the railroads they were nourishing, were the nearest available meat supply. Cody was hired by Goddard Brothers of Kansas City, which had the meat contract, to hunt buffalo at the handsome salary of $500 a month. In return he was supposed to kill a minimum of twelve buffalo a day, only the hump and hindquarters of each animal being regarded as edible and the rest of the carcass left to rot on the prairie. In eighteen months under contract to Goddard Brothers he slaughtered, by his own estimate, 4,280 buffalo.

Naturally the Indians were outraged by the wastefulness of the white hunters. The buffalo was their staff of life, supplemented by other wild game. "It is almost impossible," as General Richard I. Dodge reported to the War Department, "for a civilized being to realize the value to the Plains Indian of the buffalo. It furnished him with home, food, clothing, bedding, horse equipment—almost everything. . . ." And the white men knew well what they were doing by annually decimating the great herds, killing off millions of buffalo in one decade between the end of the Civil War and 1875; they knew they were destroying the ecological basis of the Indians' livelihood and forcing them into dependence on, subservience to, the Great White Father in Washington. In a self-congratulatory mood, General Sheridan, addressing a joint session of the Texas Legislature in 1875, proposed that a medal be struck for the buffalo hunters with a dead buffalo engraved on one side and a "discouraged-looking" Indian on the other. White hunters, he added, had done more in a few years to "settle the Indian question" than the regular Army in its thirty years on the frontier.

During that wholesale slaughter Will Cody, then twenty-two years old, began gathering renown for his marksmanship with his breech-loading 50-caliber Springfield rifle. Actually it was the speed and efficiency with which he operated, his knowledge of the buffalo, and its helpless stupidity which were responsible for his success. Shooting a buffalo with a slug the size of a heavy machine gun bullet was simple enough, and safe enough, provided you took care not to be caught in a panicky stampede. The buffalo offered no resistance and was too slow afoot to escape. One afternoon, in a shooting contest with another hunter, he gunned 69 of the beasts. There was no more adventure or sportsmanship to hunting buffalo, or much greater element of risk, than in shooting up a dairy herd.

At any rate his systematic butchery on the Kansas steppe attracted the first discoverable attention in a newspaper of large circulation. A St. Louis paper early in 1868 reported that, "At Hays City—says the *Tribune* of the 14th instant—considerable anxiety exists in regard to the safety of a party of citizens who were out buffalo hunting. There were ten in all, among whom were George and Henry Field, brothers of Mr. Samuel Field of Lawrence, and Mr. Parks, the traveling correspondent of the *Journal*, all under the direction of Cody the noted guide. They left Hays twelve days since and were to return on the 7th, but have not been heard of." The party turned up safely a few days later, and how Will must have salivated over that designation as "the noted guide." It must also have taught him the value of association with "dudes." If a mere contract hunter for Goddard Brothers had been missing in the wilderness for months instead of days, no metropolitan newspaper would have concerned itself with the matter. The fact that he was guiding a group of respectable citizens made the event newsworthy.

A few months later, in May, he abandoned hunting, the Kansas Pacific construction having come to a temporary halt, and returned to the vocation of Indian fighting.

Fort Hays, instead of being the railhead of the Kansas Pacific, was now the headquarters of General Sheridan's campaigning against the dissident tribes. That spring the Army of the West reported that 6,000 tribesmen on the Southern plains were "off the reservation" and looking for trouble. To cope with that swarm of hostiles, Sheridan had only 2,600 federal troops plus five companies of volunteer cavalry raised by the State of Kansas. As commander of the Department of the Missouri, Sheridan was responsible for making 150,000

square miles of territory in western Kansas, eastern Colorado, Indian Territory, and New Mexico safe for the white
man's exploitation, and all that stretch of country had to be
patrolled by the Seventh and Tenth Cavalry, the Third and
Fourth Infantry, and a battalion of another infantry regiment. General Sherman, then general-in-chief of the Army,
stated the problem with brutal simplicity: "We have now selected and provided reservations for all [Indians], off the
great roads. All who cling to their old hunting grounds are
hostile and will remain so till killed off. . . . The country is
so large that we cannot make a single war and end it. From
the nature of things we must take our chances and clean out
the Indians as we encounter them." Equally blunt, General
George Crook, one of his subordinates, posed the corollary:
"How are you going to surround three Indians with one
soldier?"

At Fort Hays, the forward post where Sheridan made his
headquarters, Will again signed an Army contract to act as a
scout and guide and occasionally as a dispatch rider between
Hays and other frontier forts.

It was as the Army's messenger boy, in fact, that Cody
caught General Sheridan's attention by riding 350 miles in
three days. A remarkable feat, which not even the most pica-
yune detractor could fault, not if Sheridan's account was
accurate.

One of Sheridan's chief assets as a commander was his keen
appreciation of military intelligence; he wanted to know
where the enemy was and what he was doing twenty-four
hours a day, though in his time many generals affected a
lordly indifference to the opposition. Thus he greatly valued
anyone who could keep him supplied with the latest information, who could help in coordinating the movement of his
undermanned forces. That was where his courier service was
invaluable.

It was late in Autumn, 1868, when Will Cody distinguished himself in speeding up communications on horseback. As Sheridan recalled in his memoirs, Cody first

brought an important dispatch from Fort Larned to Fort Hays. The information he brought necessitated a change in orders to be dispatched to Fort Dodge, 95 miles to the south. "This being a particularly dangerous route—several couriers having been killed on it—it was impossible to get one of the various 'Petes,' 'Jacks' or 'Jims' hanging around Hays City to take my communication. Cody, learning of the strait I was in, manfully came to the rescue, and proposed to make the trip to Dodge, though he had just finished his long and perilous ride from Larned. I gratefully accepted his offer, and after four or five hours' rest, he mounted a fresh horse and hastened on his journey, halting but once, and then only for an hour, the stop being made at Coon Creek, where he got another mount from a troop of cavalry. At Dodge he took six hours' sleep, and then continued to Fort Larned with more dispatches. After resting twelve hours at Larned, he was again in the saddle with tidings for me at Fort Hays, General Hazen sending him this time, with word that the [Indian] villages had fled to the south of the Arkansas."

Cody's reward was his appointment by General Sheridan as chief of scouts for the Fifth Cavalry, which was then commanded by General Eugene A. Carr. His pay would be equivalent to a colonel's. In later life Cody, inferring that if he got a colonel's pay he was entitled to a colonel's rank, always styled himself as Colonel Cody. It was purely a self-promotion, but there were a lot of self-styled colonels swanning around with less claim to the title than Cody.

Immediately after the Fifth Cavalry arrived as a reinforcement for hard winter campaigning, it was dispatched, with its long column of troopers and their swallow-tailed guidons, its supply train of 76 mule-drawn wagons, ambulances, and pack mules, to drive about 600 Indians north across the Platte. There were several skirmishes but no serious fighting until the first snows came. In that time General Carr, as he later testified in his memoirs, came to value most highly his chief of scouts.

"He was the best white trailer I ever saw," wrote General

Carr. "On my first expedition we soon learned to understand one another. He saw that I knew the direction I wanted to go and I saw that he knew how to take me there." He considered Cody "a natural gentleman" with "none of the roughness of the typical frontiersman." Cody, the general observed, seemed to have been born for the job of cavalry scout. "His eye is better than a good field-glass . . . he is the best judge of the 'lay of the country'—that is, he is able to tell what kind of country is ahead, so as to know how to act. . . . His trailing when following Indians or looking for stray animals or for game is simply wonderful. He is the most extraordinary hunter."

General Carr continued to esteem his chief scout, though with a few qualifications arising whenever Cody made connection with his old drinking companion Hickok and a plentiful supply of firewater, such as occurred during the winter campaign against the Cheyenne in the Indian Territory. Hickok was scouting for the vanguard of 300 men under General Penrose which plunged into the snow-covered Canadian River country while the rest of the Fifth Cavalry, under Carr, refitted at Fort Lyon. Despite the heavy snows, Cody managed to pick up Penrose's trail through the Raton Mountains. It was hard going, with the supply wagons having to be slid down icy slopes by wrapping chains around their wheels. When blizzards struck, the command was forced to hole up in the nearest canyon. Finally, with several other scouts, Cody rode on ahead for 24 miles until they located Penrose's force on a tributary of the Cimarron.

That winter campaign was distinguished mainly by the hardships of living under canvas, in rough country, with "blue northers" howling down from the Arctic Circle. Cody simply endured those hardships with hundreds of other men.

But that wasn't enough for those who fabricated the legendary West, a land as fabulous as Cockaigne, a neo-Homeric mythology which served to conceal the brutal facts of conquest.

Such pseudo-historians as J. W. Buel (*Heroes of the*

Plains) and those who rewrote him, busily inflating the greatest legend of them all, had to place Cody in the center of things. That winter the center of bloody action was the Seventh Cavalry's campaign against Black Kettle's band of Cheyenne on the Washita. It was the My Lai of 1868, as Wounded Knee would be the My Lai of 1890, a demonstration of the superiority of firepower posed against human flesh. Late in November Colonel Custer and his troopers swooped down on the disease-stricken winter camp of Black Kettle and slaughtered the chief, 103 of his warriors, and an uncounted number of women and children. According to Buel and other history fakers, Cody and Wild Bill Hickok were leading participants in the massacre on the Washita. In his widely read book, Buel related that "Buffalo Bill and Wild Bill did almost the work of a regiment; braver men never went into action. . . ." Buel pictured Hickok stabbing Black Kettle to death, but that would have been the end of Hickok "had not Buffalo Bill ridden with impetuous daring into the very midst of fully fifty Indians, which had surrounded Wild Bill. . . . The two daring and intrepid scouts plunged furiously into the midst of the Indians, each with a revolver in either hand, and literally carved their way through the surging mass of redskins. . . ."

Buel ended his account of that horrendous affray, published fifteen years after the "battle" of Washita, time enough certainly to get a few facts straight, by declaring that the two Bills "deserve inscription on Fame's enduring monument." Anyone who could "literally carve" his way through a wall of human flesh with no sharper instrument than a revolver barrel obviously deserved the accolade.

Actually, while historian Buel had Cody and Hickok wiping out Black Kettle's village double-handed, those two gentlemen were plotting nothing more genocidal than the hijacking of a pack train loaded with beer. Furthermore, they were hundreds of miles away, or to be precise, lying in ambush, with raging thirsts, just twelve miles from a new supply depot called Fort Evans. Hickok had learned that a supply train carrying beer brewed by Mexicans was coming from New Mexico for the soldiers at Fort Evans, and he and Cody decided that they and the Fifth Cavalry had better claim to refreshment than a bunch of quartermasters.

So Cody and Hickok "requisitioned" the beer train, or as Cody put it, the beer "found a better market without going so far." After drinking some of the beer and finding it potable, they went into business and sold it by the pint to the troopers of the Fifth. "The result," as Cody added, "was one of the biggest beer jollifications it has ever been my misfortune to attend."

One jollification led to another, which ended with Chief Scout Cody in disgrace with his superiors. He and Hickok had repaired to the sutler's hut several days after the beer bust. Hard liquor inspired them to even scores with fifteen Mexicans who were serving with the scouting detail attached to Penrose's command. "The Mexicans often threatened to clean us out," as Cody later explained, "but they postponed execution of the threat from time to time." More likely the Mexicans had been subjected to insult, "greaser" and "spick" then being the ordinary Anglo designation of any and all Latin Americans. Whatever the cause of hostilities, Cody admitted that he and Hickok "imbibed a few more drinks than we needed that evening." They were the leading participants in a brawl between Mexican scouts and the 100-percent Americans. Fortunately there was no gunplay, but there were more than a few broken heads. The sutler's establishment was reduced to a tangle of broken barrels, boards, torn canvas, and a pond of spilled whiskey.

General Carr was outraged, hauled Cody on the carpet, and decided that he and Hickok would have to be separated before they entirely disrupted the discipline and morale of the command. Hickok was given dispatches to carry to Fort Wallace. As for Cody, General Carr starchily informed him, "There are plenty of antelopes in the surrounding country. I suggest that you work off your excess energy by hunting for fresh meat for the camp for the rest of our stay here."

Until the Fifth broke camp in March, 1869, Cody busied himself killing from 20 to 25 antelopes a day. General Carr was so pleased with his efforts that he gave Cody a thirty-day furlough to visit Louisa and their daughter in St. Louis.

Louisa hardly knew him when he showed up at her parents' house on Chateau Avenue. Clean-shaven until his service with the Fifth Cavalry, he was now wearing his hair down to his shoulders, with a goatee and a long-handled mustache to match. Mrs. Cody's horror at the spectacle her husband presented could hardly have been less than that of a modern wife returning from a summer vacation to find that her husband had gone hippie and adopted a similar hair style. "Shear it off!" she ordered, until he explained that it was a point of honor with men such as Custer, Hickok, and himself to grow their hair long in defiance of the Indians' scalp-removing tradition. Louisa relented, and before he journeyed back to the Fifth Cavalry she tailored the first of the fringed and beaded buckskin jackets, which made him look even more picturesque.

The next time she saw him he would be something of a celebrity, which is to say a more complex man, and their marriage would never be the same. Soon enough she would find herself sharing her husband's affections with other women, a situation she would not suffer gladly or silently.

His brief immersion in family life apparently did not have a particularly sobering effect. Shortly after he reported to General Carr, the Fifth was ordered to Fort McPherson, Nebraska, with Cody and the equally bibulous Major W. H. Brown in charge of one detachment on the march. One day they left their cavalry troop to go to the nearest town and buy supplies for the cook wagon. They returned late that night in hilarious condition. Next morning the cook informed them that the only provender they brought back to camp was a five-gallon demijohn of brandy and two cases of Old Tom Cat gin.

3

Idylls of the Border King

THAT autumn, 1869, after the Fifth Cavalry and Major North's Pawnee scouts tracked down and severely punished Chief Tall Bull's band, Will Cody was discovered by Ned Buntline, and the fame-making machinery, not yet supplied with Madison Avenue techniques, began work on the product to be known evermore as Buffalo Bill. There was need for a new Western hero to keep the image of Western exploitation alluring; someone to replace Daniel Boone, Davy Crockett, and the late Kit Carson. The presses of Street & Smith's pulp magazines and of Beadle & Adams Dime Library were waiting to go on overtime to produce such works as *Buffalo Bill and His Daring Adventures in the Romantic Wild West* by Nebraska Ned, *The Dread Shot Four, or My Pards of the Plains* by (supposedly) Buffalo Bill, and Ned Buntline's effusions, not to mention the first of 203 Buffalo Bill novels turned out by Colonel Prentiss Ingraham, the most prolific of all the hacks engaged in the glorification industry.

A hero of imposing stature was particularly needed at the time because certain aspects of the Western drama were beginning to make the Eastern public suspect that something more than high adventure and the noble tasks of civilization were involved.

In May, 1869, the Union Pacific and the Central Pacific were joined in Utah by the rather symbolic golden spike. Already some people were beginning to suspect a golden spike had been driven into the national honor, especially after the holding company of the Union Pacific, Credit Mobilier, organized by financial and political insiders including a future President and three Vice Presidents of the United States, had somehow passed a 100-percent dividend. A lot of skeletons began rattling in their closets in Washington and on Wall Street, and soon the electorate would learn that $44,000,000 had been siphoned off the construction costs of the Union Pacific alone, all at the cost of the U.S. Treasury and the stockholders. Then, too, certain Eastern humanitarian groups were beginning to be organized on behalf of more liberal treatment of the Indians. Aside from such qualms and doubts, the American public was becoming more fascinated daily by the West and the illusory golden aura it cast; the railroad and the telegraph, not to mention the roving correspondents of the Eastern newspapers (Henry M. Stanley first gained attention by interviewing Wild Bill Hickok), were bringing the Wild West closer to the ordinary man. Everything printed about the Indian wars and the heroism of the border men found an eager readership. It served as an antidote to the national fatigue and depression still lingering after the Civil War; how much more salutary to read of whites from North and South united in decimating the redskins than slaughtering each other over the emancipation of the black men.

Fortunately for the makers of the Buffalo Bill myth, the reading public was less skeptical than today's. For one thing, there was a mass of people who could read and write—just barely. The semiliterates heavily outnumbered those with a full understanding of what they read and provided a huge market for the ten-penny dreadfuls and the burgeoning daily newspapers which tried to outdo the pulps in sensationalism. Such a readership demanded stainless heroes and deep-dyed villains and refused to distinguish the gray areas of human conduct such as they could observe in daily life; they wanted bravery unqualified by doubt and plenty of gore on every page. It was also necessary that a hero be Anglo-Saxon, preferably blond and blue-eyed; few people realized that the Ninth and Tenth Cavalry regiments were all-black except for the officers, though they were among the most efficient fighting forces on the frontier; the role of blacks in subduing the Indians was played down then as much as it is now, but for different reasons.

William Frederick Cody qualified, though he was half Irish (the "fighting Irish" were also becoming part of the American legend). Even without the embellishments of Buntline and his successors, he was brave and good, modest in demeanor (when sober), kind to children. What he really did was enough to qualify him, even though there were men like Major Frank North who were more qualified. Yet from the beginning his legend, like an avalanche, rolled up and swept along the detritus of other legends.

In Buntline's *Buffalo Bill: The King of the Border Men*— the pattern for everything else written about him, including Cody's various autobiographies—he was portrayed as fighting "Jack McKandkess, the border ruffian," and his gang and wiping them out with a bowie knife. This was a barefaced plagiarism from the legend of Wild Bill Hickok—the episode, greatly enhanced in the telling, that made Hickok famous on the frontier. In 1861 Hickok was a stock tender at a Russell, Majors & Waddell stagecoach station in Nebraska when he became involved in feuding with a violent Southerner named Dave McCanles and his quarrelsome family. One day Hickok shot and killed McCanles from behind a curtain and mortally wounded two of McCanles' friends. It was surprising how many celebrated gunfighters preferred not to meet their enemies face to face and how many of their obscure victims died with a bullet or a shotgun blast in the back.

But there was also more serious expropriation of other men's deeds than the borrowing from the Hickok anthology. Buntline credited Cody with having killed Chief Tall Bull, even though Cody had not even accompanied the Fifth Cavalry expedition that resulted in the death of the chief and 68 of his followers. Cody not only acquiesced in taking the credit for killing Tall Bull but in various accounts compounded the felony.

In the ultimate version of his autobiography, published posthumously, he related that he pursued Tall Bull, rode around him, and lay in wait for the chief in a ravine. "It occurred to me that if I dismounted and crept up the ravine, I could, as he passed, easily drop him from the saddle with no fear of hitting the horse. Accordingly I crept into the ravine and secreted myself there to wait till Mr. Chief came riding by. When he was not more than thirty yards away I fired. The next instant he tumbled from the saddle, and the horse kept on his way without a rider. . . ."

Carelessly enough, in other versions he or his ghost-writers variously asserted that Cody killed Tall Bull "at a range of fully four hundred yards," that he rode up to Tall Bull and stabbed him with a long knife. Even more incredibly, in one account, he pictured himself "entertaining the chief's wife and family at tea" after the battle was over and asserted that Mrs. Tall Bull "esteemed it quite an honor that her husband, a great warrior himself, should have met his death at my hands."

The oddest part about all this was that Major Frank North, the real killer of Chief Tall Bull, apparently never resented the theft of whatever glory there was in the deed. No doubt this was a tribute to the overpowering geniality of the Buffalo Bill persona. Later he and Cody were partners in a ranch, and still later Major North accepted a co-starring role in Buffalo Bill's Wild West Show. Day after day, smiling sardonically perhaps, he stood by and watched Cody "reenact" the killing of Tall Bull as part of the program. His brother Lute North later told a writer that he did not learn until three years after the event that Cody was claiming credit for the deed, by which time Cody had become an actor of sorts. "When I first heard it," he said, "I resented it and said to Frank, 'Why don't you correct that?' He just laughed and said, 'I am not in the show business.' "

It was going too far, though, when Ned Buntline pictured Cody as a pious member of the Cold Water Army, who took time out from rescuing pioneer women and golden-haired tots from the rampaging redskins to pause and deliver homilies on the evils of drink. Apparently Buntline had so many temperance lectures stored in his head that he simply had to discharge some of them through the mouth of his new hero.

"There is more fight, more headache—aye, more heartache in one rum bottle than there is in all the water that ever sparkled in God's bright sunlight," Cody was quoted as saying. "And I, for the sake of my dear brothers and sisters, and for the sweet, trusting heart that throbs alone for me, intend to let the rum go where it belongs, and that is not down my throat, at any rate."

Nor was Cody, as distinguished from Buffalo Bill, the law-and-order fanatic pictured by his idol makers.

Late in 1869, when unknowingly he was poised on the threshold of fame and fortune, the Fifth Cavalry was sent into winter quarters and Cody and the other scouts were severed from the Army payroll. It looked like a hard winter, with the only employment available "shooting for the pot"— that is, for the family larder. He built a cabin on a stretch of prairie near Fort McPherson, Nebraska, and sent for his wife and daughter, as well as his two younger sisters. There, the following year, his son, Kit Carson Cody, was born.

Until he established himself on a larger ranch, Cody spent his vacations on the spread, and there he once harbored a fugitive from justice, a rather serious offense even in those haphazard days, but it was all in keeping with the code of the West. Helping a friend was more important than any legal niceties; the rule of law could await better days. It all came about when the younger brother of Ben Thompson, the

notorious Texas gunfighter and gambler, shot a citizen of
Ogallala, Nebraska, and the townspeople proposed to stretch
Billy Thompson's neck without waiting to impanel a jury.
Ben Thompson had once saved the life of Bat Masterson,
former buffalo hunter and presently the sheriff of the county
in which Dodge City, Kansas, was located. He collected on
that debt by asking Sheriff Masterson to go to Ogallala and
rescue Billy from the lynch rope.

Masterson, who was also a friend of Cody's, found Billy
Thompson suffering from a bullet wound and being kept
under guard at a hotel in Ogallala. He rescued Billy by brib-
ing the guard and spiriting him away on a westbound train
leaving Ogallala at midnight. They traveled as far as North
Platte, where Cody was waiting with a spring wagon to drive
them to his ranch house. The fugitive was harbored on the
Cody spread until he recovered from his wound a month
later.

Intimations of immortality began occurring to Will Cody,
now more widely known as Buffalo Bill, thanks to Ned Buntline's exertions, in the spring of 1870. His name was becoming known throughout the Eastern states, but fame was not
at the moment a paying proposition.

With two sisters, a wife, a child (and another on the way)
as his responsibility, Cody scratched out a living through various pursuits. He kept the larder filled with the wild game he
shot, took on an occasional piecework scouting mission for
the forces garrisoning Fort McPherson, and served as justice
of the peace of the town of McPherson. In the latter post, he
said, he regarded his 50-caliber rifle "the best writ of replevin
I can think of." Justice as administered by Judge Cody was
evidently of the rough-and-ready sort, with little guidance
sought from Blackstone. In the case of a horse theft, the mag-
istrate went out and recovered the horse and collared the
thief. After levying a $20 fine, he recalled, "I pocketed the
$20 of course. Some people might think it was not a square
way of doing business, but I didn't know any better just

then." Once he was called upon to preside over the marriage of a sergeant at Fort McPherson, a job for which he braced himself by "imbibing rather freely of stimulants." By that time, obviously, he had begun reading his own publicity, for he ended the ceremony with the words, "I now pronounce you to be man and wife, and whomsoever God and Buffalo Bill have joined together let no man put asunder."

Already on his way to becoming the great American folk hero of the nineteenth and part of the twentieth centuries, he still had to piece together a living for himself and his family by taking any sort of job that offered itself. Late in 1870 he acted as guide for Professor Othniel Charles Marsh of Yale University, who wanted to hunt for fossils with a party of other scientists and twenty-five Yale undergraduates in the badlands of the Big Horn Basin of Wyoming. The Army arranged for horses and Cody's services. A year or two before members of Major North's Pawnee scout battalion had unearthed the fossilized bones of huge prehistoric animals in the Big Horn Basin. At the moment the basin was a sort of Shangri-La unknown to settlement because of its shelter behind the Big Horn Mountains to the east and the Wind River Mountains to the west.

In between watching Professor Marsh and his colleagues digging up old bones with a paleontologist's zeal, Cody listened carefully when Marsh prophesied that the Big Horn Basin would be the last great Western area to be settled but that its fertility would one day make it prosperous. Years later, with the passage of the Carey Irrigation Act, 1,000,000 acres of Wyoming land was thrown open to claimants. Using his influence to the utmost, Cody obtained a 200,000-acre tract in the basin, established the town of Cody, Wyoming, along the line of the proposed irrigation canal, and in 1896 located the route of a wagon road to be built into what became Yellowstone National Park.

All that aggrandizement was far in the future, however, and Cody was still teetering on the knife edge between poverty and respectability. Meanwhile prosperity, though as yet unglimpsed, was just around the corner. The West was now regarded as civilized enough for Easterners, known west of the Mississippi as dudes or tenderfeet, to venture out West in search of sport and adventure. A man wealthy and well connected enough could arrange a hunting party well guarded by soldiers and with all the comforts of home laid on. Even humbler travelers could take a crack at the buffalo, a huge and lumbering target that even a cross-eyed astigmatic could hardly miss. Pot-shooting at buffalo from train windows was, in fact, one of the joys of Western travel. As a roving journalist described the scenes from sporting life out West, "All over the plains, lying in disgusting masses of putrefaction along valley and hill, are strewn immense carcasses of wantonly slain buffalo. . . . Probably the most cruel of all bison-shooting pasttimes is that of firing from the [railroad] cars. During certain periods of the spring and fall, when the large herds are crossing the Kansas Pacific Railroad, the trains run for a hundred miles or more among countless thousands of the shaggy monarchs of the plains. The rate per mile of passenger trains is slow upon the plains, and hence it often happens that the cars and buffalo will be side by side for a mile or two. . . . During these races the car windows are opened, and numerous breechloaders fling hundreds of bullets among the densely crowded and flying masses. Many of the poor animals fall, and more go off to die in the ravines. The train speeds on, and the scene is repeated every few miles until Buffalo Land is passed."

Real sportsmen, society gentlemen from New York and titled gentry from Europe, wanted to taste the real thing, shoot from horseback, mingle with uncurried plainsmen, rub up against the wild and woolly, and patronize a few tame Indians. It soon became the in-thing to "rough it" in style, and in the early 1870's a number of glamorous caravans wended westward from the railheads, providing the new sensation for jaded aristocrats of sipping iced champagne while taking in the splendor of a prairie sunset. Long after those wine-laden wagons stopped trundling, General H. E. Davies, who to his displeasure was required by orders from the War Department to outfit and protect a number of the hunting parties, remarked that their campsites were marked for years afterward by a litter of empty champagne bottles. An archeologist exploring the West in some future century, thought General Davies, might guess that the plains were once inhabited by a race which occupied itself with the ritual of drinking out of "black vases bearing the names of Mumm or Roederer."

Cody's friendly rival, Wild Bill Hickok, got into the dude-guiding business first, earning a $500 fee for escorting Senator Henry Wilson, soon to be Vice President, and a party of friends from Washington on a tour of the prairies west of Hays City.

An old patron, General Sheridan, at the same time was trying to arrange a similar expedition with Cody in charge of the entertainment. He was certain that Cody could outflash and outtalk the rather reticent Hickok and provide more spectacular entertainment. Between campaigns, when Indians were out of season, General Sheridan indulged in high living at his mansion in Chicago, nominally his headquarters as commander on the Western frontier, and swanking around the White House and the society resorts on the Atlantic shore. Rich food, as General Crook acidly commented, had fattened the cavalry leader until he "looked like a low comedian" from the side view. General Grant was now President and habitually surrounded himself with the railroad tycoons, industrial magnates, and Wall Street speculators who found his administration so congenial to their interests—the same men, in fact, who were profiting so enormously from the exploitation of the West.

Among those whom Sheridan met at the summer White House on the shore at Long Branch, New Jersey, was James Gordon Bennett, Jr., the publisher of the New York *Herald*. Bennett was a spoiled young man but had inherited from his father not only the *Herald* but an instinct for the newsworthy. For several years he had sent correspondents West to cover the Indian campaigns and interview the leading figures of the border fighting. Now he wanted to have a look for himself; even more, he was determined to meet the fabulous Buffalo Bill he had been reading so much about. Sheridan agreed to arrange a buffalo-hunting expedition, courtesy of the U.S. Army, with Buffalo Bill acting as guide. Their plans were delayed in the summer of 1870 when President Grant dispatched Sheridan to Europe as observer of the Franco-Prussian War.

When the general returned to the United States during the following summer, he immediately began making arrangements for a hunting party to include what one New York newspaper (not the *Herald*) called the "fastest society set." He made the wires crackle with orders that nothing be spared to make the expedition as luxurious as possible. Cody accepted the invitation to take charge of what he later called "a nobby and high-toned outfit." Various post commanders were alerted, and Army quartermasters from Chicago to Hays City were urged to provide every comfort. The Fifth Cavalry, then stationed at Fort McPherson, was commanded to provide protection with as many troopers as were regarded necessary. No one thought to question the propriety of temporarily turning the U.S. Army's Department of the Missouri into a tourist agency for the benefit of General Sheridan and his friends.

One morning in mid-September, 1871, a special train pulled out of Grand Central Station in New York with Sheridan's party aboard. It included Leonard and Lawrence Jerome, venturesome speculators on Wall Street and leaders of fashion (Leonard Jerome's daughter became the mother of Sir Winston Churchill); James Gordon Bennett, Jr., their closest friend and commodore of the New York Yacht Club; Anson Stager of Western Union; Charles Wilson, editor of the Chicago *Journal*; J. G. Hecksher, Carrol Livingston, J. Schuyler Crosby, M. Edward Rogers, and Quartermaster General John J. Rucker, General Sheridan's future father-in-law.

Waiting at Fort McPherson when the party detrained was

a supply train, including sixteen wagons to haul the tents and supplies and two wagons to carry ice for the wine, not to mention a hundred troopers of the Fifth Cavalry assigned to make sure no Indians unsportingly tried to interfere with the excursion.

And there was Buffalo Bill in full regalia to greet them at the station. He well understood that he had a dramatic role to play, that of the picturesque plainsman, and he was more than adequately costumed for the part. The visitors were dazzled at the gorgeous sight: Buffalo Bill mounted on a snow-white horse chosen because he was a "gallant stepper." He wore a white buckskin suit that Mrs. Cody had made for him, a crimson shirt, and a big sombrero.

The Nebraska prairie had never seen such a procession as left Fort McPherson with 100 troopers fanning out to flush any lurking hostiles. At the head rode General Sheridan, followed by his guests and the orderlies who would act as gun bearers and camp servants. They were followed by four ambulance wagons to carry the weapons and accommodate any members of the party who wearied of riding. The supply wagons with food, wine, and ice followed.

Two days out, near Medicine Creek, the first buffalo were sighted and all the Easterners banged away, with predictable results. Several days later they crossed the Republican River and found a larger herd. Scores of buffalo were slain and left to rot, lumpishly giving up their lives as a booster shot to the masculinity of the Easterners.

Buffalo Bill was not only a great success as a guide, but at night around the campfire he was the star attraction. The Easterners listened avidly to his discourses on the habits of wild game, on his adventures as a hunter and scout, and thought him the greatest fellow alive.

Socially he shone so brilliantly that the visitors were certain that he would be a smash hit in Eastern drawing rooms. He was a wild Westerner, all right, but had decent enough manners for polite society. He was capable of domestication.

What a pet he would make for New York society, at least for a season or two. James Gordon Bennett, as ripe a character as New York society or journalism would ever dredge up, the man who participated in the last recorded duel in the United States, was especially taken by the gregarious plainsman. One night around the campfire he was seized by an inspiration. The party had just dined long and well on a menu which included:

Buffalo tail soup
Broiled Cisco; Fried Dace
Salmi of prairie dog; stewed rabbit; Filet of buffalo
aux champignons
Sweet potatoes, mashed potatoes, green peas
Tapioca pudding
Champagne frappe, Champagne au naturel, claret,
whiskey, brandy and ale
Coffee

While they were all puffing away on Havana leaf and having a few snifters of brandy, Bennett broached the subject of Cody's coming East to be placed on view. And lionized. Or, possibly, buffaloized.

"Ever been East, Cody?" the sportive young publisher asked.

"Sure, I've been to Omaha."

"That's not East. I want you to come to New York."

"Not on your life, sir!"

"Why not?"

"I came near not to getting back," Cody explained, "when I went to Omaha. I got busted there."

"Don't worry about the expense," Bennett reassured him. "I want you to come."

Ever since childhood Bennett got what he wanted, and the plainsman was something like a new toy. Later in the evening he spoke to Sheridan about arranging a New York visit for Cody. Young Will was made. At the age of twenty-five he had come under the patronage of some of the most influential men in America. All he had to avoid was making some monstrous gaffe or insulting one of his eager benefactors.

The hunt ended with all the society gentlemen proclaiming themselves more than satisfied with the experience. They had had a fling at Western adventure without brushing against danger, they had slept warm and dined well, and now they could return to the Union Club and boast for many a year of having hunted and frolicked with Buffalo Bill in the untamed wilderness.

Undoubtedly they came closest to danger the last night when Cody provided a guided tour of Hays City, then one of the frontier Gomorrahs where the town marshal conducted a body count every morning before breakfast. "Hays City by lamplight," as a contemporary journalist described it, "was remarkably lively but not very moral." The saloons were filled with men not adverse to gunplay and "gaudily dressed women striving with paint and ribbons to hide the awful lines which dissipation had drawn on their faces. These terrible marks were not confined to the women, for many of the men had noses painted cherry-red by whiskey. To the music of violins and the stamping of feet the dance went on, and we saw in the giddy maze old men who must have been pirouetting on the very edge of their graves. . . . Disturbances were frequent in all of them, and these were usually settled with six-shooters. . . ."

The visitors survived Hays City by lamplight, and their special train had hardly disappeared down the tracks when it occurred to Cody that dude nursing for fun and profit could be a lot more lucrative, and certainly less hazardous, than scouting for the cavalry. Thus he caught the first wave of Western tourism.

Shortly after Sheridan's party had left he took out a New Yorker named McCarthy and several of his wealthy English friends. Since McCarthy was related to General W. H. Emory, then in command of Fort McPherson, the group was provided with a cavalry escort of three companies plus Frank North and a company of the Pawnee scouts.

For McCarthy, at least, Cody provided an unsought thrill, an insight into Western humor, which tended toward the violent practical joke. He persuaded Major North to take his Pawnee scouts and lay in ambush along the banks of a creek about eight miles out of camp. Cody led McCarthy and the Indians to the place on the pretense of looking for game. The Pawnees suddenly appeared, howling like demons, flapping their red blankets, and waving their scalping knives.

"Shall we run or fight?" Cody shouted to McCarthy.

McCarthy wheeled his horse and fled at the gallop back toward the camp. Cody tried to catch up with him and explain that it was all a prank, but McCarthy continued his flight at full tilt. Now the joke had turned inside out. General Carr was back at the camp, and Cody knew he would be alarmed by McCarthy's report of an Indian ambush. Cody hurried back to camp himself and arrived just as General Carr was preparing to lead two troops of cavalry out on a rescue mission. General Carr, who could recall several other instances of Cody's fun-loving tendency, "was fond of a joke himself and did not get very angry."

A short time later Cody played white-hunter for an English sportsman, Lord Flynn, who had been sent along by General Sheridan. It was obvious that his lordship knew how to live. One night they found they had drunk the camp dry and rode thirty miles to the nearest water hole. The only saloon in town was closed, but Lord Flynn awakened the proprietor and bought the place for $500. After he and Cody had slaked their thirsts, Lord Flynn presented the saloon to one of Cody's assistant guides.

The English nobility, it was apparent, took to Cody's breezy personality. The Earl of Dunraven and his lady had come out West to hunt and liked the atmosphere so much they built a ranch house on the prairie. One day the Earl and Lady Dunraven came calling on the Codys after spending the morning out on the hunt with Will and some of the Pawnee scouts. Meanwhile Mrs. Cody, flustered by the social event of the season at Fort McPherson, was cooking sage chicken and antelope and baking pies and cakes for dinner.

Mrs. Cody left her steaming kitchen to greet her guests, unaware that her husband had invited the Pawnees to go around the back and help themselves to some food. Cody was boasting of what a superb dinner Mrs. Cody would serve them. His wife excused herself to return to the kitchen. Then, as she later recalled, "I opened the kitchen door, to stand a moment aghast, then to rush forward in white anger, seize the big coffee pot and slosh the whole contents of it across the room. For where dinner had been was now only a mass of messy, mussed over dishes. The kitchen was full of Pawnees! And the Pawnees were full of the dinner that had been cooked for royalty!" Mrs. Cody then attacked with a broomstick and drove the Pawnees out of her kitchen. There was nothing to do but take the Dunravens over to Fort McPherson and dine at the officers' mess.

Buffalo Bill's greatest touristic and social triumph—one publicized in newspapers through the country—was still to come. Late in 1871 the Grand Duke Alexis of Russia, the handsome young third son of the reigning czar, arrived in New York aboard one of the warships of a Russian Imperial Navy squadron on a goodwill mission. New York society flung itself en masse at the grand duke's feet; some sturdy republicans complained that it "groveled" before a scion of the despotic Romanovs. But the enthusiasm for Alexis was more widespread than that. The Russian Empire and the American democracy then were engaged in a passionate love affair. Alone of the European powers, Russia had demonstrated its sympathy for the Union during the Civil War. Two years later the United States had grandly relieved Russia of its burdensome and expensive colony of Alaska and generously paid Russia $7,000,000 to boot. Russian gratitude was being expressed through the grand duke's visit.

Alexis was a trifle more venturesome than most Romanovs

and was fascinated by accounts he had heard and read of one Buffalo Bill, particularly the tales told over dinner tables by General Sheridan and others who had gone hunting with Cody. Nothing, Alexis told Sheridan, would please him more than a buffalo hunt with the celebrated plainsman.

Sheridan went into action immediately and dropped plans for the ducal junket only temporarily when he had to hasten to Chicago and oversee the martial law imposed on that city after the Great Fire. By early January, 1872, however, preparations were going forward at speed. Half the general officers west of the Mississippi seemed to have been enlisted to ensure the comfort and safety of the grand duke and his retinue on their excursion. Sheridan kept the wires humming with orders to General John Pope, commander of the Department of the Missouri, to send daily reports on the movement of the Southern buffalo herd; to General George W. Forsyth to take charge of the commissary; to General John Palmer to assume direct charge of the travel arrangements; to Omaha Barracks to convert itself into the supply base for the hunting expedition.

In addition to Buffalo Bill, there would be another native star attraction. The grand duke wanted to see some Indians close-up. So Cody was detailed to select a tame and cooperative chief to provide local color; his choice was the Sioux Spotted Tail, who had been accounted a "friendly" for some time and presumably would not be tempted to lift Alexis' luxuriant black-haired scalp. "By way of giving their distinguished guest a real taste of the Plains," as Cody related, two members of Sheridan's staff "asked me to visit the camp of the Sioux chief, Spotted Tail, and ask him to bring a hundred of his warriors to the spot on Red Willow Creek, which, at my suggestion, had been selected as the Grand Duke's camp."

Without lingering over the irony of the Indians' being forbidden to hunt buffalo while a Russian princeling was handed the privilege on a silver platter, Cody further explained, "Spotted Tail had permission from the Government to hunt buffalo, a privilege that could not be granted to Indians indiscriminately, as it involved the right to carry and use firearms. You couldn't always be sure just what kind of game an Indian might select when you gave him a rifle. It might be buffalo, or it might be a white man. But Spotted Tail was safe and sane. Hence the trust that was reposed in him."

One day early in January, 1872, the grand duke and his retinue arrived at North Platte in the Pullman cars of their special train. General Sheridan and Buffalo Bill, gorgeous as always on such occasions, were there to meet them. They continued on to Denver, where a formal ball was given for Alexis by the newly rich of that city to whom only recently a Saturday night hoedown in a mining camp had been a glittering social event. About midnight a courier arrived with a telegram, the music stopped, and there was a hush of expectancy over the ballroom. A buffalo herd had been sighted in Kit Carson County, Colorado. That ended the festivities. The grand duke, his retinue, and his American guides, all in formal dress, streaked for the railroad station. Overwrought journalists later described the scene as something like the ball at Waterloo when the British officers were informed that Napoleon and the Grand Army were approaching.

The whole American nation, it was asserted, was holding its breath until Grand Duke Alexis dropped his first buffalo; Russo-American amity was imperiled until Buffalo Bill maneuvered the czar's son into position for the kill. As the party traveled on horseback toward Red Willow Creek, it was noted that the grand duke was casting "frequent and admiring" glances at the "handsome redskin maiden" who accompanied Spotted Tail's daughter in the procession. Apparently Alexis had another sort of kill in mind. Certainly his mind wasn't on the hunt when Buffalo Bill guided him to the fringe of the buffalo herd. The grand duke, mounted on Cody's favorite horse, fired six revolver shots at a bull and missed each time; Cody reloaded for him, and six more shots went wild. "I saw that he was pretty sure to come home empty-handed if he continued this sort of pistol practice,"

Cody said, so he urged Alexis to ride in closer to the herd and use a rifle next time. "At the same time I gave Buckskin Joe [the duke's borrowed mount] a cut with my whip which sent him at a furious gallop to within ten feet of one of the biggest bulls in the herd. 'Now is your time,' I shouted to Alexis. He fired and down went the buffalo."

Great was the rejoicing. General Sheridan had been watching through field glasses from a nearby hill and dictated a telegram to the Secretary of War: "The Grand Duke killed his first buffalo today in a manner which elicited the admiration of the party with me." By nightfall the bulletin was published in newspapers throughout the United States.

At General Sheridan's order the camp servants broke out a case of champagne and the grand duke was toasted repeatedly. That night Chinese lanterns were strung on the trees around the campsite and a gala dinner celebrated the grand duke's feat. The *pièce de résistance* was a slab of the hump from Alexis' victim.

The Russians took to the sport with Muscovite relish, and presently, as Cody observed, "we saw them galloping madly over the prairie in all directions, with terrified buffalo flying before them."

The grand duke, however, was proving a trifle stubborn, or behaving like a Romanov, on one point. Experienced hunters knew that it was impossible to bring down a buffalo, with its thick hide and matted fur, with a revolver. But Alexis kept insisting that it would be more sporting to kill a buffalo with his little pistol. Cody even managed to bring that off with a little help from the Indians. While Alexis banged away with his pistol, Cody stationed a warrior named Two Lance to bring down the target with his bow and arrow.

Before the three-day hunt was over, Grand Duke Alexis managed to bump off eight buffalo. Impartial observers believed he enjoyed his flirtation with the Indian maiden even more, but history does not record how he made out with her, understanding as little of Sioux as she did of Russian.

Alexis was so pleased by his various adventures that he invited Cody to share a few bottles of champagne on his private car before returning to New York. He summoned one of his aides, who broke out a roll of greenbacks and presented it to Buffalo Bill. The latter, with an instinctive grasp of *noblesse oblige,* shook his head and refused the gratuity. Instead he accepted a tiny jeweled box and the grand duke's own fur coat. In addition, before he left New York, Alexis commissioned Tiffany's to fashion a set of cuff links and a tiepin studded with diamonds and rubies, each as big as a half dollar and shaped like a buffalo head.

Buffalo Bill was now a household name in America, in various stately old homes in England, and in the Winter Palace at St. Petersburg.

The question was how to cash in on that celebrity; the answer was not long in coming.

4

A Social Lion in New York

THE "Millionaires' Hunting Party," as Cody called the first high-class expedition he led, had not forgotten its promise to entertain him in New York. Shortly after he had conducted the Grand Duke Alexis on the buffalo hunt, he received a railroad pass, $500 in cash, and a spray of invitations from Bennett, the Jeromes, and their friends. Along with them was a note from his chief patron, General Sheridan, declaring, "You will never have a better opportunity than now. . . ."

Just what opportunity the general was referring to he did not make clear. Making Buffalo Bill a folk hero, converting him into the paradigm of the happier aspects of the Western conquest, was not the result of an organized conspiracy, but the general and his wealthy friends must have had *something* in mind. They all had a joint interest in persuading the American people to accept the brutalities and injustices generically known as "winning the West." Aside from all that—perhaps more than that—they wanted to put Cody on exhibition, with themselves ranged alongside of him and basking in his reflected glory. There is pleasure and credit in lionizing as well as being lionized.

Cody did not hesitate over accepting the invitation. In the year since the publication of Ned Buntline's first essay in hagiography, he knew, there had been three follow-up sequels from Buntline's tireless hand: *Buffalo Bill's Best Shot, or the Heart of Spotted Tail,* followed by *Buffalo Bill's Last Victory, or Dove Eye, The Lodge Queen* and *Hazel Eye, The Girl Trapper.* And the literary assembly line known as Prentiss Ingraham was revving up to top even Buntline's production. There were rumors, too, of a play about to be produced with Buffalo Bill as its central figure.

Mrs. Cody later pictured him as being reluctant to leave her and the kiddies and their little gray home in the West. This may be put down to the sentimentality of widowhood. Actually Will was never reluctant to tear himself away from Louisa, her hypercritical attitude toward his "sprees," and her rigid ideas of how a husband should behave, whether it was to hunt Indians or display himself in society. Despite the soggy prose, it is only fair to include her wifely view of Cody on his way to solidify his fame in New York. His buckskins, he realized, wouldn't do for the canyons of Chicago and New York. " 'Mamma,' he exclaimed woefully, 'I can't wear this rigout. I'll—I'll have to have something else.' With that started a feverish week for Mrs. Buffalo Bill. Hurriedly we procured some blue cloth at the commissary and, sewing day and night, I made Will his first real soldier suit, with a Colonel's braid on it, with stripes and cords and all the other gingerbread of an old-fashioned suit of 'blues'; dear, patient, boyish Will sitting anxiously to one side, then rising to try on the partially completed garment, getting pins stuck in him, squirming and twisting, then sitting down again to wait for another fitting.

"More than once as he waited his eyes would grow wistful, and there would come a peculiar downward pull to his lips, as he stared out the window into the faraway. 'Mamma,' he would say time after time, 'I wish you were going along with me. I'm going to be scared as a jackrabbit back there. I wish you were going along.' " As Mrs. Cody coyly put it, there was a "beautiful little reason" why she couldn't go along and why he was safe in being wistful: She was pregnant with their third child, a daughter to be named Orra.

On his way to New York Cody stopped off in Chicago, where he was met by General Sheridan's brother, Colonel Michael V. Sheridan, and escorted to the general's mansion on Michigan Avenue. It was obvious that Sheridan was doing right well on a general officer's pay. Cody was overcome by the splendor with which his friend surrounded himself. "Never before had I seen such vast rooms and such wonderful furnishings. It was necessary to show me how the gas was turned on and off, and how the water flowed in the bathroom."

While Cody was recovering from witnessing the miracle of indoor plumbing, his host was eyeing the plainsman's homemade uniform with concealed dismay. General Sheridan was a West Pointer and did not take readily to the idea of a man rigging himself out as a full colonel when he wasn't even a member of the armed forces. Technically, it was his duty to summon a squad from the provost marshal's office and have Cody arrested for impersonating an officer. Instead, with unusual tact, he suggested that since Cody would be the honored guest at a formal ball that evening he would require more formal dress. Cody was then persuaded to accompany Michael Sheridan to Marshall Field's department store to be outfitted with evening dress.

It was still apparent to the Sheridans that Cody would need some currying before he was thoroughly presentable in polite society, though undoubtedly his exuberant manner would appeal to many as picturesque and authentically Wild Western. With his white tie and tails, Cody insisted on wearing a Stetson and refused to allow a barber to shear off his shoulder-length hair. Cody instinctively knew what he was doing. Barbered, manicured, and adorned with a silk hat, he would have looked like any other dude. What these effete Easterners wanted, he realized, was a touch of the real thing.

Convoyed by the Sheridans, he made his strikingly hand-

some appearance at the Riverside Hotel ballroom that evening. By his own account, his immersion in Chicago society
—so lately improvised by meat packers and their imperious
wives—was not entirely successful. Getting the hang of Eastern customs, as he said, wasn't easy. "When I was escorted in,
I was told to give the colored boy my hat and coat. To this I
violently objected. I prized the coat [the one presented by
Grand Duke Alexis] beyond all my earthly possessions and
intended to take no chances with it. I was finally persuaded
that the colored boy was a responsible employe of the hotel.
. . . Then I suffered myself to be led into the ballroom.
Here I met a bevy of the most beautiful women I had ever
seen. . . . I knew no dances but square dances, so they got up
an old-fashioned quadrille for me and I managed to go
through it. As soon as it was over, I hurriedly escorted my
fair partner to her seat, then I quickly made my way to the
barroom. The man behind the bar appreciated my plight.
He stowed me away in a corner behind the icebox and in
that corner I remained for the rest of the evening."

Cody was so discouraged that he wanted to return to Fort
McPherson, but General Sheridan firmly tut-tutted him and
placed him on the train for New York the next morning.

And New York, despite the hospitality and enthusiasm
with which he was received, was even more bewildering. The
Gilded Age, as Mark Twain called it, had just dawned and
the city had entered an epoch of conspicuous spending, of
uninhibited vulgarity that would continue, with a few sobering interruptions, until the 1920's. There were new millionaires all over the place, the postwar boom was roaring
on, and an amorality new to the American scene accepted
such diversions as the cancan imported from wicked Paris
and *The Black Crook,* with girls flouncing around in black
tights. For the masses there were dime museums, cheap
music halls, prize fights, theaters in which the scale of admissions was ten-twenty-thirty cents.

Buffalo Bill was greeted on his arrival with as much ceremony as, or more than, a mining magnate from the mother

lode country. He was met at the station by two of his millionaire hunting companions, Schuyler Crosby and J. G.
Hecksher, and driven in a carriage to the Union Club. His
hosts disapproved of his Chicago tailoring and took him to
their own tailor's for a complete wardrobe.

For the next five or six weeks he was wined and dined by
his Union Club friends—Commodore Bennett, the Jeromes,
and the others—and was constantly placed on exhibition.
Reporters tagged after him, interviewed him repeatedly, and
filled the columns of the New York newspapers with his picturesque comments. Society hostesses lionized him as a thrilling specimen of the Natural Man—so tall and strong, so win-
ningly handsome, so enthralling as he modestly recounted
how he had taken on whole tribes with his gun, knife, and
bare hands—and so much in contrast to their own
pot-bellied, slack-muscled husbands. Cody was so incompara-
bly the social prize of the season that he had difficulty escap-
ing from his Union Club friends, who insisted on trotting
him around town and exhibiting him much as a Sioux warrior would show off his belt full of scalps. With good grace
he accompanied James Gordon Bennett to a performance of
The Black Crook, and with considerably less interest he
watched Edwin Booth thundering through the role of Julius
Caesar. Whenever he attended the theater, a spotlight would
be focused on the box he was occupying with his friends and
he would be given a standing ovation.

Naturally he reveled in all the attention he was getting,
though secretly he must have wondered just how he had
been singled out as the epitome of all that was valiant about
the Western frontier. It must have been Irish luck that
brought him to the attention of Ned Buntline, General Sheridan, and all his other patrons. Not being a religious hypocrite on the order of certain millionaires who were convinced
that their good fortune was a God-given reward for pious attendance at church one day a week, he managed to keep a
sense of proportion about suddenly having become a celebrity. He was keenly aware of the fact that his pocket money

came from other men, that without their patronage he could not even have made the trip, and that while he was living at the most fashionable men's club in New York and being the guest of honor at the lordly table of August Belmont, his wife, children, and sisters were making out as best they could in a prairie cabin. For all his flamboyance he was a practical man, and he must have been intensely concerned with the problem of converting his celebrity into something more substantial than newspaper headlines, garish book jackets, and social invitations. A standing ovation was flattering, but you still had to put down a nickel to buy a schooner of beer.

Cody must have been even more bemused when he visited Ned Buntline, who had established himself in style at the Brevoort Hotel on Fifth Avenue. Buntline was making a hell of a lot of money out of retailing the supposed adventures of W. F. Cody but at the moment was unable to suggest any way in which Buffalo Bill himself could cash in on his somewhat meretricious fame.

Buntline took him to see a performance of *Buffalo Bill, The King of the Border Men*, which had been dramatized from Buntline's stories by Fred G. Meader, at Niblo's Gardens in the Bowery. It was one of the hits of the season, and Cody could see for himself that somebody was finding profit in his legend, if a theater packed with paying customers was sound evidence.

He must have witnessed that performance with a turmoil of mixed emotions. The florid melodrama was about as realistic as *The Black Crook*, and Buffalo Bill was enacted by J. G. Studley with flourishes that would have got him tarred and feathered anywhere west of Kansas City. But New Yorkers swallowed it all and begged for more; metropolitan skepticism apparently was suspended for all events taking place west of the Hudson.

The critic of the New York *Herald* may have been influenced in his professional judgment by the pro-Cody prejudice of his employer, Commodore Bennett, but he had pronounced the melodrama "one of the most extraordinary and thrilling" ever produced in a New York theater. His review continued: "The laudable desire he [Buffalo Bill] exhibits to avenge the murder of his paternal ancestor and the coolness he displays when encompassed by dangers and difficulties is superb. Rounds of applause greeted him when, finding himself surrounded by Indians, he slipped like a snake into a hollow log; which log the redskins presently added as fuel to the campfire; but the trapper soon found it uncomfortably hot, so he threw his powder horn into the fire. There was a grand explosion and the Indians went yelling skyward, while the hero escaped unscathed. . . .

"This, as might be expected, was warmly applauded by the [gallery] 'gods,' but the highest pitch of excitement was reached in the third act when Jack McKandkess, a noted border ruffian, meets Buffalo Bill and a terrific hand-to-hand conflict with Bowie knives three feet long ensues. The audience was spellbound, breathless, during this fierce encounter; but when it was brought to a conclusion by the death of the villain and the victory of Buffalo Bill, the burst of enthusiasm that followed would have rivalled the roar of Niagara."

Obviously the core of Meader's dramatization was a barefaced plagiarism, following Buntline's story line, of the Wild Bill Hickok legend. It credited Cody with Hickok's murderous engagement with Dave McCanles and his supporters. Yet Cody did not rise from the seat in his box at Niblo's Gardens and denounce the performance as a pack of lies. (Nor did he mention seeing the play in his *Autobiography*, which may have been significant.) Instead he watched himself, in the person of J. G. Studley, swashbuckling through an arrant falsification of Western history and kept a modest but appreciative smile fixed on his face.

During the intermission a spotlight suddenly swiveled around and flooded the Buntline box with a blaze of light. Cody stood up and waved to the cheering audience, which insisted on a speech. He stumbled through a few awkward sentences, then sat down. Before the final curtain came down, the manager of Niblo's Gardens slipped into his box and offered him $500 a week if he would portray himself in the melodrama.

"You might as well try to make an actor out of a government mule," he told the manager.

Afterward, that first visit to New York, that first bitter-sweet taste of fame, that feeling of "thousands of eyes all staring at me," as he later recalled it, would have a dreamlike quality. There was something relentless about mass admiration, something like being made a human sacrifice. Everywhere there were avid faces, outstretched hands, demanding voices, as though his adoring public wanted to devour him— a feeling that decades later would be experienced by film stars and pop singers. Buffalo Bill was perhaps the first American idol to be made to realize that there is an element of cannibalism in mass adulation.

At least once, toward the end of his stay, he tried to escape from the devouring process. He had been invited to a dinner party by James Gordon Bennett, but "became badly demoralized and confused" on the way to the Bennett town house. What he meant was that he stopped off at a number of barrooms to brace himself for yet another encounter with the lion hunters. He showed up very late and more than a trifle unsteady, but Bennett's guests were enchanted by his explanation that he had "gone out on a scout and got lost." This only made him more colorful; he was behaving like the rowdy, rip-roaring boyo he was supposed to be.

He also lived up to his reputation when he attended the Liederkranz masked ball at the Academy of Music, which predated the Metropolitan Opera House. It was a high-toned affair, lavishly covered by the newspapers, and Buffalo Bill appearing in his buckskins attracted more attention, journalistic and otherwise, than any of the cotillion leaders and Fifth Avenue beldams. Knowing what was expected of him, he had begun swaggering through his role with greater assurance. At the height of the revelry, he later recalled, he "took part in the dancing and exhibited some of my backwoods steps, which, although not as graceful as some, were a great deal more emphatic." The climax of the ball, however, came when a pair of Russian bears appeared in the ballroom dragging a huge snowball behind them. The artificial snowball opened up to reveal a figure costumed as Grand Duke Alexis of Russia, whom Buffalo Bill strode over to embrace as the ballroom rocked with applause. Nobody had to nudge him. He had quickly learned how to make the grand, though meaningless, gesture. There was a sizable natural streak of ham in his character—of harmless exhibitionism, to be more precise—which he was beginning to enjoy exposing. Soon not even he would know where Will Cody left off and Buffalo Bill began, and in a minor variation of the Faustian theme he would trade his real self for a fabricated personality. The drawback to such transformations is, of course, that the subject surrenders reality for a series of images and postures. From all the evidence, however, no one got more pleasure out of the quasi-Faustian bargain than Will Cody/Buffalo Bill.

He was summoned away from the heady New York scene in suitably dramatic fashion. A telegram from General Sheridan arrived at the Union Club: He was urgently required to take over as chief scout for the Third Cavalry, commanded by Major General Joseph J. Reynolds, which had replaced the Fifth Cavalry on garrison duty at Fort McPherson. The Sioux had become obstreperous again, and an experienced scout was needed to guide the inexperienced Third Cavalry on a punitive expedition.

Before leaving the scene of his social triumphs, Cody hastily arranged a dinner party for his New York friends at Delmonico's, the most expensive restaurant in town. He had $50 left and reckoned that should be enough to pay the bill. When the tab was presented at the end of a vinous evening, it came to several hundred dollars. Greatly embarrassed, Cody had to borrow the money on the spot from Ned Buntline, who was one of his guests.

On his way back home, he was greeted in Omaha by about

fifty friends and well-wishers who had kept themselves well advised of his social triumphs in the big city. Since he had a twelve-hour wait between trains, they insisted on bearing him off to the Paxton Hotel and on his putting on full evening dress for their benefit. A claw hammer coat, with a stiff white shirt (not to mention the cuff links and scarf pin given him by Grand Duke Alexis), was still a thing of wonder in Omaha. Round after round of whiskey was ordered up. By train time Cody was so well oiled that he departed without his luggage but with a quart of rye on each hip and thus traveled to Fort McPherson in white tie and tails.

That frontier post had never been dazzled by such an apparition as a badly hungover Cody stumbled off the cars.

Waiting for him—the Third Cavalry having already trotted off to the westward—was an old friend and assistant scout named Buffalo Chips White, who was supposed to pick up Cody and take him to General Reynolds' advance base. There was a rather touching aspect to his friendship with Buffalo Chips White, who had served four years as a scout for Jeb Stuart's Confederate cavalry. When they first met, White was on crutches from an unhealed war wound and trying to obtain treatment at the Fort McPherson post hospital. The surgeons there told White they couldn't treat him because he had served with the enemy. Cody, however, used his influence to obtain treatment for the ex-enemy. Later, in gratitude, White looked after Cody's horses and acted as the Cody baby-sitter without pay. Eventually Cody got him on the Army payroll as a scout. "By this time," Cody said, "he had come to copy my gait, my dress, my speech, and even my fashion of wearing my hair down to my shoulders, though mine at that time was brown, and his was white as the driven snow."

At any rate, Cody in a tailcoat and a stovepipe hat (the latter having been forced on him by his New York friends) was ever afterward remembered as one of the more astonishing events in the history of the frontier army.

Many drinks later, he was finally persuaded to remember

his duty and accompany Buffalo Chips White on the trail of the Third Cavalry. There was no time to change into a more suitable costume, and besides that would have meant going home and facing Mrs. Buffalo Bill, who predictably would be much less amused by his now somewhat soiled elegance.

Late in the day he presented himself to General Reynolds looking less like a cavalry scout than a high-born wastrel just going home from an all-night binge.

Still a trifle exhilarated, he jumped off his mount, stalked up to General Reynolds, and smartly brought his right hand up to the brim of his stovepipe hat.

"General," he said, "I have come to report for duty."

"Who in thunder are you?"

He finally persuaded the regimental commander that he was indeed Chief Scout Cody and not Coal Oil Johnny. Climbing into a set of borrowed buckskins, he guided the command to a campsite on Loup Fork before nightfall. For the first time in six weeks he felt at home, with the cook fires blazing, the smell of beans and coffee, the sounds of cavalry bedding down for the night, the horses occasionally neighing from the picket lines. As on many future occasions, he wondered how he could give up all this and the company of brave men for something so paltry as the applause of the ignorant multitudes. Each time, however, the question echoed less compellingly.

Next morning he breakfasted with General Reynolds, and they conferred on how to maneuver against the hostiles. The last reports he had, Reynolds said, were that the Indians had established themselves on the Dismal River after committing various depredations and were probably waiting for other tribesmen to join them and increase the scale of their attacks on the border settlements.

Cody suggested that he and his two assistants, Buffalo Chips White and Texas Jack Omohundro, scout ahead while the cavalry column followed them in the direction of the Dismal River. Cody and his assistants picked up the trail of the war party about ten miles out of camp. He reported back to

General Reynolds, whom he quoted as saying, "I have been fighting the Apaches in Arizona but I find these Sioux are an entirely different crowd. I know little about them and I will follow your suggestions. You start now and I will have the command following you in an hour and a half."

Cody, Buffalo Chips, and Texas Jack searched the banks of the Dismal River upstream, then downstream. They climbed a sandhill, which gave a view of the countryside for several miles. About three miles away, in the valley of the Dismal, behind a stand of timber, they spotted a column of smoke and several hundred horses.

The Third Cavalry came lumbering up late that day, and over the campfire that night Cody and General Reynolds conferred on tactics. Cody would take one troop of cavalry and charge into the Indian camp, while the rest of the force, keeping behind the sandhills, moved around to cut off the Indians' escape.

Before dawn on the morning of May 22, 1873, they moved in to spring the trap. Cody was leading the way, with Captain Charles Meinhold's Troop B on his heels. A mile or so from the hostile village he took a Sergeant Foley and several troopers with him and scouted ahead of the rest of the troop.

His approach was so stealthy that he and his companions got within a short distance of the Indian camp before they were observed. Cody then gave the signal for the rest of Troop B to come up on the run and rode into the just-awakening camp whooping and firing. In a few minutes of hectic action he made himself a candidate for the nation's highest military honor.

As he told the story himself, "I finally gave the signal to charge, and we dashed into the little camp with a yell. Five Indians sprang out of a willow tepee, and greeted us with a volley, and we returned the fire. I was riding Buckskin Joe, who with a few jumps brought me up to the tepee, followed by my men. We nearly ran over the Indians who were endeavoring to reach their horses on the opposite side of the creek. Just as one was jumping the narrow stream a bullet from my old 'Lucretia Borgia' [as he had named his hunting rifle] overtook him. He never reached the other bank, but dropped dead in the water. . . . Two mounted warriors closed in on me and were shooting at short range. I returned their fire and had the satisfaction of seeing one of them fall from his horse. At this moment I felt blood trickling down my forehead, and hastily running my hand through my hair I discovered that I had received a scalp wound."

One might gather from that account that Cody had tackled the Indian camp virtually single-handed, but the subsequent after-action report of Captain Charles Meinhold indicated there were others present. In recommending Cody for the Congressional Medal of Honor, the troop commander wrote:

"Mr. Cody had guided Sergeant Foley's party with such skill that he approached the Indian camp within fifty yards before he was noticed. The Indians fired immediately upon Mr. Cody and Sergeant Foley. Mr. Cody killed one Indian, two others ran toward the main command and were killed. While this was going on Mr. Cody discovered a party of six mounted Indians and two lead horses running at full speed at a distance of about two miles down the river. I at once sent Lieutenant Lawson with Mr. Cody and fifteen men in pursuit. He, in the beginning of the chase, gained a little upon them, so that they were compelled to abandon the two lead horses, which were captured, but after running more than twelve miles at full speed, our jaded horses gave out and the Indians made good their escape. Mr. William Cody's reputation for bravery and skill as a guide is so well established that I need not say anything else but that he acted in his usual manner."

The Third Cavalry managed to round up about 250 fleeing Indians in the valley of the Dismal River that morning and return them to the Spotted Tail Agency, where they had found life too monotonous to be borne without an occasional foray against their oppressors.

Cody had suffered only a graze wound, quite possibly from a carbine fired by one of his comrades in the melee.

It was a piddling price to pay, he believed, for the Congressional Medal of Honor, which was soon awarded him. The medal became the prize possession of his long career. Eventually it was snatched away from him by an ungrateful Congress, but that was another and sadder story.

A temporary and illusory peace had settled over the Great Plains, and Cody returned to Fort McPherson with the Third Cavalry. Several fresh Indian scalps, mementos of the attack on the Dismal River, dangled from his belt. He was at loose ends again, with a wife, three children, and two sisters to support. His admiring neighbors had placed his name on the ballot, and he had been elected to the Nebraska Legislature by a margin of 44 votes. A political career did not appeal to him, however, and he never took his seat in that forum.

Later that year he received a series of urgent invitations from Ned Buntline to venture upon a theatrical career and play the role he had been shaping for some years, himself.

Book II: Showman

5

A Living God Behind the Footlights

One of the more striking sidelights of the creation of our Western mythology is that it was being fabricated, recast, and enlarged upon almost immediately after the events upon which it was based were taking place. It was Instant History, thanks to the new quickness of communication afforded by the telegraph and the daily newspaper. Another facet of this mass delusion—in which book and magazine publishers and theatrical impresarios eagerly collaborated—was that the heroes it raised up, without any false (or real) modesty, joined in the process by portraying themselves and reenacting their supposed deeds. Would Achilles, for instance, have abandoned the forces laying siege to Troy and hurried back to Athens to play himself before a crowded amphitheater? No matter, this was modern America, where a man had the right to cash in on his fame.

The gunsmoke had hardly drifted away from the scene of a gunfight or Indian skirmish before there was someone on hand to gather the details and magnify them for an enthusiastic public. The gory events which composed Western history provided entertainment, in raw living color, for the stay-at-homes back East. During the decade that followed the

Civil War, the American public demanded vicarious thrills to help them taper off from the excitement of the war; or as Mari Sandoz (*The Cattlemen*) put it, Americans yearned for "the gaudiest, the most exaggerated characters to continue, if not the violent times and deeds of a very bloody war, at least such heroics as could be whipped up to feed the public's voracious, wolfish hunger." Soon the Eastern audiences were being satisfied in their craving by various woolly and swashbuckling Williams—Wild Bill, Buffalo Bill, Pawnee Bill—with supporting casts.

Late in the autumn of 1872 Ned Buntline had arrived in Chicago to set himself up as a fire-insurance agent and a theatrical producer. It seemed a good bet. In the aftermath of the Great Fire, Chicago had come to value insurance coverage and to need entertainment to forget their losses of the year before. An entrepreneur named Jim Dixon had run up a jerrybuilt amphitheater with board sides and a canvas top, which Buntline shrewdly refused to insure but envisioned as the site of a theatrical triumph starring Buffalo Bill, his friend Texas Jack Omohundro, and himself.

Cody found it hard to picture himself as an actor. He was certain that he would be paralyzed by stage fright. As Louisa Cody recounted her husband's struggle with the temptation offered by Ned Buntline:

" 'Mamma, I'd be awful scared,' he said to me more than once. 'I'd get out there and just get glassy-eyed from looking at those lights. I couldn't do it. I'd just naturally be tongue-tied.'

" 'Oh, you could do it all right,' I answered with that confidence that a wife always has in her husband, 'but is play-acting just the right thing?'

" 'Shucks, play-acting is all right and—' Then he stopped and looked at the children, Arta growing up to young girlhood; Kit Carson, his ideal and his dream, just at the romping age, and Orra, a tiny baby. 'And—' he said at last—'if there was money, it would mean a lot for them, Mamma. It would mean that we could send them to fine schools and have everything for them that we wanted. You know, I didn't get much chance to go to school when I was a boy. And I want them to have everything I missed."

There was much that was self-serving in that rumination. Aside from providing for his children's education, he was beckoned, as Mrs. Cody did not fully realize then, by the importunities of celebrity: cheering audiences, clamoring journalists, champagne suppers, important men, and beautiful women gathering around him as though he were a living god. He just couldn't trade in those prospects for a seat in the Nebraska Legislature. Early in December he packed up his wife and children and their negligible belongings and, along with Texas Jack, set out for Chicago.

On arrival there were a few bitter words with Ned Buntline. Each party had failed to live up to an agreement made by mail. Buffalo Bill was supposed to bring with him twenty authentic redskins to appear in the drama which Buntline was supposed to concoct. On his part, Buntline had failed to write a line of the script, though the show was supposed to open less than a week from then.

The dramaturgic problem was solved instanter when Buntline holed up in a hotel room with a ream of paper. Ever afterward he boasted that he wrote *Scouts of the Plains* in four hours. Actually he scrawled down all the dialogue and stage directions he could remember of Meader's *Buffalo Bill* as it was staged at Niblo's Gardens in New York and simply added one character, Gale Durg, whom he was going to portray himself. Since Meader's play was adapted from Buntline's dime novel of the same title, this was not quite plagiarism. In any case, the show was thrown together in exactly four days, despite the fact that its three stars— Buffalo Bill, Texas Jack, and Buntline—had never appeared behind the footlights. Even professional actors would have been dismayed by having to learn their lines and rehearse in only four days.

"Bill," Buntline asked Cody, "how long will it take to commit your part?"

"About seven years, with good luck."

Buntline was a whirlwind of activity, engaging an obscure Italian actress named Mlle. Morlacchi to play the role of Dove Eye (whom the Chicago *Tribune* critic described as "a beautiful Indian maiden with an Italian accent and a weakness for scouts") , hiring ten down-and-outers from the lakefront to play the Indians, and rehearsing the company.

Somehow, on the night of December 16, the company stumbled onstage and gave what may have been the most wretched performance in the annals of the American theater. As Mrs. Cody recalled the rehearsals, most of which were conducted in Buntline's hotel suite, "from the outside it sounded like the mutterings of a den of wild animals. . . . Every few minutes bellboys would rush up the hall with ice clinking in pitchers, hand the refreshments through the door, then hurry away again."

In a state of overrefreshment and profound shock, Cody stumbled out onstage at the rise of the curtain, sustained only by the knowledge that there was $2,800 in the till of the box office. He dried up completely, with Texas Jack and Buntline standing beside him in a similar state. Finally Buntline managed to throw him a cue: "You've been out buffalo-hunting with Milligan, haven't you?" Cody managed to ad-lib a few lines, and the rest of the first act consisted of Buntline questioning him about his experiences. Just before the curtain fell, Buntline, knowing the show needed a hypo, shouted, "The Indians are upon us!" Onstage bounded the supers clad in cambric pantalets and streaked with war paint. Buffalo Bill and his companions, finally coming to life, managed to wipe them out to the last man.

As the bemused journalists in the audience tried to describe the scenario of *Scouts of the Plains* the next day, the second act was a turgid account of warfare between the brave scouts (Buffalo Bill and Texas Jack) , a renegade white played by Buntline, and the Indians, who again came out to be slaughtered. The climactic scene was the capture of Buntline by the Indians, who tied him to a tree and prepared to

torture him. Buntline interrupted these proceedings by delivering one of his temperance lectures. This not only
padded out the play but gave Buffalo Bill and Texas Jack
time to come whooping out of the wings and save Buntline
from his captors. The third act was mostly a repetition of the
second, except that Buffalo Bill and Texas Jack dealt more
humanely with the Indians and lassoed them instead of
shooting the daylights out of them.

The audience, believing it was witnessing the real thing
and eager to forgive any crudities in the performance,
shouted its approval of the company when the final curtain
was rung down. It was apparent that Buffalo Bill would be a
theatrical success merely by appearing on stage, so consuming was the public's interest in him. So what did it matter
what the newspaper critics said of the show? The Chicago
Tribune's man not only criticized its dramatic qualities but
characterized Buntline as "a human nightmare who managed
to get drunk for several hours without a drop of anything"
and remarked that Cody "speaks his lines after the diffident
manner of a schoolboy, fidgeting uneasily when silent, and
when in dialogue, poking out the right hand and then the
left at regular intervals." The Chicago *Times* was even more
severe: "On the whole, it is not probable that Chicago will
ever look upon the like again. Such a combination of incon-
gruous drama, execrable acting, renowned performers, intol-
erable stench, scalping, blood and thunder, is not likely to be
vouchsafed to a city a second time—even Chicago." The
Inter-Ocean was only slightly critical: "There is a well-
founded rumor that Ned Buntline, who played the part of
Gale Durg in last night's performance, wrote the play in
which Buffalo Bill and Texas Jack appeared, taking only
four hours to complete the task. The question naturally
arises: what was he doing all that time? As Gale Durg, he
made some excellent speeches on temperance and was killed
in the second act, it being very much regretted that he did
not arrange his demise so that it could have occurred sooner.
Buffalo Bill and Texas Jack are wonderful Indian killers. As

an artistic success, 'The Scouts of the Plains' can hardly be
called a season's event, but for downright fun, Injun killing,
red fire and rough and tumble, it is a wonder."

For all the quibbling of the drama critics, *Scouts of the
Plains* was a box office success and moved on to St. Louis and
the Grand Opera House, where it opened December 23. At
the opening performance, Cody peered through the hissing
and flickering gas of the footlights and spotted his wife in the
audience. "Oh, Mamma," he groaned, "I'm a bad actor."
The audience thundered its applause; the spontaneous remark made him realer and more human, and people came to
see Buffalo Bill the man in all his homespun humor. The
ticket buyers, if not the newspaper critics, enthused over
Scouts of the Plains for what they conceived to be the natu-
ralism of its performers—and never mind that one journalist
described Buffalo Bill as "a beautiful blonde." The show
kept drawing standing-room-only crowds in St. Louis, then
in Cincinnati, Albany, and Boston, as part of its pre-New
York tryout.

There was only momentary consternation when the three
stars were arrested by an overzealous peace officer in St.
Louis who came to their hotel with a warrant for Buntline's
arrest on an indictment of pre-Civil War vintage charging
him with having taken part in a riot. For good measure the
officer took along Buffalo Bill and Texas Jack, perhaps on
the logical theory that anyone associated with the notorious
Ned Buntline must be guilty of something. Cody and Omohundro were freed, but Buntline was held until an unwise
friend put up bail, which Buntline promptly jumped. In
Cincinnati there was more bad luck when a member of the
company died after one of the scrimmages onstage. No mention of it was made in the Cincinnati papers, and there is no
record of any police investigation, but there was a brief dispatch in one of the New York journals: "W. J. Halpin, actor,
died at noon today from the effects of injuries received last
Thursday night when playing his part as Big Wolf with Ned
Buntline's Company." Presumably the unfortunate Halpin

was clouted by one of the scouts during one of the three Indian-attack scenes: a fatal case of overacting.

The *Scouts of the Plains* company hastily decamped from Cincinnati and finally fetched up in New York at the end of March, 1873, ready to dazzle the metropolis. Even Cody had learned his lines.

New York just then was ready to buy anything in the Western line. Westernism was the current craze. The presses at Street & Smith and the Beadle Dime Library were on a round-the-clock production. The New York newspapers carried several columns daily on the progress of campaigns against the Apaches and Modocs. Western investments were booming on Wall Street. Even the statelier forms of literature had caught up with the possibilities of the Western scene, Mark Twain having published *Roughing It* to general acclaim the previous year, and Bret Harte had come to New York to take commercial advantage of his growing popularity, only to be arrested for nonpayment of a tailor's bill.

In this receptive atmosphere, *Scouts of the Plains* opened at Niblo's Gardens on the Bowery on March 31. The audiences went wild, but there were still the jejune attitudes of the newspaper critics to be confronted and shrugged off. The New Yorkers were somewhat more trenchant than their colleagues in Chicago, even though the *Scouts* company had had three months on the road to learn the rudiments of stagecraft.

The New York *Herald*'s critic, unrestrained by publisher Bennett, who was away attending his mother's funeral, described the production as "so wonderful in its daring feebleness that no ordinary intellect is capable of comprehending it. . . . Ned Buntline represents his part as badly as is possible for any human being to represent it. The Hon. William F. Cody, otherwise 'Buffalo Bill,' occasionally called by the refined people of the eastern cities 'Bison William' is a good-looking fellow, tall and straight as an arrow, but ridiculous as an actor. Texas Jack is not quite so good-looking, not so tall, not so straight, and not so ridiculous." The play itself won the contempt of the *Times* critic: "The characters are always either fighting or getting ready to fight. Most of them seem to be shot down in the course of the action, and come miraculously to life again in the sequel, to the infinite satisfaction of the audience." The *Times* man, however, was willing to concede that Cody himself "exhibited a surprising degree of aplomb, a notable ease of gesture and delivery and vocal power quite sufficient readily to fill a large theater." The New York *World* critic was even more percipient in noting that the vehicle was unimportant; it was the real-life personalities it trundled onstage who counted. "As a drama it is very poor slop. But as an exhibition of three remarkable men it is not without interest. The Hon. W. F. Cody enters into the spectacle with a curious grace and a certain characteristic charm that pleases the beholders. He is a remarkably handsome fellow on the stage, and the lithe springy step, the round uncultured voice and the utter absence of anything like stage art, won for him the good-will of an audience which was disposed to laugh at all that was intended to be pathetic and serious."

Both from the newspaper reviews and from audience reactions, it was apparent that Buffalo Bill was a salable commodity so far as show business was concerned. He couldn't act, but no one expected him to. He had only to appear as himself, with all his natural grace, to satisfy the customers. On the other hand, Ned Buntline, as playwright, impresario, and actor, was a distinct liability. His bombastic style only cast an aura of phoniness over "The Great Scout."

Cody and Buntline were "pards," Buntline was Cody's discoverer, but Western pardship, like Broadway palship, sometimes succumbed to commercial pressures. Furthermore, Cody was irked by the fact that his share of the take from a highly successful tour was only $6,000. A partnership was about to be dissolved.

Fortuitously another flamboyant character had just come into Cody's life, the one who would nurture and cultivate the Buffalo Bill legend for the next forty years, who took up where Buntline left off, and who made Cody more famous than most Presidents and richer than any other performer of any kind.

His name was Major John M. Burke, also known as Arizona John. He had never been anywhere near Arizona, and where the title of major came from no one could determine. He would serve as Cody's press agent in chief, advance man, fixer, and perhaps his best and most loyal friend. Until he met Cody, Burke had served a valuable apprenticeship as a newspaperman, a stock company actor, and the manager of an acrobatic troupe. He knew show business, and his newspaper experience fitted him for the public relations role. Until Ivy Lee came along and performed miracles with the public image of John D. Rockefeller, Sr., John Burke undoubtedly was the unrivaled genius of publicity who invented much of what Hollywood and Madison Avenue would later build on and develop. With whatever damage it did to historical truth, he established Buffalo Bill in the public mind as the epitome of the plainsmen who were credited with conquering the West, though that credit belonged as much to any immigrant swinging a pick on the roadbed of the transcontinental railroad.

The odd thing is that Burke, who must have been as cynical as any ex-newspaperman, really believed in what he was doing. As proof of that dedication, he stuck to Cody long after the money tree withered and the applause died down. "I have met a god," he said simply after first being presented to Cody. He could make that statement because he was a Western buff, a type, still with us, which succumbs readily to any virulent untruth so long as it promotes a hallucinatory vision of the Old West; thus he wore his hair long, like a scout, and called himself Arizona John, long before meeting Cody.

Some of his newspaper friends said he had "nothing but brass and wind as a stock in trade," but beneath all the blarney there was the bedrock of hero worship—he was a salesman who believed in his product, a medicine man who swigged his own remedies. Near the end of his life he wrote of his first meeting with Cody, though he did not say where it took place; apparently it was sometime during the pre-New York tour of *Scouts of the Plains*. "For once realization excelled anticipation. Physically superb, trained to the limit, in the zenith of his manhood, features cast in nature's most perfect mold, on a prancing charger that was foaming and chaffing at the bit, and in his most picturesque beaded buckskin garb, he was indeed a picture. When he dismounted I was introduced to the finest specimen of God's handiwork I had ever seen, and felt that for once there was that nearest approach to an ideal human, a visual interpretation given to the assertion that man was indeed a replica of His Maker. . . . I thought then that he was the handsomest, straightest, finest man that I had ever seen in my life. I still think so."

It is quite probable that without the heroic and relentless endeavors of John M. Burke the Buffalo Bill legend would have withered as so many others did. He stuck to his task through good times and bad, never wavering in his devotion when Cody brought misfortunes on himself and his enterprise through alcoholic capers, misadventures with women, and quixotic ideas about handling money. The mountain range of press clippings—and the image they created in the public mind—was the most prominent feature of the terrain of Buffalo Bill country. Essentially Buffalo Bill was a hallucination. Burke was able to foster it because he was the first to be hallucinated. Everybody in the newspaper business considered him lovable, if slightly deluded, and they published his preposterous stories about Buffalo Bill without necessarily believing them. His personal charm was employed to rent theaters when they had already been committed to other productions, to engage transportation when the railroads were occupied with more important business than moving a Wild West show. An associate of Burke's named David A. Curtis remarked that Burke had few of the lesser virtues but was peerless as a transmitter of enthusiasm, which is certainly a cardinal virtue in a press agent. "You cannot think of him as punctual, for instance," Curtis wrote of Burke, "or as prudent or economical, or decorously and exquisitely choice of speech, or punctilious in any of those small niceties that make the Puritan and the prig. But when it comes to cardinal points of character the liveliest imagination cannot conceive of John M. Burke as derelict in the smallest particular.

"Is the endorsement of the government necessary, or some special privilege in regard to the wards of the Nation? Burke secures it. Is it desirable to obtain a notice from a newspaper, whether it be the London Times or the Podunk Gazette? Burke sees the editor. He is a press agent, but it is hard to apply the word to him, for there is no other press agent of his kind. I doubt if he has written a notice in years. He does not need to. What he can do, and does, is to inspire enthusiasm in the minds of those who write, or rather, to infuse them with some of his own, and in this he never fails."

At first Burke replaced Buntline as manager of the company. The show could be kept going, he and Cody agreed, only if it were revamped for the new season of 1873-74. *Scouts of the Plains* was accordingly rewritten, if not strikingly improved. The Buntline character was dropped and Wild Bill Hickok, as a luminary of Western heroics with a candlepower then equaling Cody's, was persuaded to come East and play himself. Hickok at that point had gained wide renown as the town-taming marshal of Abilene and Hays City. The prairie suns had blighted his vision—his affliction was diagnosed as ophthalmia, an inflammation of the eyeball —and Abilene had dismissed him as town marshal after he accidentally gunned down one of his own deputies. Hickok had no hankering for show business, as he indicated plainly enough to Cody, but he agreed to have a try at acting only because he had acquired expensive tastes.

Regarding "play-acting" as unmanly and theatrical traditions as ridiculous, Hickok was a trial to his old friend and new employer from the moment he set foot in New York.

By now Cody had begun taking his new career seriously. He had been infected by John M. Burke's evangelical faith in his destiny—Burke, who, as one authority said, "had the imagination to see the place Buffalo Bill would occupy in show business." Much too optimistically Cody believed he could transfer that enthusiasm to Hickok.

Knowing that Wild Bill would be as confused by the metropolis as he himself had been on his first visit to New York, Cody had provided Hickok with precise instructions on what to do from the moment he arrived: "I am staying at the Brevoort Hotel, and you will land in New York at the 42nd St. depot. To avoid getting lost in the big city, take a cab at the depot and you will be driven to the hotel in a few minutes. Pay the cabman two dollars. These New York cabmen are regular holdup men, and your driver may want to charge you more, but do not pay more than two dollars under any circumstances."

Hickok had memorized Cody's instructions, but unfortunately they did not include suggestions on how to dress. Later John Burke wrote that Wild Bill arrived "dressed in a cutaway coat, flowered vest, ruffled white shirt, salt-and-pepper trousers, string tie, high-heeled boots and a broad-brimmed hat."

On arrival at the Brevoort he handed the hansom cab's driver the recommended two dollars.

"Wait a minute," the cabbie snarled. "My charge is five dollars."

"Two dollars is all you're going to get," Hickok stoutly replied.

The cabbie climbed off his box, fists cocked in the contemporary bare-knuckle tradition. "Well, you long-haired rube," he said, "I'll take the rest out of your hide."

There was a flurry of roundhouse swings, at the end of which a badly bruised cabdriver lay in the gutter. Hickok blew on his knuckles, picked up his satchel, and strolled into the lobby. The manager, who had witnessed the scene outside, rushed up to Cody's room. "Say, Bill, I think the gentleman you've been expecting has arrived." Cody listened gravely to a description of the brawl and said, "Yeah, that must be Wild Bill all right." A few minutes later the old drinking companions were reunited.

They would maintain their friendship until the day three years later Hickok was shot in the back of the head in a Deadwood saloon, but there was a measure of disillusionment coming soon to both of them. Hickok saw that Cody had changed, that he was no longer willing to drink and brawl when there was nothing better to do, that in fact he had become part of a loathsome species, the businessman. Cody had also become something of a ham and was taking this theatrical nonsense seriously.

On his part, Cody was dismayed by Hickok's refusal to comply with the demands of the profession which was paying them handsomely for their amateurish efforts. From his first co-starring appearance with Cody, Texas Jack, Mlle. Morlacchi, and the rest of the *Scouts* company, Hickok refused to follow the script or obey the scenario. Anarchy prevailed whenever Hickok was onstage. "Although he had a fine stage presence," as Cody would recall, "and was a handsome fellow, and possessed a good strong voice, yet it was almost impossible for him to utter a word. He insisted that we were making a set of fools of ourselves, and that we were the laughing-stock of the people."

Yet Hickok may have been right in a sense, though he did not claim to be a connoisseur of the theatrical arts. *Scouts of the Plains* may well have been the most wretched exercise in playwriting of that generally depressed era. Writhing with embarrassment, Hickok was required to deliver the line: "Fear not, fair maid! By heavens, you are safe with Wild Bill, who is ever ready to risk his life and die, if need be, in defense of weak and defenseless womanhood!" Even nineteenth-century melodrama rarely attained the thundering banality of that line.

Hickok, in fact, disgraced himself at the first performance when the show reopened at Niblo's Gardens. A stagehand manipulated the spotlight from his post in the gallery. Whenever Hickok appeared onstage, usually delivering the vaguest approximation of the dialogue assigned to him, the spotlight followed his every movement. Being greatly embarrassed every moment he was onstage, Hickok angrily gestured toward the gallery to direct that beam of light elsewhere. During his "Fear not, fair maid" scene with Mlle. Morlacchi, he produced a curious effect, bellowing encouragement at the girl while simultaneously waving off the spotlight. He even tried to hide behind some scenery while finishing the scene. Finally, in total exasperation, he ripped his pistol out of its holster, hurled it at the spotlight, and scored a bull's-eye. The audience was delighted, but Burke and Cody were not.

Both in New York and later on the road, Hickok relieved the tedium of the performance by various Katzenjammer antics which distressed his fellow players. "Wild Bill," as Cody recalled, "was continually playing tricks on the members of the company, and it was his especial delight to torment the 'supers.' Quite frequently in our sham Indian battles, he would run up to the 'Indians,' and putting his pistol close to their legs, fire and burn them with the powder instead of shooting over their heads. This would make them dance and jump, although they were paid twenty-five cents each for performing the 'dying business.' "

Hickok's first biographer (J. W. Buel, *Life and Marvelous Adventures of Wild Bill*) became infatuated with his subject after attending one of the first performances in New York. Hickok was so distracted by the uproarious applause greeting his first entrance that he dried up completely. One of his fellow actors primed the pump by inquiring, "Where have you been, Bill? What has detained you so long?" Hickok struggled momentarily for an ad-lib. "Thereupon Bill," his biographer related, "who is an excellent story teller, knew just how much ornamentation to give his recitals that a curious-loving audience could desire, and upon concluding the story there was an encore which shook the house like an explosion."

It was magnificent, his friend Cody might have agreed, but was it show business? Then there was the matter of Hickok's boozing onstage and in his dressing room. In one of the play's early scenes, Buffalo Bill, Texas Jack, and Wild Bill were sitting around a campfire, telling tall stories and swigging out of a supposed whiskey bottle. The bottle, by tradition, was filled with cold tea. In an ornery mood one night Hickok took his turn at the bottle, then spewed tea all over the stage. "You must think I'm the biggest fool east of the Rockies," he blurted out, "that I can't tell whiskey from cold tea. This don't count, and I can't tell a story unless I get real whiskey."

Hickok refused to allow the play to continue until Buffalo Bill hissed to the stage manager to get a bottle of the real stuff from Hickok's dressing room, which was more than adequately stocked. From then on, Hickok's performances grew less inhibited and more unpredictable. The shapely Mlle. Morlacchi was especially discomforted because he "grew fonder of the heroine on-stage than the script stipulated."

Hickok's onstage lechery was viewed by jealous watchers in the wings with a distaste bordering on the homicidal. The delicious Italian, it seems, was the center of an emotional storm system. By the time Hickok joined the company both John Burke and Texas Jack were bitter rivals for her affections. Wild Bill was considerably upset when she spurned his attentions as unwelcome and superfluous. Eventually she made her choice and married Texas Jack.

When the company began its tour of various Eastern cities early in 1874, Hickok asked to be released from his contract, but both Cody and Burke told him that he was too big a draw to be allowed to ride off into the sunset. Often, however, they were beset by second thoughts about Hickok's value to the company. Wild Bill simply refused to learn the art of dealing with the public on or offstage. His touchy disposition was a distinct liability when they appeared in Titusville, Pennsylvania, when it was the center of the first American oil fields. The town was filled with roughnecks spoiling for a fight, which eventuality Cody and Burke hoped to avoid by strenuous diplomacy, if only Hickok could be persuaded to keep his temper on a leash.

Immediately after checking into one of the Titusville hotels, which was next to the theater where they were to appear, the manager stopped him, as Cody recalled, "and said there was a party of roughs from the lower oil regions who were spreeing and had boasted that they were staying in town to meet the Buffalo Bill gang and clean them out. The landlord begged of me not to allow the members of the company to enter the billiard room as he did not wish any fight in his house. To please the landlord, and at his suggestion, I called the boys into the parlor and explained the situation. Wild Bill wanted to go at once and fight the whole mob, but I persuaded him to keep away from them during the day."

That evening, while Cody was overseeing the ticket sales in the box office next door, the hotel manager rushed over and informed him that Hickok was brawling with a half dozen or more ruffians in his barroom. One of the drillers had gone up to Hickok and accused him of being Buffalo Bill. With ominous politeness, Hickok denied the charge.

When the driller charged him with lying, as Cody later reconstructed the imbroglio, Hickok "instantly knocked him down, and then seizing a chair, he laid out four or five of the crowd on the floor, and then drove the rest out of the room. All this was done in a minute or two, and by the time I got there, Bill was coming out of the barroom, whistling a lively tune."

Cody upbraided his co-star, adding, "I thought you promised to come into the Opera House by a private entrance."

"I did try to follow that trail," Hickok solemnly replied, "but I got lost among the canyons, and then I ran into the hostiles. But it's all right now, they won't bother us any more."

The oil field roughnecks had indeed been taught a salu-
tary lesson, and the *Scouts* company completed its Titusville
stand without any more trouble, but it did seem that Wild
Bill was incident-prone. Farther along their route, in Portland, Maine, Hickok retired to his bed at the United States
Hotel but was awakened by a noisy party next door. He
knocked on the adjoining door to find five of Portland's leading citizens drinking whiskey and playing poker. Though he
was clad only in his nightshirt, without his notorious six-
guns strapped to his waist, he was recognized immediately as
the celebrated cow-town marshal. "Forget about sleeping,
Mr. Hickok," he was told. "Pull up a chair, pour yourself a
drink and take a hand in the game." When dawn broke,
Hickok was ahead by $700. "Let this be a lesson to you, gen-
tlemen," he yawned as he rose from the table. "Never wake
up a stranger, destroy his sleep, and then invite him to play
poker with you. Good morning."

The company proceeded to Rochester, New York, to open
a long engagement at the local opera house. Mrs. Cody had
accompanied the tour with their three children but had not
succumbed, as her husband did, to the fascination of theatrical life. She thoroughly agreed with Wild Bill Hickok that a
man ought to find something better to do than paint his face
and make-believe. Rochester was a quiet, orderly, and respectable city; it reminded her somewhat of St. Louis during
her girlhood, and it was decided that she would rent a house
and stay there with the children when the company continued its ramblings.

It was in Rochester, too, that Hickok finally detached himself from *Scouts of the Plains*. One night a lamp in the bank
of footlights exploded, and the flash of light seared his already oversensitive eyeballs. He was forced to undergo treatment by a specialist and wear glasses with thick blue lenses
when off the stage. That misfortune only further convinced
him that it was time to jump the show and vanish westward
with his savings.

One night he was awaiting the cue for his entrance, with

Mrs. Cody standing nearby. Onstage Texas Jack and Mlle. Morlacchi were playing an excessively sentimental love scene.

"Ain't they foolish?" Mrs. Cody heard him mutter. "What's the use of getting out there and making a show of yourself? I ain't going to do it."

After the performance that night, Hickok left a message for Cody with one of the stagehands. "Tell that longhaired son of a gun I have no more use for him and his damned show business."

He blew town that night. As the senior in Western celebrity, as a model for costuming and deportment in attracting public attention, as an exemplar in what might be called plainsmanship, he had done much to shape the personality of Will Cody. The Will Cody who had become Buffalo Bill—a logical extension of Hickok's own pioneering efforts—he could not abide.

Cody himself was making too much money to consider following Hickok back out West. The *Scouts of the Plains* company continued its road tour, finished the season, and went out again the season of 1874-75 with a repertory of Western dramas including *Life on the Border, Buffalo Bill at Bay, The Red Right Hand, From Noose to Neck,* and *Buffalo Bill's Pledge.* All were written by various Bowery hacks on a piecework basis.

Cody boasted that he now "had money to throw at the birds," and no doubt, given his improvident nature, he did. He was aware, however, that he hadn't found the proper medium for his style of showmanship. "Will," as his wife would remember in later years, "never looked upon the stage as anything but transitory."

He and his chief adviser, John Burke, were still trying to find the right formula. The theatrical stage was too confining; it could not provide the physical space or the dramatic latitude necessary to convey the Western experience, and Buffalo Bill was too expansive a presence to be compressed under the proscenium arch. Somehow they had to take the personification of that myth outdoors and place him against a more fitting background than the painted cyclorama of a theater.

Such problems were driven from his mind in the early spring of 1876 after three seasons on the road. The company was appearing in Springfield, Massachusetts, one night in mid-April when a telegram was delivered to Cody's dressing room. It was from Mrs. Cody and informed him that their son was desperately ill.

6

Buffalo Bill Lifts a Scalp

CODY would never claim to be a model father or husband. He was somewhat a stranger in the Rochester household, where he hung his Stetson only between theatrical tours. Then and in later years, he showered his wife and children with money and lavishly furnished houses and costly gifts but rarely gave of himself. A living legend rarely finds much comfort in home life, among people who can remember him, or insist on regarding him, as an ordinary human being.

Cody's feelings toward his only son, the bright and handsome six-year-old Kit Carson Cody, were of a more intense order. Propped on his dressing-room table was a photograph of the boy, his curly hair falling to his shoulders in ringlets, à la papa, posing with a rifle in his hands. When the family had accompanied him on the road, Kit had always occupied a box overlooking the stage and when his father appeared below would call out, "Good house, Papa!"

The boy had contracted scarlet fever. So had his two sisters, but they appeared to be recovering. Kit had always been delicate.

By the time Cody arrived at his Rochester home the boy was dying. The doctor told him there was nothing more to be done. All night Cody, his eyes as feverish with despair as his dying son's, sat at the bedside. Sometimes he took the unconscious boy in his arms, as though hoping to transfer some of his own abundant vitality to the child.

Kit died shortly after dawn, and he took a part of his father—perhaps the best part—with him. Much of the ambition, the determination to succeed in a profession in which he was a stranger, which Wild Bill Hickok had found so distasteful, had been derived from his hopes for the boy. Secretly, according to his sister Helen, he hoped that the boy would become President of the United States. Now all those hopes were buried under a small mound in Mount Hope Cemetery, and Cody had lost his psychic balance wheel.

After the funeral he announced to Louisa that he couldn't bear the thought of returning to his theatrical trouping, that he was going back out West to forget his grief by plunging into the action. There was big trouble in Indian country—it was a summer never to be forgotten on the frontier—and his services would be needed.

Louisa's subsequent report of that conversation was a little hard to believe, but perhaps people really talked that way in mid-Victorian America:

"Mamma, I can't go back to that—that mockery. It's always been a joke to me—those plays. And I can't joke now. I can't go on the stage and act—remembering—remembering. . . ."

"Will, it's spring. They're starting the expeditions now, back—out home. It's your land out there. I'll stay here and wait, and hope. We've got enough money; we can live. I want you to go back out West again and ride and fight and—well, I know you won't forget."

"No, I won't forget."

One can only gather that the prescribed method of assuaging grief in a decent white American household was for the breadwinner to go and kill some Indians.

Cody disbanded his troupe and then hastened westward. Every dispatch in the newspapers told of quickening activity on the frontier. In the Dakotas, Wyoming, and Montana, thousands of Sioux and their Cheyenne allies were swarming like wasps from a broken hive.

The reason for the Indian rage was simple enough: another broken treaty. Time after time the government in Washington had promised the Sioux that the badlands of the Black Hills, bleak and eroded country that appeared worthless from the white man's viewpoint, would always be reserved for the Indians. The Indians believed that the Black Hills were the dwelling place of the Great Manitou; they were sacred ground. Then came rumors that the wind-sculptured hills were veined with gold. In 1874, Custer and the Seventh Cavalry had invaded the Black Hills ostensibly to survey for a military post to be located there; but the real purpose of the expedition was indicated by the fact that it was accompanied by two gold miners and a geologist. Soon word leaked out that the Custer force had discovered gold in large quantities, and the stampede to the Black Hills was on. The government made desultory attempts to halt the rush, reminding everyone that the Indians repeatedly had been guaranteed sole rights to the territory.

But you could no more stop white men heading for the goldfields than you could halt thirsting cattle from stampeding toward fresh water. "The day came," as the late Robert J. Casey noted (*The Black Hills*), "when pioneers more determined than cavalrymen were ranged along the Cheyenne frontier. And there were other rapidly growing mobs at Sidney and Fort Laramie and Sioux Falls City and Yankton and Fort Pierre. Rumbles of rising indignation among the Sioux tribes didn't cool them off any while they waited. They drew encouragement from their increasing numbers and began to boast of a day when they would pour into the Hills in spite of the military. . . . That a lot of them were going to be found by their associates presently, dead and without their scalps, went without saying."

Having deliberately opened that Pandora's box, the Washington government then tried to buy the Black Hills from the Sioux for $6,000,000. The Sioux demanded $100,000,000, knowing their price wouldn't be paid, wanting only to keep the white men out of their sacred lands. Washington's response was to withdraw the cavalry patrols, let the gold rush proceed, and prepare for one hell of an Indian war.

Under Sitting Bull, Crazy Horse, and other leaders, the Sioux and the Cheyenne gathered thousands of warriors early in 1876 and prepared to resist. Until now the Indians usually fought with the utmost bravery but without cohesion or direction. Sitting Bull's strategy, however, was to persuade the tribes to fight as one, to strike at the cavalry columns whenever and wherever the Indians were assured of superiority. When the Third Cavalry attacked an Indian encampment on the Powder River in March, it suffered severe losses and was forced to withdraw in astonishment.

By then General Sheridan had hurried out to coordinate the campaign against the dissident tribes and force them to accept the invasion and settlement of the Black Hills. His plan was to trap Sitting Bull, Crazy Horse, American Horse, and their followers—whose numbers and capabilities were greatly underestimated by the white commanders—between converging columns commanded by Generals Custer, Crook, and John Gibbon. The success of his operations depended on the three commands converging with precise timing; the flaw in the plan was in the character of Custer, with his ravenous appetite for fame and his fatal determination to attack as quickly as possible and gain all the glory.

The trouble, too, was that the Indians wouldn't stay put and allow themselves to be surrounded by converging superior forces. On June 17, while Cody was beginning his journey West, Crook was badly cut up by Crazy Horse on a stream called the Rosebud. Sitting Bull's strategy was to strike at each enemy force before they could combine and overwhelm him.

Cody stopped off in Chicago to report at the Army's headquarters there. His offer to enlist again as a scout was joyously welcomed. His old outfit, the Fifth Cavalry, was being summoned from Arizona Territory to reinforce the effort against the Sioux, and Cody would serve under its new commander, Major General Wesley Merritt. He had also been commissioned by the New York *Herald* to act as its special correspondent, and from Chicago he dispatched a bulletin that may have lacked something in journalistic grace but exuded his eagerness to get back into the Indian fighting.

"There is going to be the damnedest Indian war ever known," he telegraphed the *Herald*. "No man can say when it is going to end. The Indians thus far have whipped every command they have met."

He arrived in Cheyenne just after the Fifth Cavalry detrained and prepared to take the field. His costuming was more dazzling than ever, having come from the wardrobe trunks of the Buffalo Bill theatrical troupe. It was a black velvet and gold uniform, of vaguely Mexican design, decorated with silver lace and topped by a white-brimmed, plumed sombrero with one side pinned up.

Despite his theatrical apparel, he was assigned to duty as chief of scouts. The Fifth Cavalry proceeded to Fort Laramie, where General Sheridan ordered it to scout the country between the Sioux agencies and the Black Hills and to interpose itself between Cheyenne war parties heading for the Little Big Horn country and their Sioux allies. It was an 80-mile march, begun on June 22, to the trails northward from the Spotted Tail and Red Cloud reservations. The Fifth Cavalry, now commanded by General Wesley Merritt, assumed a blocking position.

There were no telegraph lines in that country, and the cavalry was operating with only the vaguest information on what was happening elsewhere. The Fifth Cavalry drove back several bands of Cheyenne who were trying to reach Sitting Bull's forces on the Little Big Horn. That accomplished, it was supposed to join General Crook's column in operating against the main body of the hostiles.

The Fifth was just preparing to move out and join Crook when a messenger rode up with the news that sent a galvanic shudder throughout the entire white nation: news demonstrating that destiny did not dictate that the white man would win every battle with the redskins; news that conditioned white attitudes toward the Indians for almost a century. Custer had recklessly attacked the greatly superior Sioux and Cheyenne forces on the Little Big Horn, without waiting, as ordered, for Crook and Gibbon to join him. Custer and five troops of the Seventh Cavalry had been wiped out the afternoon of June 25. The savages had destroyed the forces of civilization. "The news of the massacre, which was the most terrible that ever undertook a command of our soldiers, was a profound shock to us all," Cody recalled. "We knew at once that we would all have work to do, and settled grimly into the preparations for it."

On the heels of that message about the Custer disaster came word from the Red Cloud Agency that 800 warriors were leaving the reservation to join Sitting Bull. If the Indian forces grew much more powerful, it would take the whole U.S. Army to contain them. General Merritt, risking a court-martial, decided to disregard his orders to join General Crook and instead cut off the 800 Cheyenne before they could join up with Sitting Bull.

Hard campaigning followed. The Fifth had to reach War Bonnet Creek and its trail crossing before the Cheyenne. The command marched all day, halted at 10 P.M., was awakened five hours later, and resumed the march before first light. It arrived on War Bonnet Creek at 8 P.M. on July 16. The following morning Cody was ordered to guide Company K, commanded by Lieutenant Charles King, later a writer who considerably enhanced the Buffalo Bill legend, to establish an outpost which would warn the main body of the Cheyenne's approach. It was rolling country in front of the outpost, with a line of bluffs marking the course of the War Bonnet to the rear.

At the outpost, on the summit of a sand hill, several Indian scouting parties were observed two or three miles away shortly before dawn. General Merritt was sent for. Just as the general was studying the situation through his field glasses, the regimental wagon train was coming up the Black Hills trail, with two troopers riding ahead. The wagoneers could not see the Indians, who were concealed by the rolling terrain. It was a ticklish situation. General Merritt didn't want to spring his ambush before the bulk of the Cheyenne had arrived on the scene; he also did not want his wagon train attacked. It was obvious that the Indians, about fifteen or twenty of them, were preparing to cut off the two troopers riding ahead of the supply train.

As Cody later told the story, he suggested to Merritt—he never hesitated to advise his superiors no matter how many stars they wore—"General, why not wait until the [Indian] scouts get a little nearer? When they are about to charge down on the two men, I will take fifteen soldiers, dash down and cut them off from their main body. That will prevent them from going back to report, and the others will fall into your trap."

General Merritt, he said, told him to proceed with the plan. Cody and a dozen troopers rode out to intercept the Indian scouting party before it could attack the wagon train. A running battle ensued in which three Cheyenne warriors were killed. After the Indians had been driven off, hundreds of Cheyenne suddenly appeared on the ridge ahead, a scene to be reenacted countless times in Western films.

The Fifth Cavalry and the whole Cheyenne war party now confronted each other. Then, incredible as it seems, both forces settled back to watch a duel between contending champions, Buffalo Bill and a young chief called Yellow Hand. It was like something out of the Wars of the Roses.

Yet General Merritt's after-action reports, Lieutenant King's account (*Campaigning with Crook*), and other sober witnesses certify that it happened. But Cody told it best, though his colorful account, of course, was refined by his ghost-writers.

Chief Yellow Hand rode out and challenged Cody to personal combat, shouting, "I know you, Pahaska. If you want to fight, come out and fight with me."

"Pahaska," a title in which Cody thereafter rejoiced, meant "Long Yellow Hair." The chief may have been color-blind, because Cody's hair was brown. Cody, at any rate, was enraged by the spectacle Yellow Hand presented. The young Cheyenne chief was wearing the American flag as a breechcloth, and from his belt dangled the scalp of a blond woman. The saucy fellow was a walking advertisement of Indian aggression.

As Cody told the story of the "Duel with Yellow Hand," which was to figure so largely in his future endeavors and to loom so magnificently in his publicity: "The chief was riding his horse to and fro in front of his men, in order to banter me. I concluded to accept his challenge. I turned and galloped toward him for fifty yards, and he rode toward me about the same distance. Both of us rode at full speed. When we were only thirty yards apart I raised my rifle and fired. His horse dropped dead under him, and he rolled over on the ground to clear himself of the carcass."

By some accounts Yellow Hand was armed only with a tomahawk and in that case must have issued his challenge with the understanding that Buffalo Bill would confront him with a knife, not, unsportingly, with a rifle. Cody, however, claimed that Yellow Hand was armed with a rifle.

"Almost at the same instant my own horse stepped into a hole and fell heavily. The fall hurt me but little, and almost instantly I was on my feet. There was no time to lie down and nurse slight injuries. The chief and I were now both on our feet, not twenty paces apart. We fired at each other at the same instant. My usual luck held. His bullet whizzed harmlessly past my head, while mine struck him full in the breast.

"He reeled and fell, but I took no chances. He had barely touched the ground, when I was upon him, knife in hand, and to make sure of him drove the steel into his heart."

But that wasn't the end of it. A good Indian was not only a

dead Indian but a scalped Indian. The practice, which constituted a surefire body count, had long been popular among plainsmen.

Cody afterward described the process in one chilling sentence: "Jerking his war-bonnet off I scientifically scalped him in about five seconds."

Then he rode back to his cheering comrades, waving his grisly trophy and shouting a line that sounded as though it had been composed by Ned Buntline:

"The first scalp for Custer!"

Later the scene was recaptured by Western muralists for the benefit of connoisseurs of saloon art, one of the more memorable paintings, by Robert Lindneux, later being consigned to display at the Buffalo Bill Museum in Cody, Wyoming.

There was a curious domestic sequel to the killing and scalping of Chief Yellow Hand. Always the sentimentalist where his feats of valor were concerned, Cody sent the scalp home to Rochester. He evidently believed that Louisa might fancy it as a conversation piece, possibly displayed under a glass dome in her parlor with other ornaments of a lively career.

The package was sent express from Fort McPherson and evidently was delivered so swiftly that Mrs. Cody had not even heard of the Indian gentleman whose topknot was being presented to her or of her husband's hand-to-hand encounter, which would soon overshadow the whole Fifth Cavalry campaign on the War Bonnet. After prying open the box with a hatchet, she later recollected, "a terrific odor caught my nostrils. . . . I reeled slightly—then reached for the contents. Then I fainted. For I had brought from that box the raw, red scalp of an Indian!"

When Cody returned home weeks later, his wife upbraided him for sending such a grisly souvenir of his adventures.

"What on earth did you send me that old scalp for? Aren't you ashamed of yourself? It nearly scared me to death."

"Why," he guilelessly replied, "I thought you'd like it. I was so excited that I just said to myself that I'd send this scalp home to Mamma and let her know how fine a time I was having out there, because it was about the best fight I ever had."

Then he provided Mrs. Cody and their little daughter with an exuberant account of how he had dispatched Yellow Hand, sparing none of the gory details. Such was life in an Indian fighter's family.

The death of Yellow Hand had been followed by a chase across the prairies. The Cheyenne lost heart after the death of the chief and broke for their reservation, abandoning large stores of arms, ammunitions, food, blankets, and other supplies they had brought for the abortive campaign with Sitting Bull. Once the chase was over, there was a flurry of dispute over who had really killed Yellow Hand. One Sergeant Jacob Blaut dared to assert that he had fired at the young chief at the same time as Cody and claimed that his shot killed Yellow Hand. Cody's version, however, was substantiated by Lieutenant King and a Sergeant Richardson, who were also close by.

When the command returned to Fort Laramie Cody remembered that he was supposed to be acting as a special correspondent for the New York *Herald*. Perhaps overcome by modesty, he asked Lieutenant King to compose the dispatch for him. It was written in the style of a military communiqué, but Lieutenant King did not neglect to mention his friend's exploit in stirring prose: "Yellow Hand, a young Cheyenne brave, came foremost, singling out Buffalo Bill as a foeman worthy of his steel. Cody coolly knelt and, taking deliberate aim, sent his bullet into his horse's head. Down went the two, and before his friends could reach him, a second shot from Bill's rifle laid the redskin low. . . ."

By the time that and other stories on "The Death of Yellow Hand" were published, Buffalo Bill's fame was considerably enhanced. The feat helped to ease some of the shock over the Custer disaster and to reassure white Americans that there were still heroes around capable of doing in the redskins, with their bare hands if necessary. The Great Sioux War ended with the Indians outnumbered and dispersed, Crazy Horse a fugitive in the Black Hills, Sitting Bull in flight with some of his followers across the Canadian border.

Cody did not care to participate in the donkey work of rounding up the remaining hostiles. Besides, he was saddened by the deaths of two close friends. Buffalo Chips White was killed when the Fifth Cavalry raided one of Crazy Horse's villages at Slim Butte. And Wild Bill Hickok—in reality a much more spectacular character than Cody, but one who lacked the pliability to profit from his fame—died ignominiously from a bullet in the back of the head while playing poker in a Black Hills saloon. It must have occurred to Cody that it was better to be a live hero, and a rich one, than a defunct legend.

John Burke had been urging him to return East posthaste to capitalize on the publicity he had been getting, and Cody agreed, going straight to New York City without making a detour for a reunion with his wife and daughters in Rochester. His theatrical company was reassembled, this time without Texas Jack and Mlle. Morlacchi. His new co-star was Captain Jack Crawford, billed as "The Poet Scout of the Black Hills."

Crawford was a curiosity both on the border and in the theater because he was a total abstainer. He was born in County Donegal, Ireland, and was brought to Pennsylvania as a child. He enlisted in the Union Army and was badly wounded at Spottsylvania Court House. After recovering from his wound, he served as an Army scout and dispatch rider, then as military correspondent for the Omaha *Bee*. All the time he was composing poetry of the most bathetic sort.

During the Fifth Cavalry's recent campaign he had joined Cody's scouting force. When he caught up with the regiment, he brought a present for Cody—a bottle of whiskey—from one of the latter's admirers. This astonished Cody, as he explained. "I will say in passing that I don't believe there is another scout in the west that would have brought a full bottle of whiskey three hundred miles."

Cody signed him on for a co-starring role despite a certain priggishness in the "Poet Scout's" makeup which must have often irked him. The flavor of the Crawford personality was conveyed in a Chicago newspaper interview: "We looked down at the man, with his long flowing hair, reaching far down on his shoulders, wearing a broad-brimmed hat, a wildly fringed buckskin overcoat, blue shirt and light silk necktie, more nearly representing in appearance an ideal old-school Spanish cavalier than the writer of such sweet lines."

The reporter suggested, "Let us take a drink, Captain."

"No, I thank you," Crawford replied. "I never drink but I will recite you a poem entitled Mother's Prayers."

Crawford then recited the poem that outraged misanthropes from coast to coast but delighted most of his audiences with its unabashed sentimentality:

> Mother who in days of childhood,
>   Prayed as only mothers pray;
> Keep him in the narrow pathway,
>   Let him not be led astray;
> And when danger hovered o'er me,
>   And when life was full of cares,
> Then a sweet form passed before me,
>   And I thought of Mother's prayers.

The Chicago journalist confessed that he required a number of drinks after being briefly submerged in Crawford's treacly sentiments.

There must have been times on the Eastern tour beginning in the early autumn of 1876 when Cody yearned to have

Wild Bill back breaking up barrooms in the place of the
sanctimonious Poet Jack, but the combination paid off at the
box office. They alternated between performances of *Scouts
of the Plains* and a new version of *The Red Right Hand,*
which John Burke had rewritten to include the duel with
Yellow Hand. The new melodrama was three-sheeted by
Cody's advance agents as follows:

First appearance since his return
from the Indian wars
Buffalo Bill Combination
HON. W. F. CODY
Supported by Capt. Jack
"The Poet Scout of the Black Hills"
In the new drama founded on incidents
in the late Indian War
entitled
THE RED RIGHT HAND
or
BUFFALO BILL'S FIRST SCALP FOR CUSTER

The theatergoing public mobbed the box offices, eager as
it was for dramatic evidence that Custer's death had been
avenged, somehow, by the killing and scalping of Yellow
Hand. Yet there were some chicken-hearted or redskin-loving
Easterners who objected to certain aspects of the exploitation.
Cody's advancemen rented a store window in each city in
which he was about to appear and displayed the feathered
headdress, the ornaments, and the knife and tomahawk that
Cody had stripped from Yellow Hand's body. In New England, particularly, some newspapers and various religious
groups objected to "displaying the blood-stained trophies of
his murderous deeds," and thereafter the souvenirs were not
exposed to the public eye.

For several seasons Cody and his troupe reaped a bountiful harvest at the box office. Despite the prediction that Cali-
fornians would not be attracted by his sort of showmanship,
he extended his tour to the Pacific Coast and played to

packed houses everywhere. Even the West, it seemed, was succumbing to the mythologists—and they were very busy from 1876 on. As chief legend maker, John Burke was convinced that it was impossible to overestimate the public's gullibility. He and various literary subcontractors turned out such works as *Pearl of the Prairies, or The Scout and the Renegade; Deadly Eye;* and *Prairie and Prince, the Boy Outlaw, or Trailed to His Doom.* To some extent, apparently, Cody collaborated on these endeavors. His implication in the myth-making process was attested by a letter he wrote to one publisher while suffering qualms of modesty:

"I am sorry to have to lie so outrageously in this yarn. My hero has killed more Indians on the war trail than I have killed in all my life. But I understand this is what is expected of border tales. If you think the revolver and Bowie knife are used too freely, you may cut out a fatal shot or stab wherever you think wise."

So far as can be determined he was sometimes the hero of the dime novels issued under his imprimatur, sometimes the author or at least collaborator, but always the profit-sharer. It made a lucrative sideline to his trouping, especially after Burke got the bright idea of selling the paperbacks in theaters where Buffalo Bill was appearing.

He and Burke were shrewd enough to expand the company's repertoire and also to capitalize on the public's eagerness to see dramatizations of recent and necessarily bloody events. These pseudo-documentaries were only loosely based on fact, but there were few scholarly quibblers among the paying customers and triflings with history were more than compensated for by the presence of a score of real, live Indians whom Burke persuaded to leave the Red Cloud reservation and join the Buffalo Bill troupe. No one saw anything particularly distasteful, or even ironic, in the victims of Western conquest portraying themselves as bloodthirsty savages bent on wiping out the white race. All's fair in love, war, and show biz.

The success of *The Red Right Hand* as topical drama encouraged Burke and Cody to commission a dime novelist, Major A. S. Burt, to write a play titled *May Cody, or Lost and Won*. Its background was the Mormon massacre of a settlers' wagon train at Mountain Meadow. Cody's sister was supposedly the heroine, though she had never been anywhere near Mountain Meadow, and her role was played by an actress named Constance Hamblin. The show opened at the Bowery Theater on September 3, 1877, and was the most profitable of all the productions in which Cody and Burke had participated thus far. *May Cody* was succeeded in the Cody repertoire by such dramas as *Boy Chief of the Plains* and other plays tailored to his stage personality.

During those years between 1876 and 1880 Cody was cashing in on a bonanza which might, for all he knew, be played out at any moment. Often he wearied of trouping and sometimes was disgusted by all the heroic posturing required of him off and onstage. His sister Helen came backstage to see him after a performance in Leavenworth and later quoted him as saying, "Oh, Nellie, don't say anything about it. If heaven will forgive me for this foolishness, I promise to quit it forever as soon as this season is finished."

Yet, he must have asked himself, how could he quit when the money tree kept on showering down its fruit? In seven years as a performer, according to Burke, he had earned $135,000.

Not much of that was saved, since he spent money freely on himself and his family and was always an easy touch for any down-and-outer. He did have enough, however, to satisfy Mrs. Cody's craving for a comfortable home of her own with plenty of empty space around her to guarantee privacy. In partnership with Major Frank North, he bought a large cattle ranch on the Dismal River north of North Platte, Nebraska, near the Wyoming line. He also built a large house just outside North Platte for Louisa and their two daughters, which he called Welcome Wigwam. When he came in off the road, he usually invited old friends to stay with him, hospitality that was often terminated when Mrs. Cody objected to their rough language, their marathon poker sessions, and their strenuous demands on the Cody liquor supply.

The Honorable William F. Cody, as he was locally known, was regarded with pride by his fellow citizens. Not only was he the co-owner of a large cattle spread but one of the most famous men in the country. The local Grand Army of the Republic post was named for him, and the North Platte weekly declared the town should congratulate itself on "the possession of a citizen whose prominence of position is not bounded by his township, his county or his state, but whose name is a household word, whose pictures are familiar to people throughout the nation. . . ."

Reluctantly, unable to resist the tidal pull of what he considered "immense success and comparative wealth," he went out on the road again for the season of 1880-81, this time with an epic titled *White Beaver,* with several authentic Arapaho chiefs in the supporting cast. It managed to outdraw even such great commercial successes as *East Lynne,* which was a marvel of craftsmanship compared to *White Beaver.* Burke assured him that he would continue to be a sensational attraction as long as he could haul himself onstage, and since Cody was then only thirty-five years old, a seemingly endless vista of local opera houses, anonymous hotel rooms, and squalid dressing rooms loomed before him. If Burke as creator and promoter of the expanding legend could never permit himself a moment of doubt, or break the spell of self-hypnosis, Cody himself was able to reflect wryly, even cynically, on the preposterous role he was called upon to play. "That I did not lose my life," he once said, "has always been a marvel to me—no, not from the use of real bullets instead of blank cartridges, but from some members of an irate audience."

Domestic happiness became a thing of the past, too, following a distressing scene at the end of his 1881 road tour. Louisa unwisely decided to surprise her husband by meeting him in Omaha, where the tour had just ended. It appeared to her jealous eye that Will was operating a mobile harem in the guise of a theatrical troupe.

When she arrived at his hotel, she found him kissing several of the actresses good-bye with an ardor which seemed excessive and indicated there were warmer personal relationships in the Buffalo Bill touring company than might be expected of professional colleagues.

Mrs. Cody's temper flared alarmingly, then burned with a cold rage all that summer, during which she refused to speak to her husband. He tried to close the breach between them by signing over all the Nebraska property he had acquired to her name. But she was not appeased and insisted on speaking to him through a third party. "Tell Mr. Cody to take his nose out of the decanter. . . ." And so forth. "Welcome Wigwam" now seemed to be a misnomer. When he went on the road again that fall the estrangement had not ended, and from then on their marriage was only a continuing formality.

7

Buffalo Bill Goes Outdoors

JUST how the Wild West Show developed and for many years was as indigenous to the American scene as Fourth of July oratory, ice cream socials, and torchlight parades is a matter of controversy. There were several claimants to the honor, but Buffalo Bill's, as amplified by his publicity apparatus, was the loudest and most persistent.

Cody himself provided several accounts of how that vast commercial enterprise was conceived. Once he recalled that Ned Buntline had told him, "Take the prairies and the Injuns and everything else right to 'em. That's the idea. There ain't room on a stage to do anything worthwhile. But there would be a big lot where we could have horses and buffalo and the old Deadwood coach and everything! That'd be something they'd never seen before! That'd be showing them the West!"

On another occasion Cody recalled that he had first discussed the idea with General Sheridan in 1872, when it seemed that the Army wouldn't have much more use for cavalry scouts. "One night," he said, "I went out for a walk to think it over, and the idea struck me I might get up a little show of western life and pull over some money on that. I put it up to General Sheridan and asked him what he thought about it. 'Never do in the world, Billy,' he said. 'First thing you know some of those bucking broncos would buck into the audience and kill a couple of people. Or else the buffalo would stampede and there'd be all kinds of trouble.' "

A rival claimant of equal renown was P. T. Barnum, who told a biographer that he had dreamed up the idea of a Wild West Show as early as 1860, complete with Indians, horses, and buffalo, but never got around to producing it.

Actually, like so much of his career and of the public personality he created for himself, not to forget the expropriation of the McCanles shootout, it seems probable that the Wild West Show was yet another borrowing from the legacy of Wild Bill Hickok. Indisputably Hickok had organized and appeared in an outdoor show of that sort in 1870, more than a dozen years before Cody first galloped into an arena, and even longer before such imitations as Oklahoma Ike, Honest Bill, Denver Pete, the Lamonte Brothers, and the Miller Brothers 101 Ranch took to the road in their gaudily painted caravans. And certainly Cody must have learned much from Hickok's experiences, which were disastrous from beginning to end. Wild Bill made all the mistakes from which Buffalo Bill profited. Such a venture had to be well organized, well capitalized, and well planned. Hickok's presentation, "The Daring Buffalo Chase of the Plains," was none of these.

Early in 1870, as one of Hickok's later biographers has recorded, he "began to see himself as a unique sort of institution, patented, trademarked and copyrighted. Hickok's first venture into show business was a Wild West show, the first of its kind. No matter how much debunking has been done on his career, not all of it unwarranted, even the more skeptical historians have conceded that he was the innovator of this type of entertainment. Admittedly it was a humble and unsuccessful beginning, but his conception was the seedling from which Buffalo Bill reaped several fortunes . . . presenting a blank-cartridge-riddled version of the West that never existed except in a showman's fancy."

With three cowboy assistants, Hickok had roped six buffalo from a herd on the Republican River and then took two weeks hauling, dragging, and kicking the beasts into the railroad yards at Ogallala, Nebraska. He then engaged four unemployed Comanches, who agreed to join the show only if they could bring along their pets, a cinnamon bear and a monkey. In May, 1870, Hickok took his outfit to Niagara Falls, on the Canadian side of the border, hoping to attract some of the thousands of annual visitors to the waterfalls. His only capital was several thousand dollars he had won over the cow-town gaming tables. The first and only performance of "The Daring Buffalo Chase" was a fiasco. It was staged in a wire enclosure without grandstands. Hickok got the "daring chase" underway by firing his pistol. The buffalo obliged by charging wildly around the enclosure, followed by the Comanches, then by a pack of dogs attracted by the excitement, and finally by a horde of small boys. It was more of a spectacle than Hickok could have foreseen. The buffalo broke through the fence and rampaged through a nearby residential section; the bear crashed through the gate of his cage, seized an Italian sausage vendor posted nearby and nearly hugged him to death, then gobbled up all the sausages. When the dust settled, Hickok found that his receipts totaled $123.86. He and his cowboy assistants had recaptured the buffalo, who were sold to Niagara butchers; the proceeds were just enough to buy tickets home for the Comanches. Hickok and the cowboys had to ride the freights back to Kansas.

Cody, a more cautious and businesslike man, would make certain his own debut in the outdoor extravaganza was plotted to the last detail. His experiences with a touring theatrical company had taught him the importance of logistics, scheduling, advance publicity, and advertising. Half of showmanship was the part the public never saw.

Producing a Wild West show had become something of an obsession with him by early 1882, when he brought his latest show, *Prairie Wolf,* to the Grand Opera House in Brooklyn and met the third member of the triumvirate who, along with Cody and Burke, was to make a world-famous institution of the outdoor horse opera. Appearing at another Brooklyn theater was a stock company called the Salsbury Troubadors, which was presenting *Fawn of the Glen, or the Civilized Indian.*

The manager of the rival troupe was Nate Salsbury, who was just two days younger than Cody. Orphaned in early childhood, he had run away from his brutal stepfather's home at the age of fifteen and enlisted in the Union Army. Among other military misadventures, he had spent seven months as a prisoner in the death camp of Andersonville. On his release, he broke into the theater, was an actor, manager, and playwright and trouped all over America and Australia. Nobody knew more about getting a show on the road than Nate Salsbury, and few possessed his theatrical imagination.

By his own account he, too, had conceived the idea of an outdoor Western spectacle in 1877, while journeying home from Australia. In a memorandum written shortly before his death, he affirmed that he had "mapped out a show that would be constituted of elements that had never been employed in concerted effort in the history of show business. I knew that certain circus managers had tried to reproduce the riding of the plains, by made-up professional circus riders, but I knew they had never had the real thing. . . . I decided that such an entertainment must have a well known figurehead to attract attention. After careful consideration I resolved to get W. F. Cody as my central figure."

Five years later, that conception still nagging at him, he seized the opportunity of Cody's proximity and invited him to lunch. Thus it happened that the first sizable commercialization of the Western saga was plotted in a Brooklyn restaurant. Both men had been thinking along the same lines and agreed that there was a fortune waiting to be claimed in taking the Western out of stuffy theaters and into the open air, where it belonged. They parted with the agreement that they would work separately toward that joint objective in the coming months.

That summer, in North Platte, the citizens had decided to stage an "Old Glory Blowout" to celebrate the Fourth of July. They asked Cody, naturally enough, to take charge of the program. This was his opportunity, he saw, to experiment with an outdoor show. Instead of the bronco-busting contests usually staged on such occasions, he would put on a Wild West show. He bought a stagecoach from the old Deadwood line, engaged cowboys and Indians, rounded up a small buffalo herd, arranged for horse races and sharpshooting contests. The climax of the program was to be a stagecoach holdup.

The largest crowds ever seen in North Platte, with some people coming hundreds of miles, wildly acclaimed the entertainment. Cody was confirmed in his belief that the outdoor show, Western style, could be as popular as the circus.

Almost from the moment the dust settled over the North Platte celebration, he began making preparations for a traveling Wild West show. One of the men who had participated in the "Old Glory Blowout" was a dentist named W. F. Carver, whose real vocation was marksmanship. Doc Carver, billing himself as "The Evil Spirit of the Plains," had traveled around the country exhibiting his talent with the rifle. There was no doubt of his marksmanship—he could plug a nickel thrown into the air time after time and rarely miss— but it was more difficult to substantiate his claims to having been an Indian fighter and a buffalo hunter with a record that excelled Cody's. His "Evil Spirit" title, he claimed, had been given him by the Indians in awed honor of his various talents. Cody was soon to regard him as *his* evil genius. Almost from the beginning of their association there was jealousy and rivalry.

Privately, Cody was a fairly modest man, with a sense of proportion that would not allow him to be overcome by the cloying fragrance of his own publicity. Among friends he would scoff at the claims made for him, though such claims were made by his own hirelings. Doc Carver, however, was inclined to believe his own publicity, one broadside of which read, "At five years of age he was regarded as a phenomenal rifle shot. He was the greatest curiosity among the simple frontiersmen, who regarded him as one upon whom the Almighty had bestowed a spell, and more than one old frontiersman visited young Carver and left feeling satisfied in his own mind that the child was in league with the devil. . . . With long golden hair framing his handsome face, the *tout ensemble* makes him the perfect picture of a thoroughbred, dashing, whole-souled Western gentleman. . . . With his own brain he originated rifle shooting in the air. He reduced it to a system, and came before the public eight years ago, and nearly every man in America thought him crazy to shoot nickels, thrown in the air, with rifle balls, but the performance must be seen to be believed."

For some reason, despite personality clashes, possibly because, as Carver's biographer claims, the dentist had $80,000 to invest in the show, Cody took him on as a partner and co-star. He then telegraphed Nate Salsbury, somewhat disingenuously, and inquired whether he was willing to become a third partner—if Carver didn't object. Salsbury later said he considered Carver a "fakir"—as though that weren't the name of the game—and replied to Cody that he wasn't interested in any proposition including Carver. So for the time being Salsbury opted out. Cody and Carver would be partners, John M. Burke the press agent and advance man.

The winter of 1882-83 they organized and endlessly rehearsed the show. Cody later wrote that he was pleased that the show was put together in the nearby town of Columbus, Nebraska, which served as its headquarters, because that was "the spot famed from time immemorial as the deadline between the powerful Pawnees south of it and the Sioux to the north, a place fairly entitled to its appellation of the dark and bloody ground. This nursery cradle was in a section well grassed, watered and wooded, a natural commissary depot, and in all respects suitable for the beginning of such a venture."

A mettlesome cast was assembled in support of Cody and Carver. Captain A. H. Bogardus, a champion clay-pigeon shot, was to receive third billing. Major Frank North would be presented as "The White Chief of the Pawnees," a newly concocted title. A number of Pawnees were produced for villainous services in the show by Gordon Lillie, a pudgy, self-assertive fellow who called himself Pawnee Bill and who later set himself up as Cody's rival as the rightful representation of all that was glorious about the winning of the West. For all his claims to derring-do, Lillie actually had been an interpreter on the Pawnee reservation.

Perhaps of greater value to the show than anyone but Cody among the temperamental men who claimed top billing were the young and daring riders recruited from various Nebraska ranches: Buck Taylor, who threw steers around like sacks of grain; Jim Lawson, the star roper; and Seth Hathaway, the Pony Express rider.

Another recruit, one who was to stay with Buffalo Bill till the end of his career and who became his adopted son, was the nine-year-old Johnny Baker. An orphan born in North Platte, he was to live a boyhood and youth envied by every other boy in America. Johnny had attached himself to Cody during the latter's summer stays at the Welcome Wigwam and was allowed to take care of Cody's horses and equipment. He begged to go along with the show, and Cody finally agreed that he would throw the blue glass balls in the air which Cody would shatter as part of his marksmanship act. Later he was billed as "The Cowboy Kid" and became a celebrated marksman, his head patted by Presidents and European royalty.

One of the inanimate stars of the production was the old Concord mail coach that had survived all sorts of hazards on the Deadwood run. No doubt the history claimed for the vehicle in the show's publicity was concocted at least in part by John M. Burke. Time after time, Burke wrote, that coach had been attacked by Sioux war parties and stage robbers. Once the driver was killed and Calamity Jane herself "seized the lines and brought the coach to its destination." Not only that but "When Buffalo Bill returned from his scout with General Crook [sic] in 1876, he rode in this self-same coach, bringing with him the scalps of several of the Indians whom he had met."

Early in May, 1883, "The Wild West, Rocky Mountain and Prairie Exhibition" was transported to Omaha for its first engagement at the fairgrounds on May 17. Omaha had been plastered with three sheets proclaiming: "The Grassy Sward Our Carpet, Heaven's Azure Canopy Our Canvas, No Tinsel, No Gilding, No Humbug. No Sideshows or Freaks."

Fortunately no claims had been made for the smoothness or professionalism of the performance. A lot of things went wrong, as was to be expected at a break-in performance, but the audiences were suitably enthralled. The show began with a bareback pony race between the Pawnees and was climaxed by what was advertised as the "grand realistic battle scene depicting the capture, torture and death of a scout by the savages" and the "startling and soul-stirring attack on the Deadwood mail-coach," with Cody and Carver riding in with their scouts to the rescue.

Doc Carver was something of a disappointment on that first day before a paying audience. He kept missing his shots, until the crowd began yelling, "We want Bill Cody!" Cody succeeded him in the arena and put on a splendid display of marksmanship. The incident so angered Carver that the partnership was almost sundered on the spot.

From Omaha the show headed East in a sixteen-car train. One car was a traveling barroom, loaded with scores of cases of whiskey, in which Cody himself was the leading patron. From all accounts, friendly and otherwise, he was then drinking heavily—which may have been one reason the show was so badly managed. There were also serious problems with transportation, with discipline in the company, with making the performance move swiftly from one action set piece to the next. Often the cowboys could not be found in time for the performance until all the surrounding saloons were scoured. Just when Cody needed all his wits about him, he succumbed to his more feckless traits of character. He seemed to be determined not only to outshoot Doc Carver but outdrink all comers.

The first weeks of the tour, in fact, constituted an extended spree for its chief performer. Gordon Lillie, or Pawnee Bill, as manager of the Pawnee troupe, caught up with the show after it left Omaha and later professed to have been shocked at the degradation which drink had wrought in Cody. "I had been carrying around in my mind for a dozen years or more, the picture of Buffalo Bill as I had first seen him, a fine looking man, well groomed, with a beautiful buffalo robe coat. I never was so disappointed in my life. He had been sleeping on the floor of a tent in some hay, his fur coat was missing, his hair was all matted and he was drunk. . . . Colonel Cody was drunk every day for our first five weeks out."

The show was making money, but the proceeds seemed to flow in one end of the box office and out the other, perhaps in the direction of the bar car. Another observer, Courtney Ryley Cooper, wrote that during the first weeks on the road "it was an eternal gamble as to whether the show would exist from one day to the next, not because of a lack of money, but simply through an absence of human endurance necessary to stay awake twenty hours out of twenty-four, that the birth of a new amusement enterprise might properly be celebrated. When the show got into town and the biggest saloon announced an open house for the company, it was always quite all right with Bill Cody. In fact, striving always to be the good fellow, he would be in the thickest of the celebration, whooping it up as long as anyone else—and sometimes a bit longer. Then, at the last possible moment there would be a rush to the show lot, and as much attention paid to business as possible under the circumstances."

Mostly the show played at fairgrounds or in vacant lots large enough to accommodate an arena, grandstand, stables, and corral. Whatever the troubles backstage, whatever the degree of sobriety achieved by the performers on any given occasion, it was an eye-popping marvel to the people of the Eastern cities. It was acclaimed in Boston and in Newport, where the summer colony turned out en masse and Lord Mandeville rode in the Deadwood stage and pretended to be wounded during the pursuit and attack by the Indians. In Hartford the *Courant* declared the exhibition was the best outdoor show ever seen there. No matter how much liquor was boiling around inside, Cody, with the professionalism he had acquired in the theater, always managed to spruce up and make a splendid appearance when it came time to ride into the arena. The Hartford *Courant* described him as "a perfect model of manly beauty. Mounted on his blooded horse, he rode around the grounds, the observed of all observers. Cody was an extraordinary figure, and sits on a horse as if he were born in a saddle. His feats of shooting are perfectly wonderful. . . ."

By the time the show trouped on to Coney Island, where it settled down for a five-week stay, Cody and Carver were hardly speaking to each other. Carver, a teetotaler, believed that Cody's boozing—and, not least, the example he set for the rest of the company—was going to bring about the enterprise's collapse. Cody, on the other hand, was disgusted by Carver's arrogance and his outbursts of temperament. Whenever Carver had an off day with his marksmanship, he vented his spleen on the hired hands. One day at Coney Island, after missing a number of shots, he broke his rifle over his horse's head and punched the assistant who tossed the nickels into the air.

Early that autumn the show turned westward, played Chicago, and continued on to Omaha, where it was disbanded for the winter. It was seriously questioned whether it would ever take the road again; certainly it would not under the joint management of Cody and Carver. In Chicago, Nate Salsbury and his stock company happened to be appearing in one of the theaters when the Cody-Carver exhibition made its stand. Salsbury went out to catch a performance, which was ragged and haphazard, still lacking in discipline, and predicted the outfit would go bankrupt. Cody looked up Salsbury at his hotel and confirmed Salsbury's impression of looming disaster. Cody, as Salsbury recorded, "said that if I did not take hold of the show he was going to quit the whole thing. He said he was through with Carver, and that he would not go through another such summer for a hundred thousand dollars."

Before he left Chicago, Cody signed a partnership agreement with Salsbury, even though the one with Carver had not yet been dissolved.

The showdown with Carver came several weeks later in Omaha, after the troupe was disbanded for the winter. Cody had been summoned home on a tragic errand, the funeral of his daughter Orra. There had been a temporary reconciliation with Louisa the previous year, and a third daughter, Irma, had been born in February before Cody went on the road.

Later Doc Carver claimed that when he met Cody in Omaha the latter was on another binge, possibly occasioned by his daughter's death. Carver, as he told his biographer, went up to Cody's room at the Paxton Hotel, found him surrounded by "a score or more empty bottles," and had to shake him out of an alcoholic stupor. A few harsh words were exchanged by the ill-matched partners. About the only subject they could agree on was that they had come to a parting of ways and that the only sensible method of splitting up their joint assets was to flip a silver dollar for all the horses, buffalo, rolling stock, and other assets. Then Carver departed, claiming that Cody owed him $29,000. That and other matters, not least their antipathetic personalities, caused a lifelong vendetta between the two men. Carver immediately organized his own show, Carver's Wild West, with Cody's former co-star, the Poet Scout Jack Crawford, as his chief supporting attraction.

The early spring of 1884 Cody had himself in hand again and was energetically supervising the new road show which would be billed as Buffalo Bill's Wild West with Cody as president, Salsbury as vice-president, and John M. Burke as general manager on its letterheads and posters. Salsbury was pumping money into the enterprise but had not yet assumed control of its management, since he wanted to continue with his very profitable traveling stock company.

Colonel Prentiss Ingraham, who had served his apprenticeship as an icon maker by turning out hundreds of Buffalo Bill stories for the magazines and paperbacks, had joined Burke's staff and was composing some gaudily-hued advertising.

In a manner pleasing to all those who were enriching themselves from the exploitation of the West—everyone from mining magnates and railroad builders to land speculators and corrupt Indian agents—the new promotional line stressed that anyone, by catching a performance of Buffalo Bill's Wild West, would learn all he needed to know about how the West was conquered. In a swirl of horsemanship, a charge of Indian warriors, a burst of marksmanship, a series of tableaux demonstrating how a few valiant scouts led by Buffalo Bill beat off menacing hordes of red-skinned savages, the Eastern ignoramus would be instructed in Western history.

As conceived by the shrewd Nate Salsbury, who understood that American audiences liked to believe they were being educated and entertained at the same time, the show's advertising promised all sorts of instructive delights: "The Amusement Triumph of the age. The Romantic West brought East in Reality. Everything Genuine. Each Scene Instructive. Civilization's reception to its pioneers. Amusement, Instruction and Education to All. A Year's Visit West in Three Hours. Actual Scenes in the Nation's Progress . . ."

This advertising theme, sounded year after year for almost three decades, achieved an immeasurable impact on the national consciousness. There is no more insistent drumbeat of propaganda than that of a popular medium; no government can broadcast its views so effectively. How compelling a figure was President Rutherford B. Hayes compared to Buffalo Bill, magnificent in buckskins and mounted on a white charger? Was it any wonder that the masses, now being expanded annually by hundreds of thousands of immigrants who could not read English but who could grasp the meaning of Buffalo Bill's spectacle, were willing to accept the Wild West Show as an accurate rendering of recent history? Not many Americans were eager to deny the signed statement of a Congressional Medal of Honor holder and certified national hero that this was "a true rescript of the frontier as I know it to be, and which no fictitious pen can describe." To question that "rescript" would have been un-American.

With Salsbury's sizable bankroll behind the new venture, Cody assembled a highly picturesque company to take on the road in the spring of 1884. Among them was David L. Payne, also known as Old Oxheart, Scout of the Cimarron, whose struggles to colonize Indian Territory were related in the show's program. The brochure claimed that Payne's 100,000 fellow colonists were being harassed by Washington, which hadn't thrown the territory open for official settlement yet, and by the Indians, who "have surrounded his cabin in the lonely solitude of the primeval forests, threatened his life, tried to burn down his house, and watched day and night for opportunity to murder him. . . . With his trusty Winchester he has defended his cabin against scores of his wily foes. . . . While waiting for certain developments in his still continued contest, Capt. Payne will accompany, for recreation only, his old friend Buffalo Bill's 'Wild West,' to renew again the cherished object so dear to the progressive spirit of the Oklahoma Raiders."

When you winnowed the salient facts from Prentiss Ingraham's purplish prose, you came up with an Old Oxheart determined to grab a large section of Oklahoma against Washington's feeble efforts to protect the Indians' rights.

Another ripe old character was John Nelson, the squaw man, who presided over what was billed as the camp of "genuine blanket Indians." He was the son-in-law of the great Sioux chief Red Cloud, and his wife and several of their children traveled with the show. One of Nelson's duties was to "ride shotgun" on the Deadwood stage. Con Groner, "the cowboy sheriff of the Platte," was alleged to have captured more than fifty murderers. The featured marksman was one Dr. W. F. Powell—it almost seemed that the Old West was overrun by dentists with twitching trigger fingers—who was also known as White Beaver. The show's program identified him as "chief medicine man of the Winnebago Sioux—a reckless adventurer on the boundless prairies, and yet in elegant society as amiable as a schoolgirl in the ballroom; evincing the polish of the aristocrat and a cultured mind that shines with vigorous lustre where learning displays itself."

The first engagement of this new aggregation was at the St. Louis racetrack early in May. Unfortunately Doc Carver's show had played there a week earlier, and before leaving town Carver had published an advertisement in the St. Louis papers warning the populace not to contaminate themselves by going to see Buffalo Bill: "He who loves Wine and Women, and Indulges to Excess, is not a fit Representative of Mankind to appear before the Public as an Instructor of Refined women and children."

Buffalo Bill proceeded to lend substance to Doc Carver's malicious moralizing by going on a monumental bender just before the opening day. Nate Salsbury happened to arrive just then to check on his investment. Out at the racetrack everything was in turmoil, and Cody himself was "boiling drunk," as Salsbury noted in a memorandum. "I found him surrounded by a lot of harpies called old timers who were getting as drunk as he at his expense. . . . He had taken a plug hat from someone in the crowd, and jammed it on his head, and as his hair was long and thick in those days, a more ridiculous figure could not be imagined than he cut with his arm around White Beaver while they rehearsed the exploits of the frontier to the gaping gang of bloodsuckers that surrounded them."

Salsbury went back to his hotel and wrote Cody a reproving letter, pointing out that they were partners in a considerable enterprise, that they had to behave in a businesslike way, that Cody could not maintain discipline if he continued to play Buffalo Bibulous. Cody replied by taking the pledge and humbly writing his partner, "Your very sensible and truly rightful letter has just been read. . . . I solemnly promise you that after this you will never see me under the influence of liquor. I may have to take two or three drinks today to brace up . . . that will be all as long as we are partners. . . . This drinking surely ends today and your pard will be himself, and on deck all the time. . . ."

Apparently Cody overbraced himself, and he was still struggling with the demon when the company reached Pittsburgh. He had to quit drinking there because, as he put it, "my liver flopped," and he had to take to his bed.

From there the show proceeded to New York and a long stand at the Polo Grounds. To advertise the opening, Cody, Captain Bogardus, and Colonel Ingraham, along with six newspaper reporters, rode up Fifth Avenue in the Deadwood coach and rolled onto the original Polo Grounds. Salsbury had rejoined the show to tighten up the program and give it a faster pace. Cody evidently did not want to arouse his partner's suspicions that he was still boozing on the sly, because at a party given for the New York press at least one journalist noted his evasiveness on the subject. "A large barrel and several corpulent bottles were noticeable in a corner of the tent," he wrote, "and the eyes of a number of persons in the party turned upon them during the progress of the meal. Mr. Cody, however, noticing these looks, speedily put all temperance scruples at rest by explaining that the cask was nicknamed Hiawatha and that it contained the laughing

waters of the Dreen-ken-Swell River, a stream recently discovered in the Indian Territory. The bottles, he said, contained various preparations concocted by competent medicine men. The various fluids were tasted out of curiosity by
the members of the party."

The New York papers were almost unanimously enthused
over Cody's presentation at the Polo Grounds, although
there was some caviling over how many times the Indians
had to die and then be reincarnated for another slaughter at
the hands of the scouts. The reviewer of a weekly periodical
believed there was too much shooting, that the only "artistic" aspect of the show was in its displays of horsemanship.
"Why should not Buffalo Bill engage some Comanche braves
and show us the real feats?" he asked. "The best part of his
present entertainment is not the shooting but the riding. His
cowboys, Mexicans and Indians may not be as wild as the
playbills assert, but they know how to ride. Let him take this
hint for next season and he will make Barnum and Forepaugh [circuses] shake in their shoes, despite their white elephants, gilded chariots, Roman races and triple rings. He has
hit upon one good idea already, and has only to enlarge and
perfect it in order to eclipse all rivalry. As for money, when
he is tired of touring this country, there is an immense fortune awaiting him in England."

The immense fortune accurately predicted for him seemed
to be more of a mirage than a possibility that first season of
the joint management of Cody and Salsbury. Several times
Cody would have given up, had it not been for Salsbury's
faith in the venture and his willingness to back it up with
transfusions of cash. But it was Cody, of course, who was on
the spot and personally experienced the various disasters.
Right after the New York engagement the summer of 1884
turned wet and cold, which was death to all outdoor attractions. In Connecticut the show almost foundered under the
weight of various troubles, most of them stemming from the
feud between the Buffalo Bill and Doc Carver outfits. In Hartford, while the scouts and the Indians were chasing each other

around the arena, Major North fell when his saddle girth broke. Most of the riders following him managed to swerve their mounts aside, but one trampled him. He was removed to the hospital with a crushed spine and broken ribs and never appeared as a performer again. Less than a year later he died of his injuries. It was poor recompense for the man— the real "Great Scout" Cody always advertised himself to be —who had pointed out the future Buffalo Bill to Ned Buntline fifteen years before.

The vendetta with Doc Carver also sapped the enterprise morally and financially. By the time both shows reached Connecticut, Carver and Cody had slandered each other so vociferously, each claiming the other a fraud, that their differences fell into the hands of the lawyers. Cody's filed a $16,000 libel suit against his rival, and Carver upped the ante to $25,000. Each show attacked the other. Only the intervention of peace officers prevented the cowboys and roustabouts from each attraction settling the issue with their six-shooters. The lengthy recriminations between the two showmen were finally reviewed in New Haven Superior Court, which was concerned mainly with getting the two shows out of the state before they could stage a Western-style shoot-out for real.

Cody occasionally was lacerated by Levi Blydenburgh, the razor-tongued counsel for Doc Carver. When Cody's lawyer objected to Cody being called to the witness stand on the grounds that he hadn't been served with a subpoena, Blydenburgh retorted, "Oh, yes, he has, and has been paid. The sixty cents is in his pocket now if he hasn't drunk it up."

The brisk and sensible Nate Salsbury hurried up to New Haven and cut short the legal wrangling. A settlement was arranged in which Salsbury paid the court costs and also handed over $10,000 to Carver in settlement of his claims. Five years later the showmen clashed again, but that time it was a problem for the police of Hamburg, Germany.

By the time they finished their disastrous tour of New England, the show was in the red for about $100,000. Cody and

Salsbury agreed that the only way to recoup was to keep the show on the road that winter. They would proceed to New Orleans, stopping along the way to play any engagements that could be hastily arranged. There was an exposition in New Orleans which might make a lengthy stay profitable.

A new advance agent had to be hired to arrange the dates on the route to New Orleans and also to procure transportation. Burke, who had formerly attended to such chores, was staying with the show and trying to straighten out its financial affairs. Cody had a weakness for "old pards" and hired as his advance man Bob Haslam, who had been a splendid Pony Express rider but knew little or nothing about scheduling a road show.

Haslam leased an old Mississippi riverboat in Cincinnati, and the show with all its equipment was placed aboard. It threatened to sink every time it struck a snag in the river. The riverside towns Haslam had selected for Buffalo Bill appearances turned out to be too uninterested, underpopulated, or hard up for cash to patronize the show. It was losing thousands a week by the time the old tub reached the lower Mississippi.

Cody left the boat as it approached New Orleans and went ahead to determine what sort of arrangements Haslam had made for the exposition engagement. He found that his friend had rented a vacant lot, which was now under several feet of water. The Metarie racetrack, near the exposition grounds, was available, and Cody rented it. He was just congratulating himself on having forestalled another disaster when he received a telegram telling him the riverboat had collided with another steamer and had slowly sunk. All the animals, except some of the horses, were drowned; all the equipment except the Deadwood coach and the bandwagon was lost, but the human members of the company all had managed to save themselves.

Cody immediately wired Nate Salsbury, whose Troubadour company was then appearing at the Denver Opera

House: OUTFIT AT THE BOTTOM OF THE RIVER. WHAT SHALL I DO?

Salsbury promptly replied: OPEN ON YOUR DATE. HAVE WIRED YOU FUNDS.

In just two weeks Cody managed to round up the horses, buffalo, and other animals required to restock his outfit and to replace the equipment at the bottom of the Mississippi through agents who scoured the Southwest to meet his requirements. In such emergencies Cody was at his best because a challenge could always distract him from drinking. He stayed off the sauce until the show opened, as advertised, just before Christmas.

It was soon apparent that he might as well have taken his time about refitting. Winter rains, which neither he nor Salsbury had counted on, drenched New Orleans. For forty-four days it rained, and potential customers stayed at home. One day only nine persons bought tickets to the afternoon performance, but Cody and his 150 fellow performers went through their paces in the sodden infield of the Metarie racetrack.

On February 15, 1885, Cody was ready to hoist the white flag as he wrote Salsbury (with his usual uncertain spelling and shaky syntax), "The camels back is broken. . . . God, Christ and the devil is against me. The morning opened bright. I started with a full parade, thousands of people in the damed city. And we would surely have played to $2000 had it not been so ordained that we should not. At 10:30 it clouded up all of a sudden and poured rain until 4 P M then it cleared up again just as pleasant as before. Its plain to me now. I can read it clearly. *Fate* if there is such a thing is against me. . . . The sooner we give this outfit away the better. . . . I am a dam condemned Joner [Jonah] and the sooner you get clear of me the better for you. . . . I am an *Ingersol* man [he referred to Colonel Robert G. Ingersoll, whose atheistic lectures were then shocking the country] from this out. And a damed Joner disgusted with himself and the world—there is no *heaven*—if so it can stay there and be damed. . . ."

The "condemned Jonah" and new convert to atheism was dissuaded from folding the company, and a few weeks later the skies cleared and business improved. Cody wrote Salsbury that he would stick it out, but "next winter when the show is laid up I am going to get on a drunk that is a drunk. Just to change my luck I will paint a few towns red hot—but till then I am staunch and true."

Captain Bogardus, the clay-pigeon marksman and one of the top-billed performers, quit the show and was succeeded by young Johnny Baker, whom Cody had coached in sharpshooting and who became a star attraction. The show still needed a booster shot of some kind. Even the magnificent presence of Buffalo Bill could not sustain a three-hour performance without support from other famous or notorious names, from people with some extraordinary talent for shooting, riding, or stunting.

Better times were dawning even as Buffalo Bill and his cohorts were drying out from the Biblical deluge which had swamped New Orleans. The show's cashbox was empty and needed frequent replenishment from Nate Salsbury, but late in March it would roll out of New Orleans and begin its spring tour amid greener and dryer pastures. And within six months it would acquire two personalities who were strikingly opposite in character and disposition but who came to understand and love each other—Little Annie Oakley and Chief Sitting Bull.

8

Little Annie and Sitting Bull

ANYONE studying the legend of Buffalo Bill Cody should never lose sight of the heroic labors of John M. Burke. He not only managed the show until Salsbury took over full-time and kept the publicity mill grinding with the help of Prentiss Ingraham and other imaginative assistants but was responsible for acquiring the services of both Annie Oakley and Sitting Bull. Throughout their joint career, Burke served as Cody's buffer and apologist, retrieved his blunders, and occasionally served as the lightning rod for Cody's wrath. He was the keeper of the flame, a role he regarded as near sacred, though many others could see that his idol was as flawed as any other mortal.

His dogged devotion only was reinforced when the self-destructive element in Cody's makeup was in the ascendant. Despite his frequent pledges of abstinence to Salsbury, Cody often drank his breakfast and was swacked to the eyebrows by showtime. Even though he fired shotted shells (loaded with twenty grains of black powder and one-quarter of an ounce of No. $7\frac{1}{2}$ chilled shot) in his Winchester repeating rifle during the glassball-breaking exhibition, he sometimes missed repeatedly. The fact that he missed with a spray pattern of buckshot usually indicated he had been exercising his elbow. On such occasions he often further betrayed himself by making a dramatic speech on the glorious history of Kansas, sometimes in states hostile to Kansans. Burke would then explain to journalists who demanded to know what was wrong with Buffalo Bill that he had been overcome, not by strong drink, but by his great love for Kansas, "where his much-beloved father was the first to die in the struggle to free the slaves."

When newspapermen in Boston insisted on cross-examining Burke on rumors that Cody was indulging in sexual transactions that would have been frowned upon in Dodge City, let alone Boston, Burke would launch into a dissertation on Cody's ancestry, claiming that he was "nine-tenths Irish, descended from one of the early kings of Ireland." In Wisconsin, again confronted by scandalous rumors, Burke would inform hostile questioners that Cody was of Teutonic origin, that his family had changed its name from Koditz.

Burke was able to overawe inquisitors, to distract keen young journalists baying on the trail of truth, to protect the near-knightly reputation of Buffalo Bill from evil (though often accurate) rumors, by cultivating a presence almost as impressive as Cody's. In a Western atmosphere he could climb into buckskins and play the role of "Arizona John," but in the cities he always appeared in a Prince Albert coat and striped pants which, with his flying-buttress whiskers, his bassoonlike voice, and his portentous manner, made him look and sound like a senior partner of J. Pierpont Morgan.

Thus accoutered, Burke was sitting in the grandstand of the Metarie racetrack one day in March, brooding over his various problems. The recent resignation of Captain Bogardus was one of them. A young couple climbed up the wooden terrace around noon, long before the performance was scheduled to begin. They introduced themselves as Mr. and Mrs. Frank Butler and, though they looked more like rubes of the less offensive sort, asserted that they were the best marksmanship team in America. They had just left the Sells Brothers circus because they didn't approve of the raffish atmosphere of the big top, and besides their act had not been sufficiently appreciated by the Sells management. Buffalo Bill's outfit seemed just the right setting for their talents.

Burke listened attentively to their pitch while studying the pint-sized Mrs. Butler with increasing interest. She wasn't beautiful, but if she was half as handy with a rifle as she claimed to be, it was obvious that a sharpshooting young woman would be a novelty of the sort the show needed. Her professional name, she said, was Annie Oakley. "Little Annie Oakley"—what a billing! Already Burke's fertile mind was churning with exploitation angles. In due time he would create the legend of Annie Oakley—just as Buffalo Bill was an amalgam of Cody, Buntline, and Burke—so durable that in 1946 it would serve as the basis for a musical comedy, *Annie Get Your Gun,* with shy little Annie portrayed by un-bashful Ethel Merman, and make more money than Mrs. Frank Butler ever did by breaking glass balls from the Pacific Coast to the Bosporus.

Burke took the young lady to the target range and watched her bang away with unerring accuracy. It was astonishing. Burke was convinced she could outshoot any man with the company. Her husband was also a crack shot.

"The show could use you," Burke told the Butlers. "Trouble is, we're strapped for money at the present. We can't hire anyone, and it's all we can do to keep food on the tables in the mess tent. Things'll be easier when we start touring again. Come see us next month in Louisville."

Buffalo Bill and company moved north by rail to open its spring tour with a stand at the baseball park in Louisville. Salsbury had not only refinanced the outfit but had become its full-time general manager, while Burke devoted all his time to beating the drum for what he called "America's Greatest Entertainment." Under Salsbury's firm hand, the format of the Wild West Show was brought to theatrical perfection and its business affairs were conducted with an

equal efficiency. Salsbury made all the difference; the enterprise had lacked only a show-wise administrator to make it
paramount among outdoor attractions, and in the first five
months of 1885 it turned a profit of $100,000.

In Louisville, Mr. and Mrs. Frank Butler again called on
John Burke, who took her to Salsbury. Again she demonstrated her prowess with a shoulder gun. Could she shoot accurately, Salsbury wanted to know, from the back of a galloping pony? Yes. Just then Cody, who had been leading a
parade through downtown Louisville, appeared in the mess
tent, resplendent in white buckskin. "They told me about
you, Missie," he said. "We're glad to have you." From then
on, Cody always called her Missie and looked upon her as a
daughter surrogate. Butler himself retired from shooting and
served as his wife's assistant and manager.

She was a tiny thing, about five-feet-nothing tall, weighing
one hundred pounds or less, with brown hair flowing to her
shoulders, a winsome face, and a marvelous smile. Wearing a
modified Stetson, a blouse covered with marksmanship medals, a pleated skirt, and gaiters, she rivaled the voluptuous
Lillian Russell as the most admired of American females, and
she did it without Lillian's equipment. As one misty-eyed observer wrote, "Many a man now gray, who once perched on a
hard wooden plank and watched her through a haze that was
half powder smoke and half boyish dreaming, will still confess that Annie was his first hopeless love."

She was born to Quaker parents in Darke County, Ohio,
in 1860. Her real name was Phoebe Anne Oakley Mozee.
The Quaker aversion to firearms was not transmitted to her.
At the age of nine, a confirmed tomboy, she was able to shoot
the head off a running quail, it was said. Early in her teens,
as one of eight children in an impoverished backwoods family, she began hunting rabbits and quail for the tables of
Cincinnati restaurants. At the age of fifteen she was entered
in a shooting contest against a traveling professional, Frank
Butler, and easily defeated him. A short time later they were

married and as "Butler & Oakley" formed an exhibition shooting act.

She made an immediate and resounding hit with the Buffalo Bill show. Her virtuosity with hand and shoulder guns was, even without Burke's exaggerations, one of the wonders of the age. At thirty paces she could slice a playing card held up edgewise by her husband. With a brace of double-action revolvers she could roll an empty tin can with well-spaced shots. By sighting through a mirror she could fire over her shoulder and break a glass ball her husband whirled around his head on a string. She could break glass balls thrown in the air with her rifle held high over her head. She could lay her gun down, throw glass balls in the air, and break them before they could reach the ground. Once, using three 16-gauge shotguns, she broke 4,772 out of 5,000 balls tossed in the air for nine hours running. No wonder she was advertised as "Little Sure Shot."

Annie's extraordinary talent was inserted into the program with considerable finesse. She not only opened the show but appeared several times later, each time performing increasingly difficult and amazing trick shots. The reason for the careful showcasing was explained by Burke in his memoir: "It was our first thought, when we planned the show, that so much shooting would cause difficulty, that horses would be frightened and women and children terrified. It was when Annie Oakley joined us that Colonel Cody devised the idea of graduating the excitement. Miss Oakley comes on very early in the performance. She starts very gently, shooting with a pistol. Women and children see a harmless woman out there and do not get worried.

"Gradually she increases the charge in her rifles until at last she shoots with a full charge. Thus, by the time the attack on the stagecoach comes, the audience is accustomed to the sound of shooting, and in all our history of Wild West there has never been a horse frightened sufficiently to run away at any of our outdoor performances."

Less than three months after Annie Oakley joined the show, Burke secured the second unique attraction of that 1885-86 season, Sitting Bull, the squat, fierce-looking leader of the Sioux, who had a face like a tomahawk but who wrote rather good poetry when he wasn't scaring the wits out of white people. For his qualities of statesmanship—his determination to fight for Indian country only until it was apparent that it was impossible to resist the steamroller advance of what the whites called civilization—it could fairly be said that Sitting Bull was the greatest living American, including any number of Presidents who sat in the White House while he hunkered down in a shack on the Standing Rock reservation.

Yet Sitting Bull was a daring choice, agreed upon by Cody, Salsbury, and Burke, as a Wild West Show attraction. Most whites knew him only as "the killer of Custer." Just how audiences would react to him they couldn't be sure, but it was certain that his notoriety would attract the crowds.

Burke had a way with Indians, it was always said—possibly because he was an Irishman with some private feeling for a conquered people. Also, as he said, he always bore in mind Cody's advice on the necessity of dealing fairly and keeping your word with the Indians. Burke never forgot that during the first season of the Wild West Show he had given an Indian member of the troupe a cigar in return for a favor and promised that he would bring a whole box from town. Cody had observed the transaction, taken Burke aside, and warned him, "Don't forget those cigars. Maybe you didn't mean it. But don't ever promise an Indian anything without giving it to him. If you break a promise to an Indian you'll be no good to me or the show."

Burke journeyed to the Standing Rock reservation in June and found Sitting Bull in a bored and restless mood. Reservation life, drawing rations from the government, trying to learn farming, and looking after a few half-starved livestock did not appeal to him. Four years before he and his followers had been conned into returning from Canada; Sitting Bull

hoped that, once back in the States, he would be able to persuade the Great White Father to treat the Indians with more
justice. In 1884 a showman named Colonel Alvaren Allen
had talked Sitting Bull into going East with him with the understanding that he would be taken to the White House and
allowed to present his case to the President. Instead he was
exhibited among the waxworks at the Eden Musée in New
York.

Burke, wisely, did not make any vast promises. His offer
was simple and to the point: $50 a week and expenses. Sit-
ting Bull had a large family and needed the money. Having
acquired a certain amount of bitter wisdom about show business, he added a codicil to the brief contract: He was to
have the sole right to sell photographs of himself and would
be allowed to charge visitors to the show's camp who wanted
to be photographed with him.

The Sioux chief joined the show at Buffalo and immediately became the center of attention. His impassive presence,
seated on a horse and merely allowing himself to be seen in
the arena, stole the show from Cody and Annie Oakley.
Many in the audience booed him as an exhibition of patriotism, or racial pride, or continuing resentment over his
smashing defeat of the Seventh Cavalry. Sitting Bull simply
shrugged off the hostile attitude of the crowds; he had expected it.

Oddly enough, as John Burke observed, Sitting Bull, with
his broad face and glittering black eyes, bore a strong resem-
blance to another American statesman, Daniel Webster. This
oddity was pointed up by at least part of the chief's costume:
He wore a brocaded waistcoat, black pants, and a scarlet tie,
as well as rubber-soled, beaded moccasins. Evidently considering it part of his jewelry collection, he also wore a large
crucifix around his neck, which gave many earnest Christians
an additional reason to stare in bewilderment.

He detested being on display, but he liked two things
about the Eastern cities: oyster stew and hard candy. Fifty
dollars a week was good pay in those years, but he kept little

of it for himself. There was the necessity of sending money home for his two wives and eleven children. What was left went to poor little palefaces—newsboys, bootblacks, and other starvelings—whose plight both touched and puzzled him. With all the wealth and power he saw accumulated in the Eastern cities, why couldn't they provide for their own unfortunates?

Annie Oakley, whom he greatly admired for her shooting and who became his closest friend in the company, recalled of Sitting Bull that "Most of what he earned went into the pockets of small, ragged boys. White boys. He could not understand why all the wealth he saw in the cities wasn't divided up among the poor. Among the Indians, a man who had plenty of food shared it with those who had none. It was unthinkable for an Indian to feed himself while others were going hungry within eyesight."

That the whites allowed children of their own race to go hungry convinced him that they would never do anything for the Indians but make promises. "The white man knows how to make everything," he told Annie Oakley, "but he does not know how to distribute it."

When the show crossed the border into Canada for a series of appearances, Sitting Bull came into his own as a celebrity more appetizing to the Canadians than Buffalo Bill or even Annie Oakley. Somewhat maliciously perhaps, the Canadians greeted the chief as a great hero, not in spite of but because of the way his followers had wiped out Custer and the Seventh Cavalry; they pointed out that they treated *their* Indians (much fewer in number) with greater generosity, and conveniently forgot that they had assisted Washington in retrieving Sitting Bull by telling him that he was no longer welcome. The Canadian newspapers hailed him as "the illustrious Indian general and statesman," and the Canadian audiences bought thousands of copies of a photograph showing Sitting Bull and Buffalo Bill linked together under the caption, "Enemies in '76, Friends in '85."

Cody gave interviews in which he portrayed the Indians as

honorable men who had often been unjustly treated. "In nine cases out of ten when there is trouble between white men and Indians, it will be found that the white man is responsible. Indians expect a man to keep his word. They can't understand how a man will lie. Most of them would as soon cut off a leg as lie."

Sitting Bull was equally candid in the interviews he gave the press through an interpreter. "Nobody," he said, "knew who killed Custer; everybody fired at him. Custer was a brave warrior but made a mistake. The Indians honored him and did not scalp him. I fought for my people. My people said I was right. I will answer to my people. I will answer for the dead of my people. Let the palefaces do the same on their side."

The tour did provide Sitting Bull with a more favorable impression of his old enemies. Some, like Cody, treated him fairly and did not speak with forked tongue. Annie Oakley was so lovable that Sitting Bull adopted her as a daughter in a ceremony which Burke made the most of with lavish newspaper coverage.

Through Cody's intervention, too, Sitting Bull finally got to meet the President after a tour of Washington, which caused him to remark, "The white people are so many that if every Indian in the West killed one every step they took the dead would not be missed among you." The jovial and immense Grover Cleveland, just starting his first term in the Presidency, must have been even more impressive in their private meeting. Sitting Bull never disclosed exactly what President Cleveland told him, but he said later, "I go back in four weeks and tell my people what I have seen. They will not go on the warpath again. I have learned much. The Indian must keep quiet or die. The Great Father must protect us and give us justice."

With such sterling new attractions as Annie Oakley and Sitting Bull, the 1885 tour put the Buffalo Bill Wild West company in the black for the first time in its three seasons on the road. John Burke was extending the art of public relations to the point where he could all but commandeer plentiful space in the newspapers along their route. One innovation was the "Indian rib roast"—sides of beef roasted over wood coals, carved into thick slices, and passed around in tin basins—to which various dignitaries and selected members of the press were invited. The idea was to give them an idea of what the rough-and-ready cuisine of the Great Plains was like. At the outset of the feasting each guest was given a sharpened stick and told that was the only utensil with which he would be supplied. Watching the dudes fumbling around with their slabs of beef and spattering their starched white shirt fronts, Cody would roar with laughter and order knives, forks, and napkins to be brought in. Before, during, and after the beef-gorging, there were lashings of whiskey of various potencies, red-eye for the daring, smooth old rye for the discreet. A show-business periodical provided, perhaps with tongue in cheek, the menu of those banquets on the show's campgrounds:

SOUP
Whiskey with water
FISH
Whiskey straight
ENTREE
Crackers with pepper, salt and whiskey
ROAST
Chunks of beef ribs
SALAD
Tomatoes au Naturel
DESSERT
Whiskey, beer, Champagne
Ambulances to order.

Less distinguished visitors were received by the thousands at the campgrounds in various cities. This, too, was one of Burke's innovations. He sensed that Easterners wanted to rub up against the "real West," that they wanted to assure themselves that heroic Westerners were neither demigods

Bill Cody at the age of twelve.

(Culver Pictures)

William F. Cody at the start of
his career.

(DPL, WHD)

William F. Cody's wife, Louisa.

(DPL, WHD)

Buffalo Bill at the height of his fame.
(DPL, WHD)

Sitting Bull and Buffalo Bill.
(DPL, WHD)

Annie Oakley
(Culver Pictures)

Wild Bill Hickok
(The Granger Collection)

English lithograph poster for Buffalo Bill's show, 1903.

(The Granger Collection)

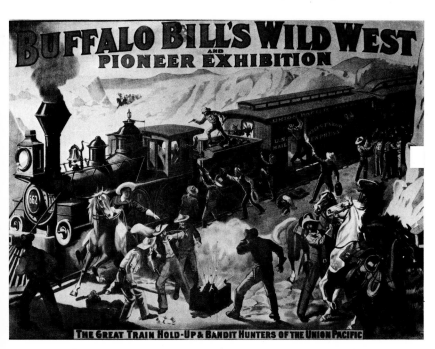

An American poster for Buffalo Bill's combined Wild West and Pioneer Exhibition.

(The Granger Collection)

Indian chiefs and U.S. officials (Buffalo Bill is standing at right center) at Pine Ridge, South Dakota, 1891.

(The Granger Collection)

Buffalo Bill and members of his troupe, 1906.

(DPL, WHD)

Cody, in what was sup-
posedly his last appearance,
about 1913.

(DPL, WHD)

Cody with his wife the year
before his death.

(DPL, WHD)

Buffalo Bill's funeral.

(DPL, WHD)

nor demons, that people who would never be able to afford
to travel very far from their hometowns, in a day when $10 a
week was a living wage, more or less, appreciated closer contact with the wild Westerners than the distance between the
grandstand and the arena. It was the best possible advertising
to throw open the campgrounds and let the public wander
around at will. They could watch the buffalo and mountain
elk grazing, the cowboys and Mexican *vaqueros* squatting
around a fire, the Indians in their tepees attending to household chores, elfin Annie Oakley fraternizing with the wranglers with Ma Whittaker, the severe-looking wardrobe
mistress, as her chaperone. Sitting Bull sat in his tent and
stared back at the rubberneckers, occasionally thrilling them
by grunting, "Hau! Hau!" which whites wrongly translated
as "How! How!" Thus the Buffalo Bill troupe was really
"offstage" only during the sleeping hours, and no one enjoyed the goldfish-bowl life more than Cody himself. It was
not only the wide streak of ham in his character, but he gen-
uinely liked people of all sorts, was as genial and courtly
with a housewife and her brood as with a society leader and
her debutante daughters. He sat in his tent and welcomed all
comers, displayed the scalp of Yellow Hand, and reenacted his
famous duel with the Cheyenne warrior; he especially delighted in taking some wide-eyed youngster over to introduce
him to Sitting Bull.

The troupe wound up its highly successful 1885 tour in St.
Louis, where the show went into winter quarters.

Just before Sitting Bull left the show, he and Cody met
General Carr, Cody's old commander and retired hetman of
the Fifth Cavalry, which had chivied the Sioux so mercilessly
for a half dozen years. Much to Cody's disappointment, Sitting Bull refused to shake hands with General Carr. He was
no hypocrite, he had a long memory, and he was tired of
looking at palefaces. With a few sacks of hard candy and an
affectionate embrace from "Little Missie" Oakley, he went
back to the Standing Rock reservation, "sick of houses and
noises and too many people," he said. The people he had met

made little impression, presumably including President Grover Cleveland. "I can not remember their talks. Some were light, foolish men, some were bad men. They were all the same to me. They talked much, but to my ears it was like the sound of the waters, which man can not stop."

Cody himself went back to the open spaces so pleased with the tour that he forgot his threat to Salsbury earlier in the year to go on a monumental bender the moment the show closed down for the winter. Instead he hurried back to Nebraska, bought more land near North Platte, and spent much of the winter building up what was later called Scout's Rest Ranch. He stocked the spread with 125 prize specimens of Herefords, polled Angus, and Shorthorns. With the newly purchased additions, he now owned almost 4,000 acres of prairie, thickly coated with buffalo grass, with a spring-fed creek and a four-mile stretch along its northwestern border fronting on the wide and placid Platte River.

When spring came, following his fortieth birthday, he was eager enough to face the crowds and read the daily box office reports. The 1886 season, from advance reports, promised to be greater than 1885. What every right-thinking man of his time wanted to be was a millionaire, and that status was no longer an impossibility for William F. Cody. But money didn't matter all that much; it was the daily immersion in public admiration, the "thousands of expectant countenances," as he once remarked during that season. "Such a sight is enough to make any man a laughing hyena with happiness."

Mrs. Cody was no longer thrilled by all the hero-worship her husband attracted. She'd had enough of trouping in their early years, and she was convinced that he traveled with a harem. Her suspicions on that score could hardly have been alleviated by the fact that for the 1886 season a troupe of cowgirls was engaged, along with other novelties. A Sioux paladin named American Horse was hired to take the place of Sitting Bull, who could not be budged from his ramshackle cabin at Standing Rock. A new spectacular had been devised for the program, "Custer's Massacre." Greater stress was laid on the riding acts, which now included a race between the cowgirls and more bronco-busting contests. Salsbury also worked long and hard on the show's logistics, which eventually reached such perfection that they aroused the interest of the Greater German General Staff. He had obtained a special train for the show, twenty-six cars painted white with BUFFALO BILL'S WILD WEST in gold lettering. The train carried all 240 of the performers and other employees, along with a portable grandstand, a huge canvas back cloth representing the Wyoming mountains, a lighting system for night performances, and all the livestock. Salsbury had also organized the backstage work force into crews, with a boss in charge of each, and drilled them until they worked with the precision and swiftness of circus roustabouts.

The crowds were bigger than ever along their route east from St. Louis. The street parades whipped up attention, with the cowboy band leading the procession and blaring "Marching Through Georgia." On June 27, the company arrived in New York for a summer-long stand at Erastina, Staten Island, where an arena seating 25,000 had been established. It seemed that the whole city turned out to cheer when they marched off the ferry at Twenty-third Street, marched up Eighth Avenue, across Forty-second Street to Fifth Avenue, then down Fifth Avenue and Broadway to the Battery, where they boarded the Staten Island Ferry.

That summer Buffalo Bill's show was the thing to see for New Yorkers and summertime visitors. It even attracted the celebrities. General William T. Sherman attended the first performance, and he was followed by Governor David B. Hill, Mark Twain, General Custer's widow, Sir Henry Irving of the English stage, Prince Dom Augusta of Brazil, and even old P. T. Barnum, who was suffering from the gout but hobbled down from his Connecticut home to wander around the campgrounds and praise the performers.

Mark Twain's boyish enthusiasm, reinforced by nostalgia for his own carefree years in Nevada and California, was especially valuable to John Burke and his publicity forces. They seized upon and broadcast a letter Twain wrote to Cody: "Down to its smallest details the Show is genuine. It brought back vividly the breezy wild life of the Plains and the Rocky Mountains. It is wholly free from sham and insincerity and the effects it produced upon me by its spectacles were identical with those wrought upon me a long time ago on the frontier. Your pony expressman was as tremendous an interest to me as he was twenty-three years ago when he used to come whizzing by from over the desert with his war news; and your bucking horses were even painfully real to me as I rode one of those outrages for nearly a quarter of a minute. It is often said on the other side of the water that none of the exhibitions which we send to England are purely and distinctly American. If you will take the Wild West Show over there you can remove that reproach."

Twain's much-quoted panegyric served a double purpose. With his status as the most celebrated American writer, he certified that the show was "genuine," that the garish tableaux it presented with a few broad strokes of tumultuous action were a worthy accounting of what the white man did in and to the West. The letter to Cody also suggested a new field of action, taking the show abroad, which would be acted upon less than a year hence. It must have occurred to Burke that it was a pity that Twain was too rich and famous to be lured into his publicity stable. Twain's deft hand at hyperbole would have been invaluable.

The SRO sign was out all summer at the arena on Staten Island, with interest constantly maintained, even increased, as the summer went on by columns of publicity planted in the New York newspapers, one of which exulted that "The Wild West came to New York like a cyclone to a Kansas town." It took all seventeen steamboats pressed into service by the Staten Island Ferry line to carry the crowds out to the Erastina Stadium.

With all those profits rolling in and public interest still unabated through early autumn, somebody, probably the canny Nate Salsbury, decided it would be a shame to close down for the winter. Indoor quarters would have to be found and the show restyled to fit into a more cramped space, and that would have to be done in a matter of weeks, but the problems were not insuperable. Besides there was no point in going into winter quarters out West if the show's next season would be spent across the Atlantic.

The massive old Madison Square Garden, occupying the block between Madison and Fourth avenues, Twenty-sixth and Twenty-seventh streets, seemed the only suitable place for restaging the spectacle, which was now titled *Drama of Civilization*. The Garden was regularly used by horse shows and circuses, so it should be able to accommodate the Buffalo Bill troupe. Steele MacKaye, who had staged many diverse performances in the Garden, was engaged to oversee the production. One end of the Garden was raised 20 feet to make room for huge prairie and mountain backdrops. An enormous wind machine was installed and proved so powerful that it blew down the flats representing miners' shacks and toppled passengers off the stagecoach.

Since Cody and Salsbury did not want to stake all their summer profits on a risky and untried indoor venture, they persuaded Adam Forepaugh, the circus operator, to put up the front money while they were billed as "managers and proprietors." The price scale was fairly stiff for those times—$1 for reserved seats, $8 to $15 for boxes.

The set piece of the new production was a miniaturized version of *Custer's Massacre*, with Buck Taylor, the Nebraska broncobuster, portraying General Custer. Buffalo Bill's role as "Custer's avenger" was not ignored; it was still more inflated until it reached preposterous proportions. After the mock battle ended and the tanbark of the arena was littered with fallen cavalrymen, Cody strode out in all his costumed glory and bathed in the confluence of spotlights. There was an expectant hush. He took off his hat and bowed his head. Then a slide was flashed on the screen with the words TOO LATE! In this revised version of military history, the paying customer was left with the feeling that if Buffalo Bill had been present at the Little Big Horn the Indian hordes would have been sent reeling away in defeat.

Drama of Civilization opened on Thanksgiving eve and was a success from the beginning. Almost 1,000,000 people passed through the turnstiles, 9,000 to 10,000 nightly, until the show closed in February. According to the always friendly New York *Herald,* it was a memorable evening: "At the Madison Square Garden, where Moody and Sankey sang their hymns, where Terpsichore and Bacchus have made such a night of it, Buffalo Bill appeared last night with his company of long haired cowboys. In one of the boxes were General William Tecumseh Sherman, in another Henry Ward Beecher. In other boxes were Congressman Perry Belmont, Mrs. August Belmont and Oliver Belmont.

"The vast interior was cut in half with a partition on the east side of it, with a proscenium arch. On this stage Steele MacKaye presented as Dream First: The Primeval Forest of America before Its Discovery by the White Man. No one could deny it being quite accurate. Frank Richmond, the silver tongued orator, appeared in a sort of pigeon loft to the left and recited words from MacKaye's golden tinged vocabulary."

The hit of the show, aside from "Custer's Massacre," was an elk being stalked by an Indian hunter. "The elk sniffed the air, and paused before Mrs. Belmont. She raised her opera glasses. The elk turned his head toward Congressman Belmont. The wily red man then approached. The elk turned on him, the redskin ran and the crowd roared."

The *World*'s reviewer was less easily pleased by the pageant, complaining that "there is no actor in the company, except Buffalo Bill, who says nothing, shoots badly, and is pretty much kept in the background . . . the border drama without actors is not a success . . . the animals are cribbed, confined and have to be whipped into a display of a little animation. We hope that Buffalo Bill, the Indians, the cowboys and the bisons will be let loose in the open again and that, when they go to Europe, all of Matt Morgan's scenery will be carefully left behind."

The moment *Drama of Civilization* closed down the preparations for crossing the Atlantic were begun. The whole array of frontier generals were solicited by John Burke for testimonials to Cody's prowess as a cavalry scout; they would be needed to convince the skeptical and irreverent English newspapers that Cody was not a fraud. In the past London had been deceived by a number of amiable charlatans pretending to be ferocious Westerners, notably the poet Joaquin Miller, who appeared at dinner parties in buckskins and a red sash and picked up a fish by its tail and swallowed it whole. The Buffalo Bill legend must not be tainted by such associations. Cody must be presented as the real thing. The trouble with the military recommendations which Burke received from Sherman, Sheridan, Crook, Carr, Merritt, Emory, King, and a whole constellation of starred epaulets was that each one of them referred to him as "Mr." Cody. That wouldn't do. A slight amount of pressure was exerted in the capital of Nebraska, with the result that Burke received a handsomely engraved certificate proclaiming that the governor had commissioned Cody as "Aide-de-Camp on my staff, with the rank of Colonel." A Nebraska colonelcy was as good as any other for the purposes of John Burke's publicity machine.*

The last two seasons had shown that the Wild West Show was big business and deserved the dignity of incorporation. On February 26, 1887, Cody's forty-first birthday, the articles of corporation were signed. One hundred shares of stock were issued, with Cody and Salsbury each holding thirty-five shares and the remainder divided among three mutual friends.

Now all was in readiness for the departure aboard the steamship *State of Nebraska*. The ship's name seemed a

* Cody was later promoted to brigadier general by the governor of Nebraska but always used the title of colonel, which seemed to have a better ring to it.

happy omen. The expert opinion held that the show would
be enormously successful abroad. Britain was said to be in a
receptive mood, its empire temporarily at peace, its economy
booming, and best of all, it was celebrating the Golden Jubilee of Queen Victoria. At last the King of the Border Men
would meet the Queen of all the British realms.

9

A Sea Change or Two

FOR the next fifteen years the Wild West Show played before most of the crowned heads of Europe—the cliché was endlessly repeated in Burke's publicity broadsides—and a goodly section of the *Almanac de Gotha*. Nothing so conclusively certified the worth of an American performer as the approval of royalty; predictably, nothing so quickly turned the head of an American, no matter how firm his republican loyalty, as the patent of royal patronage. Cody was no exception. He had not been spoiled by the attentions of Presidents, three-star generals, business and social leaders in the United States. Abroad it was a different story. It would seem that a sea change could occur in a man's character, symptomized by an expansion in the size of his hatband and an evaporation of boyish simplicity. The patronage of a duke was so much more impressive than that of the publisher of the New York *Herald*, though James Gordon Bennett's manner was lordlier than any lord's.

It was almost incredible the way the British aristocracy in particular could warm to and enfold the newcomer, the more outlandish the better. Cody might have taken a lesson from the experience of Pocahontas, who went to England as the

wife of a colonial gentleman. She was received at Bucking-
ham Palace, invited to tea by the Bishop of London, and entertained by the landed gentry. At the end of her visit, before
she could return to her native Virginia, she suddenly and
mysteriously died, whether or not of a surfeit of the British
nobility's attentions.

Immediately on arrival in England, Cody seemed to go
hog-wild for the urbanities and amenities of London life. He
not only took a suite in a luxury hotel on Piccadilly Circus
but actually employed a valet. The news that Buffalo Bill
was primping and preening with the aid of a manservant,
which Burke could not prevent leaking out, shocked old
comrades from Kansas City to the most remote cavalry post.
He took to appearing on the dais at banquets and sonorously
declaiming, "The march of civilization started on the Atlantic coast and moved ever westward, over the mountains,
across the majestic Mississippi and onto the vast buffalo pastures of the Great Plains." He developed a streak of
temperament more befitting a Shakespearean ham or an
opera tenor, grew vain and touchy, and indulged in monumental sulks when Annie Oakley or another attraction di-
verted attention from his own presence. A combination of
champagne and excessive flattery turned him into something
of a popinjay. It was a classic case of an actor playing a role
he had come to relish, coming to believe he really was the
legendary figure created largely through the efforts of other
men and no longer able to distinguish between Will Cody,
the boy from Salt Creek, and Buffalo Bill, the man who conquered the West.

The extent of the sea change was illustrated by an incident
that occurred in Italy and indicated that even so close an associate as John Burke could not always cope with his tower-
ing imperiousness, and it was fortunate for Cody that he
gradually recovered a sense of proportion or he might have
lost the services of more than one man who contributed
largely to his success. The only falling out between Cody and
Burke occurred when the former arrived in Italy and found

that Burke had neglected to make certain arrangements with customs officials on the docks. Furthermore, Burke wasn't waiting to meet him; he was in Rome at the moment, had lost his interpreter, and was trying to tell the editor of a Roman newspaper, who didn't speak English, just what was so glorious about the Wild West Show.

"Where's Old Scarface?" Cody roared. Burke had a jagged scar on one cheek. "Go out and find him. I want to know why he wasn't here when this ship came in!"

A searching party was dispatched while Cody fumed and raged on the docks of Civitavecchia.

When it finally returned with a disheveled Major Burke, Cody shouted at him, "John Burke, you're fired! Understand that? You're fired!"

Burke sadly returned to Rome and sent a cable to Nate Salsbury reading: MY SCALP HANGS IN THE TEPEE OF PAHASKA AT THE FOOT OF MOUNT VESUVIUS. PLEASE SEND ME MONEY TO TAKE ME BACK TO THE LAND OF THE FREE AND THE HOME OF THE BRAVE. Before Salsbury could hasten from London and prevent the discharge of the invaluable Burke, he received another cable stating that a reconciliation had been arranged and Burke had been forgiven. Those first years of touring Europe were, however, trying ones for Cody's associates and hirelings. Then his natural amiability resurfaced, his sense of humor was restored, and Cody was himself again.

From the moment the *State of Nebraska* discharged its cargo at Gravesend, including performers and roustabouts, the animals and equipment, and the old Deadwood coach in which kings would ride with boyish glee, the Buffalo Bill company was received in England with a wild enthusiasm.

The voyage itself had been a dismal experience, especially for the ninety-seven Indians led by such Sioux hetmen as Red Shirt, Little Bull, Cut Meat, and Poor Dog. The Indians recalled a superstition that any member of their race who crossed the ocean would sicken and die. It was a rough passage, and when they were stricken with seasickness the Indians were convinced the prophecy would come true in mid-ocean. Their only comfort was the fact that Cody and most of the whites were similarly stricken. Morale drooped so low that Cody held daily convocations at which Nate Salsbury performed his old Salsbury Troubadour routines, Cody recited passages from the plays in which he had appeared, and Frank Butler revived the juggling act with which he had once appeared in vaudeville.

A special boat train was waiting to take the company from the Royal Albert Docks at Gravesend to the exhibition grounds in Earl's Court, Kensington, where the show would occupy an area adjoining the American Industrial Exhibition, which was also part of the Queen's Jubilee. It would open when construction of a grandstand seating 30,000 people was finished. Meanwhile, its success seemed to be assured by the consuming interest Londoners took in every facet of the production, from the speed and efficiency with which the Yanks settled in at the Earl's Court headquarters to the manly beauty of Colonel William F. Cody himself. At times it almost seemed that it was Buffalo Bill's Jubilee instead of the Queen-Empress'. Burke and his henchmen had plastered London with posters and three sheets heralding the summer-long appearance, causing one London journal to comment in verse:

> I may walk it, or bus it, or hansom it; still
> I am faced by the features of Buffalo Bill;
> Every hoarding is plastered, from East End to West
> With his hat, coat and countenance, lovelocks and vest.

Within a few days after the show's arrival, Burke and his crew had little to do but hand out passes—later known to the trade as Annie Oakleys, because the punch marks on them looked as though they had been used for target practice—and paste the sheaves of clippings in the official scrapbook. The spectacle at Earl's Court even before the first performance moved a reporter for one of the London dailies to write that "One could not help recalling the delightful sensations of youth, the first acquaintance with the Last of the Mohicans, the Great Spirit, Firewater, Laughing Water and the dark Huron warrior."

The Indians gaped at Londoners, and Londoners gaped back with even more avid interest. Chief Red Shirt was as fascinating to the journalists as Buffalo Bill and with immense dignity held court in his tepee on the campgrounds near the Earl's Court Arena. Several days before the first performance, the Right Honorable William Gladstone, the Prime Minister until a few months before, came out to the Indian village with Mrs. Gladstone, the Marquis of Lorne (husband of Princess Louise), and Lord Gower. Mr. Gladstone smoked a cigar with Cody while Mrs. Gladstone chatted with Annie Oakley. Then the former Prime Minister sought out Chief Red Shirt and, according to an eavesdropping journalist, "Mr. Gladstone asked Red Shirt what he thought of the English climate. The chief said he had not had much to complain about so far. Mr. Gladstone asked if he thought the Englishmen looked enough like Americans to be kinsmen and brothers. Red Shirt wasn't sure about that." The enterprising London correspondent of a provincial newspaper wangled an exclusive interview with the Sioux chief in which Red Shirt obligingly commented that all white men weren't necessarily devils. "They are educating our children," he told his interviewer, "and teaching them to farm and to use farming implements. Our children will learn the white man's civilization and to live like him." There were many Sioux on the Dakota reservations who would have violently disagreed with Red Shirt, as events at Wounded Knee were to testify a few years later.

For London society, a little bored with the familiar pageantry and imperial trappings of home manufacture, the Buffalo Bill camp with all its barbaric suggestions and trans-Atlantic exuberances was the place to go and the place to be seen late in April of Jubilee year. The place was crawling with toffs, awash in gray toppers, ablaze with diamond-studded honorables and dames and ladies of the realm. Lord Gower, the honorary chairman of the American Exhibition, assumed a proprietary air and was present almost daily, as were Lady Alice Beckie and Sir Francis Knollys, the secretary to the Prince of Wales. Others who came calling before the opening day were Ellen Terry and Sir Henry Irving, the novelist Justin Huntley McCarthy, Charles Wyndham, the Grand Duke Michael of Russia, Lord Strathmore, and Lady Randolph Churchill, whose father and uncle had hunted with Cody.

The official opening was to be May 9, but three days before that the Prince of Wales, the future Edward VII, appeared at the arena for a special command performance. The afternoon of May 6 he and the Princess of Wales, their children, and a sizable entourage including the Princesses Victoria, Louise, and Maude, the Duke of Cambridge, the Comtesse de Paris, the Crown Prince of Denmark, and the Marquis of Lorne journeyed there in a long line of carriages. Cody showed the visitors around the camp, then escorted them to the royal box draped with the Union Jack and the American flag. In the otherwise empty arena, Cody and his fellow performers staged a preview. Annie Oakley rode in and blasted a number of targets with perfect form. The moment she rode off, a herd of buffalo charged into the arena, followed by a whooping band of Indians. From the other end, a herd of long-horned steers was driven in by cowboys and stampeded past the royal box. The Deadwood Stage made its perilous journey. Backstage Nate Salsbury kept the show moving at a terrific clip, knowing how important the Prince of Wales' imprimatur was. And the prince was enthralled; he and his children, including the future George V, were so fascinated that they stood up throughout the performance. Afterward Annie Oakley was presented to the prince and princess. Instead of extending her left hand to be kissed, as was customary, the princess democratically shook hands with Little Sure Shot.

The show was a roaring success even before it opened. At

the Prince of Wales' urging, Queen Victoria announced a command performance to which she would be accompanied by an array of reigning European monarchs.

The premiere on May 9 was attended by a capacity crowd, with every one of the grandstand's 30,000 seats filled. Special trains had been laid on to bring the crowds to the West Brompton station, and the Brompton Road was jammed by omnibuses, hansom cabs, and carriages. In the boxes were Princess Victoria of Teck, Cardinal Manning, Leopold Rothschild, Henry Irving and Ellen Terry, and other celebrated figures of the aristocratic, social, and theatrical sectors. Buffalo Bill was never more magnificent than on that day, in his masculine prime, still graceful on horseback or on foot, still deadly of aim, with his glossy auburn hair and his commanding presence. He held the audience transfixed when he rode in to shatter glass balls thrown in the air by Johnny Baker or to lead his trusty scouts in rescuing a pioneer woman from a homestead surrounded by Indians.

Queen Victoria's command performance was held on May 12. She led her entourage from Windsor Castle in the royal coach flanked by outriders. In the following carriages were the King of Denmark, the King and Queen of Belgium, the King of Saxony, the King of Greece, the Crown Prince of Austria (whose assassination was the signal gun of World War I), the Crown Prince and Princess of Germany, the Grand Duke Michael of Russia (who was supposed to be scouting for a royal English bride), and Prince Louis of Baden.

The moment the queen was seated, Cody rode into the arena bearing a huge American flag. Queen Victoria bowed from her seat. It was a stirring moment for Anglophile Americans and Americanophile Britons present. A British queen bowing to the Stars and Stripes! What Cody's Irish ancestors would have thought of the scene, with Ireland still under the British heel, was another matter. As John Burke put it in the show's publicity release for the American papers, "For the first time since the Declaration of Independ-

ence, a sovereign of Great Britain saluted the Star Spangled
Banner—and that banner was carried by Buffalo Bill."

Victoria Regina's prolonged mourning over the death of
her consort, it was further claimed by the Buffalo Bill publicity corps, was finally broken by her delight over the Wild
West Show. That wasn't quite accurate, but it was true
enough that the sixty-eight-year-old Widow of Windsor enjoyed herself tremendously. She had intended to stay only an
hour because of the long drive back to Windsor; instead she
sat through the whole performance. And when it was over
she asked that members of the company be presented to her.

Buffalo Bill and his comrades, white and Indian, acquitted
themselves nobly. Presumably they had been coached in bowing, curtseying, and addressing the queen. She held a lengthy
conversation with Cody, who looked every bit as kingly as
any of the royalty present. Chief Red Shirt was even more
imposing in his massive calm and greeted the sovereign as an
equal, which, considering that she was a mere female, was a
considerable condescension on his part. The Sioux chief informed Queen Victoria that he had "crossed the big water"
just to see her and "felt glad." This was a fair sample of the
Indian version of blarney, since the chief had never heard of
Victoria until he crossed the ocean. She was especially
pleased with Annie Oakley in her fringed buckskins and told
her, "You are a very, very clever little girl."

Lord Ronald Gower, as chief patron of the American participation in the Jubilee, wrote excitedly in his diary that
evening that the queen's visit had been a triumph. "Some of
us went in the Deadwood coach, which, driven at great speed
around the arena, is attacked by mounted Indians, and much
firing takes place from within and outside the vehicle. . . .
The Queen seemed delighted with the performance; she
looked radiant. At the close of the performance, Buffalo Bill,
at Her Majesty's request, was presented, as well as the Indian
Chief, 'Red Skin' [sic], and two of the squaws with their 'pa-
pooses,' whose little painted faces the Queen stroked. . . .
Her Majesty, who had driven into the Exhibition in a car-

riage-and-four, with outriders in scarlet, left soon after six en route for Windsor."

After that, of course, the Buffalo Bill Wild West Show was the sensation of the Jubilee summer. Londoners called it "the Yankeries," *Punch* magazine christened it the "Buffalo Billeries" with characteristic whimsy. Every day the Earl's Court location, now the scene of the British automobile show, was packed with 30,000 to 40,000 spectators, many of them standing, while the rest of the American Exhibition dwindled into what one London newspaper unkindly characterized as "an exhibition of dental surgery by distinguished Americans."

The royal patronage, coming as it did in the autumnal glow of European royalty, with hereditary rulers everywhere presiding over peaceful and prosperous realms from one end of the Eurasian continent to the other, was invaluable. It brought in 2,500,000 customers before the summer was over, and it attracted publicity equally as negotiable as the half crowns, florins, and shillings that poured into the box office.

There was the shooting match arranged by the Prince of Wales between Annie Oakley and the Grand Duke Michael of Russia, for instance. It was supposed to be a private affair, but John Burke saw to it that the London newspapers were advised. Grand Duke Michael was paying court to Princess Victoria, but the courtship was opposed both by her father, the Prince of Wales, and the majority of the British public. Since the Prince of Wales arranged the contest, it was widely suspected that he was scheming to discredit the Russian suitor. One morning the Grand Duke, the Prince of Wales, and a covey of princes, princesses, dukes, and duchesses appeared at the empty arena to watch him shoot against the American girl and what the newspapers called her "magic gun." It wasn't much of a contest, though the Grand Duke Michael had prided himself on his marksmanship. Each fired at 50 clay pigeons, with Annie breaking 47 of the targets, the Grand Duke Michael 36. Burke saw to it that the event was covered by all the London papers, and as Annie herself later recorded, "The papers that were against his courting expedition were pink with sarcastic comments of this dashing cavalier who was outdone at his own game by a little girl from America, of this Lochinvar who was no match for short dresses and whose warlike career faded before the onset of the American kindergarten. Whether all this had anything to do with what followed, I of course can only guess. But about that time the engagement was broken off and the opposition papers announced that 'Annie Oakley of the magic gun' had won two matches at once from the Grand Duke—the shooting trophy and the hand of the Princess."

The royal patronage extended still farther, and the glow it engendered reached blinding magnitude when Queen Victoria announced that she simply had to see the Wild West Show again. The second command performance—an unprecedented gesture, as the newspapers reported—would take place June 20, the day before the climax of Jubilee ceremonies at Westminster Abbey. The show would move to the grounds of Windsor Castle, and the queen's special guests would include all the kings and queens and other royalty who had gathered for the celebration.

Undoubtedly the climax of that special performance at Windsor was the dash of the Deadwood Stage into the impromptu arena, surrounded by whooping Indians, with Buffalo Bill and the Prince of Wales on the box and four royal personages riding inside as passengers. Cody ordered the Indians to make the ride as exciting as possible, slather themselves with war paint, and fire off all the blank cartridges they could.

Cody described the most celebrated run the Deadwood coach ever made in an excited letter to Mrs. Cody: "What do you think, Mamma? I've just held four kings! And I was the joker! It wasn't a card game either. You remember the old stage coach? Well, I got a request from the Prince of Wales to let him ride on the seat with me, while inside would be the kings of Denmark, Saxony, Greece and Austria. Well, I didn't know just what to say for a moment. I was a little worried and yet could I tell the Prince of Wales that I was afraid to haul around four kings, with Indians shooting blanks around? So I just said I was as honored as all get out, and we made the arrangements.*

"And, Mamma, I just had to have my joke, so I went around and told the Indians to whoop it up as they never did before. We loaded all the kings in there and the Prince got up on the seat with me, and then I just cut 'er loose. We sure did rock around that arena, with the Indians yelling and shooting behind us, fit to kill. And Mamma—I wouldn't want to say it out loud—but I'm pretty sure that before the ride was over, most of those kings were under the seat. It sure was fun."

Buffalo Bill provided a little prairie humor when the royal passengers dismounted from the coach. The Prince of Wales, whom Cody had taught how to play draw poker on one of their social evenings, asked him whether he had ever held four kings before. "I've held four kings," Cody replied, "but four kings and the Prince of Wales makes a royal flush, and that's unprecedented." The prince then tried to explain the joke to the other personages, in three different languages, but it didn't survive translation.

Against all the royal competition—and that from distinguished Americans representing the United States at the Jubilee, including Secretary of State James G. Blaine, Joseph Pulitzer, Chauncey Depew, Lawrence Jerome, and Senator Simon Cameron—Buffalo Bill was the social lion of the season. It was said that Oscar Wilde was petulant with envy over the amount of attention given Cody. Nightly he was wined and dined, and both the wine and the flattery went to his head. It was incredible that a boy from the sodhouse frontier should be clapped on the shoulder by noblemen and statesmen, that he should be admitted to the intimacy of the Prince of Wales, yet didn't that prove he must be some kind

---

* Seems a shame to ruin a good story with nit-picking, but in the interests of historical accuracy it must be noted that there were only three kings in the stagecoach. It was the crown prince, not the king, of Austria.

of natural-born aristocrat himself, not forgetting the family legend that he was descended from the first kings of Ireland?

In the giddy course of the summer he moved out of the Piccadilly hotel suite and into more expansive quarters in Regent Street, in the West End, where he could entertain on a grander scale. The rooms were found for him by Ralph D. Blumenfeld, the London correspondent of the New York *Herald*, who doubtless had received instructions from Publisher Bennett to act as Cody's social guide and mentor.

Blumenfeld alone among the various observers of Cody's careening course through London society that summer of 1887 maintained that Buffalo Bill was still the same simple, unpretentious plainsman whom everyone admired for his democratic attitudes. "Cody," he cabled the New York *Herald*, "can now wear evening dress and adjust a white tie as easily as he could skin a buffalo calf. He has a fine sense of humor and laughs at himself when he sees his mantel covered with invitations." He quoted Cody as remarking to him, "I've been reading about Bret Harte and Tom Thumb. They were lionized here for a while, too, but only while there was excitement about them."

Correspondent Blumenfeld insisted that Cody was unspoiled by all the adulation. "Everything was done to make Cody conceited and unbearable, but he remained the simple, unassuming child of the plains who thought lords and ladies belonged in the picture books and that the story of Little Red Riding Hood was true." But it couldn't be said that Cody's social triumphs and dining out in Mayfair delighted everyone. There were those mossbacks who regarded the aristocracy's adoption of Buffalo Bill as its current pet as a sign of debility, a symptom of the sort of decadence that inspired Marie Antoinette and the ladies of her court to play at being milkmaids. Trout-faced dukes childishly entranced by what was, after all, only a commercial entertainment enterprise and marchionesses throwing themselves at the feet of an American roughneck did not encourage faith in the durability of the empire. James Russell Lowell, who had just finished a term as American ambassador to the Court of St. James's, acidly wrote a professor friend in Boston that "I think the true key to this eagerness for lions—even of the poodle sort—is the dullness of the average English mind." That didn't really explain the Buffalo Bill phenomenon, since Cody had been equally lionized in the United States and would be in various European capitals.

There were few exceptions taken to Cody's lionization by English journalists, who could not ignore the fact that he had received the cachet of the royal family from Queen Victoria down to her smallest grandchild. One of the more waspish London periodicals, which was striving to maintain standards in London and county society—a difficult task with the Prince of Wales associating with shady entrepreneurs and female commoners of dubious morals—did openly view some of the idolatry with misgivings. "On the whole, I cannot but consider it a mistake," one of its columnists wrote, "for Lord Beresford to have given the Yankee showman a mount on the box seat of his drag at the Coaching Club meet. *Noblesse oblige*, there is a want of congruity in the companionship of an illustrious officer who fills an important position in the Government with a gentleman chiefly famed as an adroit scalper of Indians. I do not blame Buffalo Bill; my censure is confined to the fashionable throng who pay their devotion at such a shrine."

But that wasn't the view of the establishment. If there was something a trifle kinky about the leaders of government and fashion seeking vicarious thrills in Buffalo Bill's arena or in his company, it was not visible to that organ of the established, the *Times* of London, which preferred to think that there was a parallel between England's reception of the Wild West Show and the current effort to establish a court of arbitration for the settlement of disputes between Britain and the United States. The *Times* conceded that "it might seem a far cry from the Wild West to an International Court. Yet the connection is not really remote. Exhibitions of American products and scenes from the wilder phases of American life certainly tend, in some degree at least, to bring America nearer to England. . . . Those who went to be amused often stayed to be instructed. The Wild West was irresistible. . . . Civilization itself consents to march in the train of Buffalo Bill. Colonel Cody can achieve no greater triumph than this, even if someday he realized the design attributed to him of running the Wild West Show at Rome. . . . It is true that Red Shirt would be as unusual a phenomenon on Broadway as in Cheapside. But the Wild West, for all that, is racy of the American soil. We can easily imagine Wall Street for ourselves; we need to be shown the cowboys of Colorado. Hence it is no paradox to say that Colonel Cody has done his part in bringing America and England nearer together."

Cody's opinion of himself was soaring at the moment the *Times* chose to describe him as leading the march of civilization. Therefore he was unable to understand how Crown Prince Wilhelm of Germany could invite Annie Oakley, alone, to appear at a shooting exhibition in Berlin. The invitation led to a falling out between Cody and Little Annie. Let the girl go her own way. Burke and Salsbury begged him to arrange a reconciliation with the number-two attraction of the show, but Cody stubbornly shook his head and dipped into a beaker of scotch. Thus she was lost to the show for a whole season and toured with Pawnee Bill's rival outfit after fulfilling the Berlin engagement, until Cody's self-esteem assumed more comely and sensible proportions.

Without "Little Missie," the show moved on to Manchester, where it played all winter in a huge hall. When it returned to the States in the early spring of 1888, Cody was informed by Salsbury that he was $500,000 richer. And that was before the imposition of the federal income tax. Considering the purchasing power of that amount of money in 1888, Cody's earnings were by far the greatest ever recorded by an American entertainer in England. He came away not only much richer but with awed respect for the drinking capacity of the English upper classes. "My genial hosts' capacity for the liquid refreshments," he said, "would have made me envy them in the Sixties"—that is, when he was doing his drinking in frontier saloons—"and led me to suspect that there might be accomplishments in England in which even western pioneers are excelled."

The Buffalo Bill company returned to New York aboard the chartered steamship *Persian Monarch* to a warm welcome from their fellow citizens and the press, who agreed that Buffalo Bill had done them proud as an unofficial ambassador of goodwill. As the New York *World* described it: "The harbor probably has never witnessed a more picturesque scene than that of yesterday, when the *Persian Monarch* steamed up the quarantine. Buffalo Bill stood on the captain's bridge, his tall and striking figure clearly outlined, and his long hair waving in the wind; the gayly painted and blanketed Indians leaned over the ship's rail; the flags of all nations fluttered from the masts and connecting cables. The cowboy band played 'Yankee Doodle Dandy' with a vim and enthusiasm which faintly indicated the joy felt by everybody connected with the 'Wild West' over the sight of home."

The company settled down for a summer-long stand at the stadium on Staten Island, where the attendance was even better than during the 1886 season.

And still relying on a stalwart constitution, Cody continued a style of living which had begun to alarm his associates in England. He took a suite at the Waldorf-Astoria and threw open its doors nightly for wassail. His fellow revellers were a curious combination of New York society and hairy old Western pards in town for a binge. There were women as well as men present at the nightly routs, word of whom undoubtedly seeped back to Welcome Wigwam, North Platte, Nebraska, where Louisa Cody was making a brave pretense for her daughters and the neighbors that the marriage was still sound and secure.

Newspapermen, hardened veterans of the Park Row saloons, marveled at his ability to appear daily in the Staten

Island arena, clear of eye and steady of hand, and yet preside over nightly booze-ups. And what did Mrs. Cody think of his excesses? Cody maintained that Louisa, though a temperance advocate, actually indirectly encouraged his drinking.

One night back in North Platte, he said, he went home early and without a drop in him. The door was locked, and he had to awaken Mrs. Cody, calling out in an unslurred voice, "Let me in, Lulu." Mrs. Cody refused to believe that it was her husband outside. He immediately repaired to the sutler's at Fort McPherson, got roaring drunk, and staggered back home at 4 A.M. "Then," he related, "I fell up against the door like a bale of hay and shouted for my wife. 'Oh, is that you, Willy? I'm so glad you're home,' my wife said, and she let me in." The story was always good for a laugh, but Nate Salsbury, his partner and the keeper of a long-forgotten pledge of total abstinence, rarely found it amusing.

10

The Further Adventures
of Buffalo Williamus

EARLY in the spring of 1889 preparations were going forward for another tour overseas, this time on the Continent,
where every capital west of the Carpathians was clamoring to
experience the world-famous thrills of watching the Wild
West re-created and neatly packaged for civilized consumption. The European fascination was cogently explained by
James Bryce in *The American Commonwealth*. "For the
West," he wrote, "is the most American part of America, that
is to say, the part where those features which distinguish
America from Europe come out in strongest relief."

From James Fenimore Cooper, Washington Irving, Bret
Harte, Mark Twain, and other American writers, Europeans
had conjured an image of a primitive America which keenly
whetted their curiosity. Many intellectuals were inclined to
adopt Rousseau's romanticizing of the "noble savage," and
undoubtedly for European audiences the Indian contingent
of the Buffalo Bill show, though not individually celebrated
on equal terms with Cody or Annie Oakley, was at least half
of the attraction.

The juxtaposition of the semibarbaric splendors of the
New World with those of European antiquity—and a sugges-

tion of the culture shock that might result—was facetiously anticipated in a newspaper poem published shortly before Buffalo Bill and company sailed for Europe:

> I'll take my stalwart Indian braves
>   Down to the Coliseum,
> And the old Romans from their graves
>   Will all arise to see 'em.
> Prepare triumphal cars for me,
>   And purple thrones to sit on,
> For I've done more than Julius C—
>   He could not down the Britons!
> Caesar and Cicero shall bow,
>   And ancient warriors famous
> Before the myrtle-wreathed brow,
>   of Buffalo Williamus.

After the Staten Island stand of summer 1888 and the following tour of the South, Cody went home to North Platte for the first time in several years. He divided his time between the Welcome Wigwam, listening to Louisa's strictures on the sort of life he had been leading, and the Scout's Rest Ranch, where his sister Julia had been installed. Home life quickly palled, and he hastened back East to help Salsbury and Burke with the preparations for a European tour. Their first measure was to retrieve Little Annie Oakley from Pawnee Bill's show, which had been lurching from one disastrous stand to another, and sign her to a new contract.

"Little Missie!" Cody cried when the contract was signed and he took Annie in his arms. From then on there were no more rifts in their relationship, no more professional jealousy to disturb their seventeen-year association. She got to know him as well as anyone else connected with the enterprise, and her estimate of his character, formed by a knowing and perceptive mind, was a touching testimonial to the private as well as the public Buffalo Bill.

"He was the kindest, simplest, most loyal man I ever knew," she wrote. "He was the staunchest friend. . . . Like

all great and gentle men he was not even a fighter by prefer-
ence. His relations with everyone he came in contact with
were the most cordial and trusting of any man I ever knew.
. . . The same qualities that insured success also insured his
ultimate poverty. His generosity and kindhearted attitude toward all comers, his sympathy and his broad understanding
of human nature, made it the simplest thing possible to handle men. But by the same token he was totally unable to resist any claim for assistance that came to him, or refuse any
mortal in distress. . . . The pity of it was that not only could
anyone that wanted a loan or gift get it for the asking, but he
never seemed to lose his trust in the nature of all men, and
until his dying day he was the easiest mark above ground for
every kind of sneak and gold-brick vendor that was mean
enough to take advantage of him.

"I never saw him in any situation that changed his natural
attitude a scintilla. None could possibly tell the difference
between his reception of a band of cowboys and the train of
an emperor. Dinner at the camp was the same informal,
hearty, humorous, storytelling affair when we were alone,
and when the Duchess of Holstein came visiting in all her
glory. He was probably the guest of more people in diverse
circumstances than any man living. But a tepee or a palace
were all the same to him, and so were their inhabitants. He
had hundreds of imitators but was quite inimitable."

Success in the first stages of the European tour was practically guaranteed by the fact that the Wild West Show would
make a six-month stand in Paris the summer of 1889 while
the Universal Exposition was being held. The French government sponsored an industrial and cultural exposition
every eleven years, but the 1889 event would be bigger and
better than ever because it celebrated the founding of the
French Republic. The exposition grounds covered more
than 200 acres, spreading along the Seine and over the
Champ de Mars, the Trocadéro Park, and the Esplanade des
Invalides, right in the heart of Paris and in the shadow of the

Eiffel Tower, the recent construction of which made it a contemporary wonder of the world. Buffalo Bill's camp would be set up on the edge of the Bois de Boulogne in the Parc du Neuilly within sight of the Arc de Triomphe.

A Parisian triumph was further assured by the efforts of John Burke's band of press agents and promotion experts. Parisians were salivating for their first glimpse of the fabulous Indian fighter and his noble savages long before the company sailed from New York. Even the conservative Paris fashion houses had taken up the Western motif. Fashionable young men bought American and Mexican saddles for their morning rides in the Bois de Boulogne. The shops along the boulevards were well stocked with souvenirs and other merchandise which disfigured provincial homes for generations—statuettes of Buffalo Bill, pottery, Indian baskets, moccasins, cowboy hats, toys modeled after bucking horses, buffaloes, cowboys, and Indians.

Cody and his company landed at Le Havre early in May and proceeded to the thirty-acre site off the Avenue de la Grande Armée. There, within a few days, the Parc du Neuilly was converted into a sector of the Wild West. At one end of the U-shaped arena rose a huge canvas background depicting the forks of the Yellowstone with the Montana mountains rising behind them.

Twenty thousand persons crammed the arena at the opening on May 18, with President Sadi Carnot and his wife and the members of his Cabinet in the Presidential box. Queen Isabella of Spain was in another box. Also present were visiting American dignitaries—Whitelaw Reid, the American ambassador to London, and Thomas A. Edison, who would make a pioneer film actor of Buffalo Bill—and the American ambassador to Paris, Louis MacLean. In the stands were celebrated artists, Rosa Bonheur, whose genre was not far removed from the spectacle she witnessed in the arena, E. Meissonier, celebrated for his sports paintings, and Édouard Detaille, whose subject was military life.

At first there seemed to be little reaction from the French

audience. It listened respectfully, but with some bewilderment, to the blaring tunes of Bill Sweeney's cowboy band. It watched in amazement as the whole company made the grand entry and rode around the arena but stayed silent and rooted in the seats. Usually a tremendous cheer went up when the company made its dashing, prancing appearance. Cody and Salsbury eyed each other in dismay. Were they about to be faced with a tremendous flop? Actually the reason for the lack of response was simply a cultural gap. Unlike the English, the French knew little about the American West; as always they were self-absorbed, and for years they had been fighting on their own overseas frontiers in North Africa, the Middle East, and Indochina. They could only gape in wonder at the rickety old Deadwood Stage, the hundred whooping Indians, and the hard-riding cowboys.

It was Little Annie Oakley who saved the day. Many in the audience were army officers, ex-soldiers, and sportsmen. One thing they could understand was fine shooting, and Little Missie was in splendid form that day. She ran into the arena, which remained silent; no doubt she was conscious of the oppressive weight of Gallic skepticism, that collectively morose suspicion of 20,000 individuals that they had been diddled out of their francs. Calmly she waited while two assistants rode out to hold her targets. With pistol and rifle, she broke the glass balls held up for her. Then in rapid cadence she snuffed out the flames on a revolving wheel of candles. There was a rustle of interest from the stands. Wielding a shotgun, she broke two, then four discs before they could reach the ground. Then came the *pièce de résistance* of her act. She threw two balls into the air, reached for the gun on her table, turned, and fired in one fluid motion and broke both targets while they were still in the air. No one could withstand the grace and precision of her performance, the self-deprecating air with which that slight, girlish figure accomplished her feats.

"*Vive! Vive!*" the audience thundered. "*Vive* Annie Oakley!"

She topped it off with the riding part of her act. As a spotted pony galloped into the arena, she leaped onto his back, then leaned down to pluck a pistol off the grass, and shattered six glass balls while riding hell for leather. *Now* the French understood what the Wild West was all about, epitomized for them by that small, energetic figure whirling and darting and shooting against the huge backdrop of the Montana mountains.

With Annie Oakley in the lead, the show swept on to enthusiastic acceptance by the French. Buffalo Bill did not capture their imagination as Little Sure Shot did; they had not read the dime novels which made him fascinating no matter what he did in the arena for English-speaking audiences. And Cody had learned his lesson. With some audiences he would always be overshadowed by Annie Oakley; and a good thing it was for the show as a whole.

The Wild West Show was the rage of Paris and the camp itself a magnet that drew distinguished visitors. Cody presided over Indian breakfasts and rib roasts attended by the French aristocracy and leaders of fashion. His guests included the Sultan of Turkey, the Shah of Persia, and the King of Senegal. The Senegalese monarch, being confronted by a plague of tigers in his homeland, tried to buy Annie Oakley from Cody for 100,000 francs, but the offer was declined.

Rosa Bonheur, a weathered lady of seventy in her black smock and beret, practically lived in the Buffalo Bill camp that summer. She set up her easel in the corrals, on the shooting range, and in the Indian camp, sketching busily away at everything she saw. The most famous painting she produced was a life-sized canvas of Cody mounted on his white charger, reproductions of which were later used in the show's advertising. The original was presented to Cody, who shipped it home to Mrs. Cody. Perhaps it served to remind Louisa what her wandering husband looked like. Later it was widely exhibited in the United States.

Other artists followed Mlle. Bonheur's example, and soon

a forest of easels appeared in the Parc du Neuilly and the place looked like an outdoor studio. A man couldn't scratch himself without half a dozen daubers from Montparnasse immortalizing the scene. Another summer-long guest of the camp was Prince Roland Bonaparte, who was the leading French anthropologist. Fascinated by the Indian village, he endlessly questioned the Sioux and Cheyenne about their customs, myths, and superstitions and filled notebooks with precise observations on the texture of their skin, the color of their eyes, the tone of their sinews. Some of the braves even pulled out strands of their black hair, which Prince Roland carefully filed away in envelopes.

Occasionally a distinguished visitor, particularly in the case of the Shah of Persia, proved to be a resounding disappointment. The shah behaved as though he were the reincarnation of Darius the Great condescending to walk among Roman barbarians. As Nate Salsbury later recorded his impressions of the Shah-in-Shah's descent on the Buffalo Bill establishment, the visit was arranged by the mayor of Neuilly, whose *arrondissement* included the show's arena and encampment and therefore was a man to be placated. "I readily assented," as Salsbury recalled, "and in return he [the mayor] said he would take much pleasure in presenting Cody and myself to the Shah. Cody got into his buckskins, I pushed myself into a spike-tailed coat, and soon the mayor appeared. Covered with decorations, spattered with medals and resplendent in the uniform of a Major General of the French Army, he was calculated to make the most extravagant picture of Solomon look like a soiled deuce in a new pack. The equerries of the Republic dashed into the grounds followed by a state carriage in which was seated the most unimpressive man I ever saw. The postillions stopped the horses, the footmen flung the carriage doors open, and the Shah descended to the ground, where he was met by the Mayor, who addressed him. . . . The Shah never stopped to hear the finish of the speech, but waved him away with petulant disdain and passed into the grandstand. And to this day neither Cody nor I has ever been presented to the Shah of Persia. The Mayor, strutting and fuming, strode away."

After six months of booming business in Paris, the show undertook a profitable tour of the cities of southern France and then invaded Spain, where everything went wrong. No one had taken into account the winter weather of erstwhile sunny Spain, nor had anyone reckoned on the stubborn Spanish belief that any outdoor spectacle that didn't include a bullfight was a waste of time and pesos.

A brave beginning was made in Barcelona when the company debarked on an early December day. John Burke, stirred to oratory by a crowd of Spanish journalists and by the historical associations of the quay on which he stood, pointed out that "on this very spot Christopher Columbus landed from his caravels upon his return after discovering America." He gestured dramatically toward the nearby statue of Columbus and declaimed, "There stands our advance agent, four hundred years ahead of us."

"Damn bad day for us," one of the Indians remarked in cultivated tones, "when *he* discovered America."

And it was a damn bad day when the Buffalo Bill troupe discovered Spain. Influenza and smallpox epidemics were raging in the port city, and poverty was endemic if not epidemic. The fact that the shows were sparsely attended was the least of their Spanish misfortunes. Instead of dukes and *marquesas,* men and women of fashion, the poor people of Barcelona descended on the Buffalo Bill camp to beg, to swarm around the mess tent and fight for the privilege of looting the garbage cans. Even the Indians had never seen such poverty on the Dakota reservations. With them the beggars brought the diseases then ravaging the slums of the city. Soon most of the company was stricken with chills and fever, all but Cody who dosed himself with so much whiskey the germs didn't stand a chance. The company's doctor was kept busy night and day making the rounds of the performers' tents, the Indians' tepees, the Mexicans' quarters, the big drafty tent where the roustabouts slept.

Salsbury cut the admission prices in half, but still the Barcelonans stayed away in droves. One day in mid-December he was summoned to the city hall and informed that the company had been placed under quarantine and would not be able to escape from Spain and its winter gales until the public health officials decided it would not spread the diseases it had contracted.

Christmas, 1889, was the blackest day in the history of the show. Three roustabouts died of smallpox and ten Indians of influenza. Then Frank Richmond, the ringmaster, also died of the flu. All were buried in a windswept Barcelona cemetery.

It was a month before they were given clearance from quarantine and Salsbury was able to charter a grimy, rust-coated Mediterranean tramp steamer to convey the company to Naples. The ship was so overloaded that the captain refused to take it beyond the harbor entrance, which was lashed by a late-January gale, until Salsbury gave him more money. And when the ship arrived in Naples after two days and nights at sea, Cody and his associates must have wondered whether the Mediterranean world was ready for American-style entertainment and honest American business practices. An enterprising Neapolitan, it seems, had counterfeited 2,000 reserved-seat tickets for the opening performance and sold them at bargain rates. The result was screeching confusion when holders of genuine and fake tickets contended for the seats—and 4,000 Neapolitans embroiled in a dispute over property rights could create more action than anything Buffalo Bill could produce in the arena. The show, in fact, was an anticlimax. Still, Naples, Rome, Florence, Venice, Milan, and Verona proved to be hospitable and receptive. Even the portals of the Vatican opened up. Italians, unlike the French, weren't especially impressed by Annie Oakley's virtuosity with firearms, but they admired her trim figure. They loved Buffalo Bill's swaggering masculinity. There were memorable moments when Chief Rocky Bear and his braves stared into the molten crater of Vesuvius, when orotund John Burke stood in the amphitheater built by Diocletian sixteen centuries before and proclaimed, "Hoary antiquity and bounding youth kiss each other under the sunny Italian skies!"

In Rome the show was a great success largely because of the Italian fascination with its bucking horses and adhesive broncobusters. The only disappointment connected with the Roman stand was that the Wild West Show could not, as announced, appear in the Coliseum, where similar entertainment, though much bloodier, had been presented centuries before. Cody surveyed the Coliseum and decided there was too much rubble and broken masonry littering the arena to permit his troupe to perform with any degree of safety.

His own gladiators were challenged by the Prince of Sermoneta, who owned a number of spectacularly untamed horses, so fierce that many Italians believed they ate people. The prince brought his wild horses to Rome and declared no American cowboy could break them. Buffalo Bill, on behalf of his fearless riders, accepted the challenge.

An American newspaper correspondent cabled a full account of how American wranglers rose to the occasion. "All Rome was today astir over an attempt of Buffalo Bill's cowboys with wild horses which were provided for the occasion by the Prince of Sermoneta. Several days past the Roman authorities have been busy with the erection of especially cut barriers for the purpose of keeping back the wild horses from the crowds. . . . Anxiety and enthusiasm were great. Over 2,000 carriages were ranged round the field, and more than 20,000 carriages lined the spacious barriers. . . . Two of the wild horses were driven without saddle or bridle into the arena. Buffalo Bill gave out that they would be tamed. The brutes made springs in the air, darted hither and thither in all directions, and bent themselves into all sorts of shapes, but all in vain. In five minutes the cowboys had caught the wild horses, saddled, subdued, and bestrode them. Then the cowboys rode around the arena, while the dense crowds applauded with delight."

Buffalo Bill and his fellow performers, including the Indians, were invited to the Vatican through the intervention of Archbishop Corrigan of New York and Monsignor O'Connell of the American College in Rome, perhaps with a genial nudge or two from publicist Burke. Some trepidation was felt regarding the behavior of the Indians who, it was feared, might fling themselves into a medicine dance or some other pagan rite on being admitted to the presence of Christ's vicar on earth. Burke, a Catholic, drilled them in the proper deportment for a Vatican audience.

It was a solemn occasion when Cody, in a dress suit, and his followers filed through the gates of the Vatican on the anniversary of the coronation of Pope Leo XIII. They were escorted by Cardinal Rampola who, as master of ceremonies, instructed them to stand in a line along the corridor leading to the papal throne. The pope was carried in his chair past the Wild West contingent, on which he bestowed a blessing in passing.

The Indians behaved splendidly until on departure they filed through the courtyard and caught sight of the preposterously costumed Swiss Guard in their striped bloomers, with halberds and two-handed swords as sidearms. For the Indians, perhaps, the pompous Swiss epitomized all the ceremonial silliness of the white race when it girded itself for war. They could accept John Burke's word that a little old man sitting on a palanquin under his triple crown was the Great Manitou's earthly representation, but they roared with guttural laughter over the idea of the Swiss Guard pretending to be warriors.

They laughed all the way back to the campsite, but there the merriment ended. When they went to the Vatican, they had left one of the braves behind because he had suddenly fallen ill. On their return, they found that he had died. The Indians immediately summoned John Burke to a council at which Chief Rocky Bear acted as their spokesman. Why, demanded Rocky Bear, had the pope betrayed them, why hadn't he protected their ailing comrade? Burke, for all his eloquence, could not find a suitable answer. And that was the beginning of considerable trouble with the Indian contingent. Possibly it started earlier when ten of them died in Barcelona. Most of the Indians, at any rate, were homesick, weary of traveling, and fed up with Europe. About this time, too, they had probably received word—either in letters from home or American newspapers forwarded to them or by some more mysterious means—that there was a great deal of trouble and disturbance on the Dakota reservations. Rumors of an impending war. Talk of an Indian Messiah. They wanted to return to their people if trouble broke out with the whites, not display themselves to crowds of palefaces in Europe. A few of the Indians, in fact, slipped away and traveled back to the United States in steerage, and more were to follow them as the show rolled through the cities of northern Italy, then into Germany.

Unlike the Latin countries, Germany was knowledgeable about the mythical, if not the real, American West. Indian lore and a somewhat distorted version of Western history were part of German *Kultur* and had been since 1830, when James Fenimore Cooper's *Leatherstocking Tales* was translated and widely read in Germany. Then a writer named Karl May—the Teutonic counterpart of Ned Buntline and Prentiss Ingraham—began producing a long series of highly romanticized "Western" novels featuring a hero named Old Shatterhand who frequently fought on the side of the Indians. There was hardly a German who did not consider himself an expert on Western history.

In April, 1890, the show began playing to huge crowds in Munich, then detoured to Vienna for a three-week stand on the edge of the Vienna Wood. The U.S. minister to Austria was Frederick Dent Grant, son of the general, who had served with the cavalry out West and acted as Cody's social sponsor. Returning to Germany, the show opened a month's engagement in Berlin on the Kurfurstendam on July 23, 1890. Berliners thronged every performance, and their number included the newly enthroned Kaiser Wilhelm II and his family. Similar enthusiasm greeted the troupe in every German city from the Rhineland north to Hamburg as it toured the Reich in the autumn.

Everywhere they were dogged by Prussian staff officers, who seemed inordinately interested in every detail of the show's operation, particularly its logistics. In France they had been surrounded by artists, in Germany by monocled military men, all brass plates and plumes, who looked as though they had wandered from a rehearsal of *Lohengrin*. At first Cody and Salsbury suspected the officers, well known for their headlong amatory tactics, were smitten by Annie Oakley or one of the prettier Indian girls. Actually the Wild West Show had become a matter of military intelligence. To the single-minded German militarists Buffalo Bill's outfit was a small army whose operations were well worth studying. Ordinary Germans were agog over the riding and shooting and pageantry, but it was the movement and victualing of the troupe that fascinated the military experts.

Late in August the show arrived in Hamburg to find that an old rival had stolen a march. Doc Carver, now billed as the "Chief of Champion Shots," had gone bankrupt with his original company. He had made a comeback, however, and during the summer of 1890 had toured eastern Europe, then the Scandinavian countries. Quite by accident Cody's old enemy appeared in Hamburg three days before the Buffalo Bill show. Once again there were threats of a wholesale slaughter between the two contingents; the same sort of thing usually happened when two Wild West outfits accidentally converged. The publicity men always made the most of such rivalries, which were good for business. The enmity between Cody and Carver was real enough, but there may have been a touch of hyperbole in the account an American correspondent cabled a New York newspaper from Hamburg:

"There is intense excitement here over a fierce row which has occurred between Dr. Carver and Buffalo Bill. The people are afraid to come out of doors after dark and the city is in a state of siege.

"The members of each troupe have openly declared their intention of fighting for their respective masters, even if the quarrel ends in a general battle. Carver's performances on the continent have been better patronized than Cody's and the latter's jealousy was aroused. Carver stole a march on his rival by arriving three days ahead of him and opening his show in fine style. When Cody got here, he found he would be obliged to pitch his tent within a few feet of Carver's show. Carver had made arrangements for an exclusive supply of electric lights, and this left Cody's place in darkness. Then the members of both companies took up the matter, and it is only through the strenuous efforts of the police that a fearful fight has been prevented."

The unfortunate reunion with Doc Carver actually was the least of Cody's troubles at the time. He was getting much more unwelcome publicity from allegations that the Indians with his show were being poorly fed and badly treated. Two members of the consular staff in Berlin investigated the charges and after inspecting their living conditions signed a statement that the Indians were "certainly the best looking and apparently the best fed Indians we have ever seen." The reports of mistreatment continued to spread, however, even the New York *Herald* reporting that "For months past the warriors have been straggling back in groups of three and five, sick and disgusted with their treatment while abroad. Fully two-thirds of the original band have returned to this country."

Actually the desertions seemed to have been caused by homesickness and by word somehow received from the reservations, perhaps along that mysterious Indian grapevine, that something important was about to take place in the West, possibly a general uprising. Neither before nor after the events of 1890 were there any complaints that the Indian performers accompanying Buffalo Bill were ill-treated in any way. As supporting evidence of Cody's fairness and responsibility in this respect there is the statement of Chief Red Fox, a Sioux and the nephew of Crazy Horse, who at this writing is still alive and prospering at age one hundred. Red Fox traveled with Cody's shows for many years as a trick roper, rider, and interpreter, and testified convincingly to Cody's keeping the faith with his Indian employees.

"I can truthfully say," Chief Red Fox has stated, "that he always took good care of the Indians in his show. When he called all of the people together before the show opened, he had each one read his contract and ask questions about anything they didn't understand. He would say, 'Remember, my Indians come first. They are the main attraction of this show. I know how some of you look upon Indians because you don't know them. If you have any trouble with them, tell Red Fox. He is in charge and will put them in their place, but don't have any trouble with them. I want everyone in this show to work together as a brother and friend.' Once a cowboy told him the show could not go on without him, and Buffalo Bill said, 'I can put a pair of boots, a big hat and red shirt on any man, and call him a cowboy, but I cannot dress anyone up and call him an Indian.' "

Cody was so troubled by the reports that when the show ended its German tour and went into winter quarters in Strasbourg, all the remaining Indians were sent home. John Burke cabled the New York newspapers and announced the move in his fanciest phraseology: "The Indians are being repatriated to give the lie to current slanders and to show the refining and ennobling influence which European travel had on them. . . . The Indian folds his tents and follows on the brine's deep blue the trail of Columbus, Vespucci, De Soto and Hendrik Hudson. Thence wandering westward he braves the bleak blizzards of the Bad Lands of Dakota and will imbibe in his wild native solitude those graces and virtues that contact with modern civilization in the intellectual centers of Europe may have blunted."

In reality, the "graces" which the Indian members of the troupe were soon to absorb were those of the Ghost Dance, and the "virtues" they were about to confront were those of rapid-firing Hotchkiss guns manned by the United States Cavalry.

Only a few days after he dispatched the last members of his Indian contingent home, Cody decided to follow them to New York. The Associated Press may not have been as efficient a grapevine as that available to the Indians, but reports of a big Indian war out on the plains where he had gained his first renown had become more and more alarming. Obviously his personal intervention would be required. Undoubtedly his public expected a grand gesture from the man portrayed as preeminent in winning the West. This time, though, he was determined to take the field as a peacemaker.

11

To Sitting Bull's Rescue

CODY'S role in the Ghost Dance disturbances, which culminated in the indelible shame of the "battle" of Wounded Knee, was a peripheral one marked by good intentions and thwarted aims. In retrospect, his much-publicized gallop across the Dakota plain with sacks full of hard candy and the usual trinkets for Sitting Bull seems quixotic at best, frivolous at worst. There was a considerable suspicion that Cody attempted an intervention on behalf of peace between the Sioux and the Army mostly as a grandstand play.

Actually his motives were probably a mixture of ego satisfaction and genuine concern for Sitting Bull and the Indians. Whatever bloodthirstiness there was in his constitution had long ago evaporated; closer acquaintance with the Indians as fellow human beings had tempered his former frontier attitudes, and he was able to comprehend the intense frustrations they experienced in the unwalled prisons called reservations. As evidence of his sincerity in 1890, there was an episode which occurred six years later, which was *not* publicized, resulting in peace between the Sioux and their ancient enemies the Chippewas. In the autumn of 1896 he arranged a meeting between the Chippewas and a Sioux delegation led by Chief Rocky Bear, a veteran employee of his, and coaxed the tribal enemies into smoking the peace pipe.

When he arrived in New York from Europe and hurried on to Washington to insist that the Indians' complaints about their treatment be investigated at once by the Indian Bureau, he learned more about the threats of trouble on the Sioux reservations of Dakota Territory. It had been fermenting for a long time. Oddly enough, it was started by the liberal organizations, the Indians' Friends, the Indian Rights Association, and the Indian Treaty-Keeping and Protective Association, which had embarked on a program of social engineering without consulting the people they were organized to protect. Through their influence on the Harrison administration, they obtained the appointment of a Sioux land commission which ordained that the Indians surrender 9,000,000 more acres of their shrinking heritage. It was all for the Indians' good. In return they would receive livestock and farming equipment; they would be forced to cultivate small farms and would become self-supporting.

What the reformers didn't know and didn't bother to find out was that small farming on the dry, dust-blown, and infertile plains simply wouldn't work. And they refused to listen to the protests of Sitting Bull, the aged Red Cloud, and other Sioux leaders. The Christian missionaries on the reservations, the earnest liberals back East, and the agents of the Indian Bureau all were intent on proving that they knew what was best for their copper-skinned brothers, who would be forced to take their medicine because it was good for them and never mind that the Sioux lands were soon grabbed up by homesteaders and land speculators.

The Sioux were still brooding over the loss of their millions of acres when, with the speed of a grass fire on the prairies, a new religious movement sprang into existence from the Western reservations to the Dakotas. A prophet had arisen among the Paiutes, a hitherto listless tribe inhabiting the wastes of California and Nevada, preaching a half-Christian, half-pagan doctrine. The prophet was a young

Paiute medicine man named Wovoka, to whom visions had appeared of a new awakening among all the Indians. If they would perform the Ghost Dance, an endless stomping around a fire which continued until many of the dancers went into convulsive trances, and certain other ceremonies, an Indian Messiah would appear among them. Wovoka preached that the Second Coming would be a vengeance on the whites for having killed Jesus Christ the first time He appeared; that all the whites would be driven off the continent and into the seas; that the buffalo herds would return, and all the Indian dead would be resurrected. The power of that creed, coming at a time when Indians all over the West were suffused with despair, was overwhelming. One of the chants that accompanied the Ghost Dance ritual ran as follows:

> My Father have pity on me,
> I have nothing to eat,
> I am dying of thirst
> Everything is gone!

In emulation of the Three Wise Men, three Sioux named Kicking Bear, Short Bull, and Porcupine journeyed westward to receive Wovoka's teachings from the source. When they returned they gathered close to 3,000 tribesmen on Wounded Knee Creek to practice the Ghost Dance and other rituals in an atmosphere of religious hysteria that ironically resembled in most of its details the white man's revival meetings. James McLaughlin, the Indian Bureau's agent at the Standing Rock agency, where Sitting Bull lived, was convinced that his charges were planning an outbreak on a scale never seen before. Equally outraged by the Ghost Dance were the Eastern Christians, who considered the new Indian religion a plagiarism, a mockery, and a perversion of their own beliefs.

The critical question, both for the Indian Bureau and the Army, was exactly where Sitting Bull stood in all this. In Agent McLaughlin's books, the old chief was a "reactionary" who had opposed the land commission's decrees and whose influence was feared by the "progressives," including the many young Sioux who had joined the reservation's Indian Police. The bitter irony of those terms as they echo in a modern context is inescapable.

An attractive widow from Brooklyn, Mrs. Catherine Weldon, the representative of the National Indian Defense Association and a courageous and idealistic woman, just then was trying to influence Sitting Bull against the Ghost Dancers. She had come to Sitting Bull's little farm on the Grand River despite the objections of McLaughlin, who told her Sitting Bull was "a coward, a savage, one who hated all white people." Sitting Bull, however, received her graciously and invited her to join his household, which swarmed with two Mrs. Sitting Bulls, eleven children, and various other relatives and hangers-on. At first there was a slight misunderstanding over Mrs. Weldon's role in the household. She pitched in and helped with the chores which, to an Indian, signified that she was proposing marriage to Sitting Bull. He advised her that he was willing to take her as his third wife, but she managed to convince him that sweeping the floor and lighting fires was not a romantic gesture. Newspapers in surrounding towns, however, published stories stating that she had become the third Mrs. Sitting Bull, and with this new sexual element, which rarely contributes to interracial harmony, she found herself a pariah among Dakota white people. Doggedly she stayed several months at Grand River, collecting data for Sitting Bull's appeal against the latest land seizure and paying for a survey of the holdings of each family living at Grand River, then went back East to write articles and otherwise enlist the support of Indian sympathizers on the Sioux's behalf. It was an effort bound to fail because the other Indian rights associations favored the reduction of the Sioux reservations and they exerted a powerful influence on the Republican administration.

Mrs. Weldon then hurried back to the Standing Rock

agency to appeal to Agent McLaughlin not to call in the Army, but he was too busy recruiting for the Indian Police, a force, incidentally, which about fifty of the Sioux who had quit Cody's show in Europe joined, to pay much attention to her appeals. She also went to Sitting Bull and begged him to stop his people from joining the Ghost Dancers, rightly convinced that a continuation would justify the government in taking harsh measures. But Sitting Bull told her, "The younger ones no longer listen to me. They join the Indian Police. They join the Ghost Dancers. They do as they please. I do not believe in the Ghost Dance myself, but I cannot prevent my people from believing as they choose. If it gives them hope, who am I to talk against it? The government takes away their food, but I will not take away their hope."

Late in 1890 the representatives of the Indian Bureau informed Washington that they could not handle the situation on the Dakota reservations; the Army would have to take over. Major General Nelson A. Miles, a vain and touchy veteran of the Indian wars, had taken over command of the frontier forces from General Sheridan. He supervised the military movements, sending the Ninth Cavalry to the Pine Ridge agency, followed by eight troops of the Seventh Cavalry, which was said to be burning with a desire to avenge the Little Big Horn. More troops were held in readiness for swift transport by rail to the troubled agencies. Meanwhile, hoping to avert an armed outbreak, General Miles ordered that the beef ration on the Sioux reservations be increased immediately. The brass hats, in fact, were less bloody-minded at that juncture than the humanitarians, who felt that the Indians had betrayed them. Senator Henry L. Dawes, for many years the humanitarians' voice in Congress, said he was washing his hands of the Sioux, that they should have stuck to their farming and not listened to false prophets.

At this juncture Cody appeared on the scene and offered his services as peacemaker. He had journeyed from Washington to General Miles' headquarters in Chicago with John Burke, and both his presence and his prestige were welcome. No soldier in his right mind would look forward to campaigning that winter over the ice-slicked Dakota plain.

Cody's scheme was simple enough: He would talk Sitting Bull into entrusting himself to Buffalo Bill and accepting protective custody by the military. He cited the fact that he and the Sioux leader had always been on friendly terms, that it was known Sitting Bull regarded as his most prized possession an old circus trick horse that Cody had given him when he quit the Wild West Show. If Sitting Bull was removed from the scene, the dissident Sioux, the Ghost Dancers, and other troublemakers would have no single figure to rally around. They would come in from the badlands and quietly go back to their homes.

General Miles agreed to give Cody a try at heading off trouble. He wrote out an order headed CONFIDENTIAL and reading: "Colonel Cody, you are hereby authorized to secure the person of Sitting Bull and deliver him to the nearest Commanding Officer of U.S. Troops, taking a receipt and reporting your actions." On the back of one of his visiting cards, Miles wrote out another passport to Indian Country: "Com'd'g officers will please give Col. Cody transportation for himself and party and any protection he may need for a small party."

Cody took off on the next train for Bismarck while Burke went around to all the Chicago newspaper offices and confidentially whispered that Buffalo Bill, single-handed, was about to head off an Indian war. At Bismarck Cody was met by Pony Bob Haslam, whose efforts as an advanceman for the first Southern tour of the Wild West Show had been disastrous and whose presence now would have caused a more superstitious man to wonder whether the auguries hadn't suddenly turned ominous. The West still looked pretty wild to Cody on that bleak day in the last week of November: a few sullen-looking Indians hanging around the depot and plentiful evidence of the military presence. He and Haslam rented a rig from a livery stable and drove out to the Standing Rock reservation, where Agent McLaughlin's headquarters and Fort Yates were located.

It was apparent from the start that McLaughlin, an ambitious young man, jealous of his authority, looked on him as an outsider rather than the man who could save the situation. Cody, brimming with confidence, asked McLaughlin only for a wagon and a team of horses; no cavalry escort, no agency officials to accompany him on the mission to the Grand River.

"I can't let you go," McLaughlin told him. "You would be killed before you got halfway there."

Cody privately agreed, as he wrote later, that crossing the Sioux reserves alone "would be the most dangerous undertaking of my career." He was unarmed and unescorted. His only protection would be Sitting Bull's friendship, provided it still existed, but that wouldn't keep him safe if he came across a party of Ghost Dancers.

He wanted to leave at once for Grand River with a wagon loaded with bushels of the hard candy Sitting Bull loved and presents for Sitting Bull's two wives. McLaughlin and the officers and Fort Yates were determined to delay him, however, while McLaughlin wired Washington for General Miles' order to be countermanded by superior authority. Cody was always partial to military companionship and yielded to the pleas of the officers at Fort Yates that he join them for a few rounds at the officers' club. It was damn cold on the Dakota steppe and a little whiskey would warm him for the journey, and Will Cody could always be persuaded to tarry for a friendly cup. What difference did a few hours make?

All the difference in the world, it developed, for the man he had set out to save.

At the Fort Yates officers' club relays had been assigned to "drink Cody under the table." Cody rose to the challenge.

He spent the night there drinking all comers under the table. When dawn came, Cody was still on his feet and calling for one more round.

While all the jollification was taking place, Agent McLaughlin composed a telegram to Washington and eagerly awaited a reply, determined that the interloper would not steal any of the credit for dealing with hostiles on *his* reservation. The telegram read: WILLIAM F. CODY (BUFFALO BILL) HAS ARRIVED HERE WITH COMMISSION FROM GENERAL MILES TO ARREST SITTING BULL. SUCH A STEP AT PRESENT IS UNNECESSARY AND UNWISE, AS IT WILL PRECIPITATE A FIGHT WHICH CAN BE AVERTED. . . . REQUEST GENERAL MILES' ORDER TO CODY BE RESCINDED.

About 11 o'clock in the morning Cody finally tore himself away from the bar at the Fort Yates officers' club, wrapped himself in buffalo robes, and took off for Grand River in a wagon stocked with presents for Sitting Bull.

He was ten miles up the wagon road when a messenger from Fort Yates overtook him with an order from President Harrison instructing him to abandon his mission. Disgruntled, he turned his mules around and obeyed. He always believed that if he had been allowed to continue on his way he would have persuaded Sitting Bull to accept protective custody and the ensuing tragedy, not only that of Sitting Bull but many of his people, would have been averted.

Agent McLaughlin and the military on the reservation, it developed, had formulated their own plan for taking Sitting Bull, one that was guaranteed to produce the violence McLaughlin had claimed he was trying to prevent. Their pretext was a letter that Sitting Bull dictated to a young Sioux educated in the white schools and sent to McLaughlin. "God made you—made all the white race, and also made the red race—and gave them both might and heart to know everything in the world, but gave the whites the advantage over the Indians. . . . I wish no man to come to me in my prayers with gun or knife. . . . You should say nothing against our religion, for we said nothing against yours. . . ." He then notified McLaughlin that, with or without permission, he would be going over to the Pine Ridge agency to "investigate this Ghost Dance religion."

McLaughlin took this to mean that Sitting Bull was going to *join* the Ghost Dancers and ordered immediate action. A forty-three-man force of the Indian Police was dispatched to Grand River, with a troop of cavalry standing by to support them. Thus Sitting Bull's own people did him in. They broke into his house just before daylight the morning of December 15; it was packed with Sitting Bull's relatives and friends, and shooting broke out. Sitting Bull was killed instantly.

That was the signal for a showdown, welcomed by the Army and the bureaucrats because it would allow them to tidy up a messy situation, break the suggestive power of the Ghost Dance, and force the Sioux to accept the dictates of the 1889 land commission. Regiment after regiment was put on trains and rushed to the Dakota agencies. With the Seventh Cavalry in the vanguard, the troops gave chase when Chief Big Foot and his band of about 400 men, women, and children made a break for freedom in hopes of joining the main body of Ghost Dancers in the badlands. Two weeks after Sitting Bull was killed—"assassinated" might be a better word—the Seventh Cavalry caught up with Big Foot and his followers on the banks of Wounded Knee Creek. They occupied high ground and trained their four Hotchkiss guns on the village. (The Hotchkiss gun was an automatic cannon which fired fifty two-pound explosive shells a minute.) On the morning of December 29 the commander of the Seventh Cavalry ordered Big Foot to surrender and sent a number of troopers into the tepees to look for weapons. Just then a medicine man, who had been shouting that the white man's bullets couldn't kill true believers in the Ghost Dance, scooped up a handful of dirt and tossed it into the air. Apparently the white troopers believed this was a signal for resistance to begin. The Hotchkiss guns opened up with their deadly chatter and the Indians fell in windrows. Many of the

Indians, including women and children, tried to flee over the frozen prairie, but the troopers rode them down. No quarter was given. No accurate body count was made, but an estimated 200 to 300 Sioux of all ages and both sexes were heaved into a mass grave. The War Department entered it on the records as the "battle of Wounded Knee," but it could have chosen a more precise description.

But there was still work to be done, more campaigning for the regiments gathered under the personal command of General Miles. All the Sioux who had left the reservation had to be bullied, coaxed, and herded back onto the reservations, where they would learn to plow a straight furrow or be damned to starvation. They couldn't be allowed to roam where they pleased; they had to be penned up and kept out of the path of civilization. The plan of operations was to herd all the Indians still on the loose toward the Pine Ridge agency, where they would be disarmed.

In the interim Cody had been brooding over the failure of his peace mission. Back in Chicago with Burke at his side, he told newspapermen that all the fighting would have been unnecessary if he had been allowed to proceed to Sitting Bull; he didn't confess that he might have made it to Grand River if he hadn't wasted a night in wassail at Fort Yates. Certainly his subsequent actions were motivated by a thirst for publicity. Probably he was prompted by Burke, who couldn't stand idly by while other men copped all the newspaper space being devoted to the "last Indian war" out on the Dakota plain. Burke hustled around and obtained a commission for Cody from the always sympathetic New York *Herald* to act as its special correspondent. Governor John Thayer of Nebraska was hurriedly persuaded to bestow on Cody the grandiose title of "Aide-de-Camp-in-Chief on the staff of the Commander-in-Chief [presumably of the armed forces of Nebraska] with the rank of Brigadier General." Apparently expecting some opposition from the regular Army, Cody also was given an order from Governor Thayer reading, "You will proceed to the scene of the Indian troubles and communicate with General Miles. You will in addition to the special service referred to, please visit the different towns, if time permits, along the line of the Elkhorn Railroad, and use your influence to quiet excitement and remove apprehensions upon the part of the people. Please call upon General Colby [the state militia commander], and give him your views as to the probability of the Indians breaking through the cordon of regular troops; your superior knowledge of Indian character and mode of warfare may enable you to make suggestions of importance."

It was a lame excuse for Cody's second intervention in the dismal fate of the Sioux, who had about as much chance of "breaking through the cordon" in their starved and frozen condition as they had of ghost dancing their way down Pennsylvania Avenue, Washington, D.C.

With Burke as his companion and consultant, Cody then hastened back to the scene of action. His feeling of self-importance was considerably deflated when one of the Indians who had accompanied him to Europe called to pay his respects and asked, "You big general now, Bill?"

"Yes," replied Cody, his chest swelling, "I'm a general now."

"Big general same as Crook and Terry?"

"No, I was commissioned by the Governor of Nebraska."

"Militia," the Indian snorted. "Oh, hell!"

General Miles' operation was proceeding slowly, cautiously, but without bloodshed. The Indians were being herded toward the Pine Ridge agency from the badlands for the mass disarmament. It was a delicate business, with the Indians sullen and resentful, the white soldiers ready to start shooting at any sign of resistance. Miles wanted no grandstand plays from General Cody. He appointed Cody as an "advisory scout," whatever that meant, to keep him under his thumb. When Cody and another scout named McGillicuddy wanted to go out and "parley" with the incoming hostiles, General Miles firmly forbade them to interfere.

In his role as journalist, or war correspondent without a

war to report, Cody was more spectacular. In a dispatch to New York undoubtedly composed by Burke, he pictured a desperate situation: "Every hour brings a new opinion. Indian history furnishes no similar situation. You must imagine about 5000 Indians, an unusual proportion warriors, better armed than ever known before, hemmed in a cordon of them about sixteen miles in diameter, composed of over 3000 troops, acting like a slowly closing dragnet. This mass of Indians is now influenced by a percentage as despairingly fanatical as the late Big Foot party, under Short Bull and Kicking Bear. . . . Such is the situation General Miles and the military confront. Anyone of this undisciplined mass is able to precipitate a terrible conflict from the most unexpected quarter. . . . In fact it is a war with a most wily and savage people, yet the whites are restrained by a humane and peaceful desire to prevent bloodshed and save a people from themselves. . . . The smouldering spark is visible that may precipitate a terrible conflict any time in the next few days. . . ."

Despite the dire Cody/Burke forebodings, the Indians were all rounded up a few days later, on January 16, 1891, and disarmed. Hundreds were taken as hostages. Among those "wily and savage" creatures, Cody and Burke, showmen once again, went on a talent hunt. They particularly wanted the services of Kicking Bear and Short Bull, as two of the leading Ghost Dancers and two of the Three Wise Men who had gone to Nevada to interview Wovoka. All in all, they signed up 100 of the hostages, including Kicking Bear and Short Bull, to reenact their supposedly ferocious careers in the Wild West Show and persuaded General Miles to release them in Cody's custody. At least they would be provided gainful employment and be distracted from any further adventures in mysticism. With more humane purposes in mind, Cody and Burke also brought East with them a little Sioux boy whose parents had been killed at Wounded Knee. He had been found wandering near the battlefield. Burke informally adopted him and named him Johnny

Burke No Neck. His new home would be the Buffalo Bill Wild West camp.

Three days after the Sioux surrender Cody wrote Annie Oakley, who was staying with the troupe in Europe, boasting that he had commanded 1,000 troops in the campaign just concluded. Presumably he meant Nebraska militia which had been called up in case the Sioux broke through the regular Army's cordon. In any case, the only man under his command had been his faithful press agent.

12

Adventures with an Expensive Soubrette

WHILE Cody had been indulging himself in a return to the heroic modes of his youth, Nate Salsbury and the rest of the Wild West company had been preparing for a resumption of the European touring which, in 1891, would range from St. Petersburg to Glasgow. In revamping the show Salsbury decided to emphasize its horsemanship, with representative styles to be contributed by riders from all over the world.

A troupe of Cossacks led by Prince Ivan Macheradze, costumed in knee-length coats, bandoleers, and silver-spurred boots, armed with long Caucasian pistols and huge daggers, was imported from Russia. The Mexican *vaqueros* and American cowboys were also joined by a band of gauchos from the Argentine. From then on the subtitle of the Wild West Show was "Congress of the Rough Riders of the World."

Shortly after Cody and Burke rejoined the company, it was further expanded by the aging survivors of the Charge of the Light Brigade, who were too brittle to challenge the Cossacks and gauchos in horsemanship but marched around the arena behind a tattered Union Jack. Uhlans from the German lancer regiments were subsequently added to the roster, and one of the more exciting new features of the performance was a hurdle race between an English rider costumed in pinks as a fox hunter, a German cavalryman, a Sioux on an Indian pony, a Mexican on a pinto, and an American cowboy on a mustang. The race was fixed. In England the winner was always the fox hunter, in Germany the uhlan, and so on.

The company stirred itself out of winter quarters in German-occupied Alsace, and once again it was mystified by the dogged surveillance of the German military. Was it suspected of harboring French intelligence agents? The mystery of the German General Staff's interest was finally cleared up, as Annie Oakley wrote in her diary: "We never moved without at least forty officers of the Prussian Guard standing all about with notebooks, taking down every detail of the performance. They made minute notes of how we pitched camp —the exact number of men needed, every man's position, how long it took, how we boarded the trains and packed the horses and broke camp; every rope and bundle and kit was inspected and mapped.

"But most of all they took interest in our kitchen. The traveling ranges were inspected and enumerated in those endless notebooks. The chefs were interviewed. The methods of storing food, of preparing it, of having necessities ready for use at a minute's notice, all these things were jotted down. Naturally we were curious as to why they were doing all this, and had our own ideas about how it would be used in some way for the army. . . . But we had no idea, of course, that the world was to listen, mouth open, twenty-five years later, to the stories of the marvelous traveling kitchens of the Teuton army, serving meals piping hot on the road to Belgium—an idea gained from the Buffalo Bill Wild West Show when we toured Germany!"

The German staff officers also absorbed valuable lessons in quick loading and unloading the show train and adapted them for their own troop movements which, along with the mobile field kitchens, were to contribute to the awesome logistical efficiency of the imperial armies.

Annie Oakley was given but did not seize upon the opportunity to eliminate one of the marplots who started World War I. Kaiser Wilhelm, who was often impelled toward reckless actions as a compensation for one arm shriveled since birth, had seen her shoot the ash off Frank Butler's cigarette during the show's second engagement in Berlin. He insisted on serving as her target in a similar demonstration. Annie nipped off the end of his cigar—the wrong end, as she later said. In 1917, after the United States entered the war, she wrote the Kaiser and asked for another chance but added that she would not guarantee the same result.

The show moved on to Belgium, gave a performance for Queen Wilhelmina in Brussels, and toured the battlefield of Waterloo, on which Sweeney's Cowboy Band played "The Star-Spangled Banner." After ranging through western Europe, the troupe returned to another round of triumphs in Britain. Following a tour of the provinces, it set up shop at the old Earl's Court grounds adjoining the International Horticultural Exhibition. And once again Buffalo Bill and company benefited from royal patronage. The Prince of Wales was often seen in the royal box with his raffish companions. Queen Victoria, fascinated by all she had heard of the Cossacks and their daring horsemanship, commanded another appearance on the grounds of Windsor Castle. Afterward the principal members of the company were invited to a reception in the quarters of the queen's equerry. Cody was on his best behavior. He had vowed not to touch a drop of the creature until the season ended. When word of his abstinence reached the United States, great was the rejoicing of the temperance societies, which inscribed his name on their banners and welcomed him to the cold-water brotherhood. He would, of course, eventually prove a disappointment to them and return to his ten-tumbler minimum daily ration of whiskey. As the *Rocky Mountain News* of Denver commented on the incredible news that Buffalo Bill had gone dry, "If Bill ever got on one of those whooping prairie tears of his, he would break up any foreign temperance community in about one hour."

During their stand at Earl's Court, Cody and Salsbury welcomed into the family circle a broad-shouldered young artist named Frederic Remington, who had come over to do an article and sketches of the Wild-West-in-London for *Harper's Weekly*. It was Prince Ivan and his Cossacks who caught Remington's eye as he worked over a sketch pad, though Burke kept insisting to him that the American cowboy could excel any of the riders from the steppes. As Remington wrote in his *Harper's* article, however, the Cossacks were incomparable as stunt riders. "They stand on their heads, vault on and off, chase each other around in a game called chasing the handkerchief, and they reach down at top speed and mark the ground with a stick. Their long coat-tails flap out like an animated rag-bag, while their legs and arms are visible by turns. Their grip on the horse is maintained by a clever use of the stirrups, which are twisted and crossed at will."

Remington, who smoked cheroots and pulled at a flask of whiskey as he worked at his sketches, was then thirty-two years old, the same age as Annie Oakley, and just at the beginning of an illustrious career. During the past decade he had worked on wagon trains and followed the cavalry from New Mexico to Montana, but he wryly remarked that anyone who wanted to obtain a glimpse of the Wild West now had to come to London, where it was encapsulated and recreated by a commercial entertainment enterprise. The frontier had been erased by the shoot-up at Wounded Knee. From then on, it would survive with increasing distortion, with garish highlights, as the property of Hollywood, U.S.A., and even later of Italian directors making American horse operas on Spanish locations.

After more than three years abroad the show returned to the States, went into winter quarters in Connecticut, and began the long preparations for a bumper harvest of dollars as a leading attraction at the Columbian Exposition and World's Fair in Chicago. That event was supposed to celebrate Columbus' voyage but actually served notice on the world that the United States was an industrial power and a cultural force to be reckoned with in the future. At the same time many of the Americans who came to the exposition were looking backward, with a wistfulness that would increase with the years, at the passing of the Western frontier. It was hard to say which emotion was stronger, pride in accomplishment or nostalgia for what could never be recaptured. But there was a strong feeling that America had lost something in its headlong lunge from the Mississippi to the Pacific.

It was one of those strikingly apt coincidences that midway through exposition summer, on a July evening in 1893, a young professor from the University of Wisconsin named Frederick Jackson Turner read an essay titled "The Significance of the Frontier in American History" to the American Historical Association, which was meeting in conjunction with the World's Historical Congress at the Chicago Art Institute. The essay was one of those "seminal" episodes, as academics would say, in the recording and reconsideration of American history. Turner pointed out that until now United States history was largely that of the colonization of the West and continued, "Since the days when the fleet of Columbus sailed into the waters of the New World, America has been another name for opportunity, and the people of the United States have taken their tone from the incessant expansion which has not only been open but has even been forced upon them. . . . And now four centuries from the discovery of America, at the end of a hundred years of life under the Constitution, the frontier has gone, and with its going has closed the first period of American history."

Almost as though to emphasize the point that opportunity was diminished, that the "great open spaces" were contracting, there had recently been a panic in Wall Street and a severe depression was beginning. The symptoms weren't bad enough as yet to keep people throughout the country from boarding excursion trains and descending on Chicago from all directions.

That summer Buffalo Bill and his cohorts were visited by 6,000,000 paying customers, and 1893 was probably the vintage year of the show. It was bigger and more exciting than ever. It almost lived up to John Burke's prose on the posters which were plastered all over the city: "AN ABSOLUTELY ORIGINAL AND HEROIC ENTERPRISE OF INIMITABLE LUSTRE . . . Its great originator now rides along Fame's Warpath . . . a holiday reflecting years of romance and the reality of imperishable deeds, making the New World and the Old appear in BRAVEST AND MOST BRILLIANT RIVALRIES."

Chicago had prided itself on being the birthplace of Cody's career as a showman, but it had grown snobbish in the succeeding decades of prosperity. The exposition on the lakefront was a grandiose conception, a plaster-of-paris White City full of pseudo-Greek temples, reflecting pools, immensely pompous statuary, all the excrescences of the American renaissance. Its biggest draw, however, was a belly dancer named Little Egypt, and other supposedly educational exhibits included the first Ferris wheel, the impressively curved torso of Lillian Russell and the musculature of Sandow the Strongman.

In such a cultural ambience, exposition officials explained to Cody and Salsbury, there wouldn't be space for the Wild West Show, despite John Burke's vociferous claims that it was a segment of living history and as educational as an evening spent with the *Encyclopaedia Britannica.* So the show was shunted off to a fourteen-acre lot just across from the main entrance of the exposition with an arena, a grandstand seating 18,000, and room for the camp.

Buffalo Bill opened a month before the exposition, and it was apparent from the SRO crowds coming on by trolley and on the new elevated railroad that the show was reaching the predictable heights of its mass popularity, no doubt aided by all the "crowned-heads" publicity with which Burke had flooded the American newspapers. Then, too, Burke was very skillful about milking the Chicago papers for feature space and timed the arrival of each contingent so that there would be almost daily interviews and photographs of the more exotic attractions. The Indians, now that they had been crushed into submission, were especially fascinating to the newspapers and their readership. There was a succession of chiefs to be interviewed and have their claims recorded. Chief Rain in the Face asserted that he was the man who slew Custer. Chief Standing Bear arrived with a bonnet made of 200 eagle feathers and boasted that, with 150 head of cattle, he was the richest Indian. Old Chief Rocky Bear, Short Bull, and Kicking Bear were still with the show, and they had been joined by Jack Red Cloud, the son of the famous Red Cloud who had forced Fort Phil Kearny to be abandoned. Reporters were also shown Annie Oakley's tent, surrounded by flowers Little Missie was growing to lend a touch of domesticity, and the bullet-splintered cabin where Sitting Bull had made his last stand. To counteract rumors that Buffalo Bill was America's leading womanizer, Burke widely publicized the fact that his youngest daughter, Irma, was spending the summer with her father.

The international exhibition of horsemanship had been augmented for the Chicago engagement. Probably it was, as Burke tirelessly proclaimed, the finest display of equitation ever seen. A troupe of Bedouins performed acrobatics on horseback which even the Cossacks could not match. But it was the European cavalry whose costuming stunned the audience and made a detachment of U.S. Cavalry look drab by comparison. There were twelve French chasseurs with brass helmets, blue tunics, scarlet breeches, and patent leather boots. A company of British hussars from the Prince of Wales' Regiment wore full parade dress in the arena. But the French and British were easily outshone in costuming, if not in horsemanship, by a detachment of German uhlans, members of the Potsdamer Reds, a regiment largely devoted to delighting Kaiser Wilhelm and impressing foreign dignitaries. The uhlans, with their fourteen-foot lances, wore red helmets plumed with horsetails, red jackets, and blue trousers.

The American cavalrymen may have been drably dressed, in their dark-blue tunics and trousers with the yellow stripe, but patriotic Americans insisted that, fancy tricks aside, they performed with greater natural ease than any of the foreign competition. Amy Leslie, the star reporter of the Chicago *Daily News,* analyzed the competing styles: "An Indian hugs the animal close, lifting the horse instead of bearing weight upon it. Every muscle of an Indian's body trembles in response to the horse's gait. He sticks to the saddle or bareback by a sort of capillary action. The cowboy and Mexican do not touch a horse, but wear him out. The rider seems winged and had his hands on ropes or reins and everything but the expected. Germans are huge, bulky riders, who bounce and shake and took good care of their horses. Cossacks ride a horse like it was stationary and cast-iron, and the Arabs whirl about, a mass of circling drapery and arms. A Frenchman is always *le beau sabreur,* but he can't ride even a rocking horse. The most beautiful, graceful and easiest riders in the world are the American cavalrymen."

The publicity coup of exposition summer, however, was the famous 1,000-mile cowboy race from Chadron, Nebraska, to the gates of the Wild West Show in Chicago. It came about through the efforts of a notorious Nebraska hoaxer named John J. Maher. Several years before Mr. Maher had distinguished himself by spreading rumors of a Sioux uprising which contributed to the tension between whites and Indians in the Dakotas and helped to bring about the "battle" of Wounded Knee. In a less harmful mood this determined funster now concocted the hoax of a race on horseback from Chadron to the Chicago exposition. So many people believed him that the businessmen and mayor of Chadron felt compelled to announce that there would indeed be such a race. Taking it from there, John Burke, always alert for publicity, made it a Buffalo Bill production.

Each rider would start out with two horses, riding them alternately, and the winner would be presented with $500 and a Colt revolver by Buffalo Bill himself. There was an outcry of protest against cruelty to horseflesh from the Humane Society and the Society for the Prevention of Cruelty to Animals, which Cody attempted to stifle by putting up another $500 prize for the rider who brought his horses through the race in the best condition. He also told reporters, pointing to one of his broncos, "This little rat of a horse can stand more pounding rides uphill and down dale than most people imagine. What would kill a thoroughbred just puts a keen edge on a pony's appetite."

Burke was stirred to hyperbolic frenzy and proclaimed it "The Greatest Horse Race of All Time."

Ten riders, only two of them genuine cowhands, were enlisted to make the 1,000-mile run. One of the real cowboys was a local celebrity known as Rattlesnake Pete, on whom the loyal citizens of Chadron recklessly wagered their bottom dollars. A less serious contestant was one Doc Middleton, who relished publicity identifying him as the "gentlemanly horsethief"; the West was getting so tame that a rustler could actually attain gentility by tipping his hat to the ladies, when formerly he would have been hanged to the nearest cottonwood.

There was considerable squabbling among the contestants during and after the race, some of it doubtless caused by the alcohol consumed along the way. Several riders, with too much whiskey aboard, literally fell out of the race. Soon there were charges of skulduggery, malingering, and other misconduct eagerly reported by newspapers along the route of the race. Doc Middleton was caught riding the cushions of a day coach; puffing on his cigar, he explained to the reporters that he had joined the contest only to publicize himself. It was also alleged that several contestants were seen guzzling beer in farm wagons while their mounts trotted along behind. One contender was accused of sending fresh horses ahead by rail and maintaining his own relay system. Several competitors claimed they would have won the race if they hadn't got lost in the Chicago suburbs.

The first man to finish, two weeks after the starting gun was fired, was John Berry, who made the mistake of admitting he won because he knew the route and had taken various shortcuts. This admission raised such a clamor from the other riders that Cody finally divided the prize money among eight contestants. But it was all good for sheaves of press clippings.

For all the millions who saw the show that summer, including President Grover Cleveland, the Princess Infanta of Spain, the Duke of Veragua, Lillian Russell, and Diamond Jim Brady, the commanding figure in all that swirl of activity was still Buffalo Bill. At the age of forty-seven, it was true, he was showing signs of wear. His long mahogany hair was thinning, his face was marked by dissipation and the sagging tissue of middle age, but he was still a magnificent figure on horseback. He was a presence. An aura surrounded him. Perhaps it owed much to showmanship, to artificiality, to expectation. Seen with a cold eye, he may have been just another actor on horseback, a creature of his press agents' imagination, a magnificent blowhard capable of enchanting only those who came entranced by his legend. Even the most cynical felt a thrill, however, when that buckskinned figure rode into the arena at the start of the show and boomed out, "Ladies and Gentlemen, permit me to introduce to you a Congress of the Rough Riders of the World!"

Amy Leslie, of the Chicago *Daily News,* was not an easily impressed young woman, but she wrote, "Cody is one of the most imposing men in appearance that America ever grew in her kindly atmosphere. In the earlier days a hint of the border desperado lurked in his blazing eyes and the poetic fierceness of his mien and coloring. Now it is all subdued into pleasantness and he is the kindliest, most benign gentleman, as simple as a village priest and learned as a servant of Chartreuse. All the gray that has been thrust into his whirlwind life has centered itself in the edges of his beautiful hair."

If Buffalo Bill limited his activities in the arena to dashing in occasionally to save a white settler from an Indian attack and breaking a few glass balls with buckshot, the artistic mainstay on the show was still Little Annie Oakley. She kept perfecting her marksmanship until it seemed miraculous in its speed and precision. More than that, she stood for something in her own right, especially among her fellow American women, who were beginning to clamor for equal rights and who could point to her as a symbol of feminine superiority in a masculine endeavor. "She stood quite alone in her celebrity," as Stewart H. Holbrook observed, "which cannot be likened to that of any currently famous female. Her flavor was unique and of her time. It was a sort of combination of Lillian Russell and Buffalo Bill, a merger of dainty feminine charm and lead bullets, the whole draped in gorgeous yellow buckskins and topped with a halo of powder-blue smoke." Perhaps what fascinated her contemporaries as much as anything else was the combination of masculine efficiency and sweet domesticity which she radiated. Amy Leslie went to interview her and found her comparing embroidery patterns with Mrs. Nate Salsbury, just like any other housewife. "She welcomes us royally," Miss Leslie wrote. "Her tent is a bower of comfort and taste. A bright Axminster carpet, cougar skins and buckskin trappings all about in artistic confusion. She has a glass of wine waiting and a warm welcome."

Before they struck their tents that autumn, Cody and his associates had cleared more than $1,000,000. Salsbury and Burke were still keenly competitive, always keeping an eye on rival attractions. No matter how successful and lucrative the show was, they were determined to make it better, move faster, and include more attention-grabbing performers. "It is our intention," as Salsbury said, "to keep on enlarging Buffalo Bill's Wild West Show until we include in our performance a glimpse of every variety of wild life."

For their partner Cody, however, money and success and adulation seemed to be an increasing burden. His life was circumscribed by the show when he still had the urge to wander as he pleased. The money pouring in almost seemed a nuisance at times, one which he disposed of by spending, loaning, giving, and investing with a careless hand. He built a sixteen-room mansion at Scout's Rest Ranch and stocked the spread with 3,000 head of cattle. He lavished money on Louisa and their daughters, with the guilty feeling that it couldn't really make up for his absenteeism as a husband and father. When his sister Helen married a newspaperman, Cody bought him a printing plant in Duluth and established him as editor of the Duluth *Press*. Other old friends were set up in businesses that rarely succeeded in anything but acting as a drain on Cody's finances. Dr. Frank Powell, an early co-star in the Wild West Show and now the mayor of La Crosse, Wisconsin, was supplied the financing to manufacture a cereal substitute for coffee.

But Cody was jaded. The only thing he really wanted, a legitimate son to bear his name, was beyond his reach. Louisa wouldn't hear of a divorce, though Cody had acquired a candidate for the role of a second wife.

Often he was seen sitting in his tent alone at midnight with a bottle of whiskey on the table beside him. Dexter Fellows, later the most flamboyant of circus press agents, had started serving his apprenticeship under Burke about this time. He noted that Cody often looked "tired and harassed" and quoted him as saying, "As a fellow gets old he doesn't feel like tearing around the country forever. I do not want to die a showman. I grow very tired of this sort of sham worship sometimes."

But the show rolled on, and the money rolled in, through the nineties. Year after year he trouped across the country in the long, gaudily painted show train. The summer of 1894 the show played Ambrose Park, in South Brooklyn, on the shore of New York Harbor. It was a disappointing season; the morale of the performers seemed to sag, and something of the dash and excitement went out of the show.

Late in the season Buffalo Bill, Annie Oakley, and two of the Indian members of their troupe made their debut in a pioneering form of motion pictures, a medium which was to become more fascinating to Cody later in his career, when all else seemed lost. The producer was Thomas Alva Edison, who had just perfected the prototype of the movie camera, a device he called the kinetograph, which took a series of "galloping tintypes" displayed in slot machines in penny arcades and amusement parks. Hollywood was just glimmering on the horizon, but its present locus was the Edison laboratory at the foot of Orange Mountain in West Orange, New Jersey.

Cinematically, it was a historic occasion on September 24, 1894, when Cody, Annie Oakley, Short Bull, and Lost Horse were conveyed in two carriages to Edison's impromptu studio, with John Burke in charge of the exploratory expedition. They were taken into a room which Edison called Black Maria, a square, black-walled room with a glass-paneled roof through which the sun provided the lighting. Here they met the kinetograph without realizing that it was the forerunner of competition that would destroy much of outdoor show business and eventually replace it with drive-in movies. While one of Edison's assistants cranked the kinetograph, Annie Oakley pantomimed her shooting act, Lost Horse stomped through the Buffalo Dance, and Cody and Short Bull exchanged small talk in sign language. The premiere was held a few weeks later in a dark room at 1155 Broadway: the first of thousands of Western movies. Oddly enough, with all his vision Edison saw no future in motion pictures projected on a screen instead of shown in a nickel slot machine. "If we make this screen thing," he told Cody and Burke, "it will spoil everything. We are making these peepshow machines and selling a lot of them at a good profit. If we put out a screen machine there will be a use for maybe about ten of them in the whole United States. With that many screen machines you could show the pictures to everybody in the country—and then it would be done for. Let's not kill the goose that lays the golden egg."

One year seemed to blur into another . . . travel all night on the show train . . . roll out at dawn and set up for that day's performance . . . pack up again and roll on to the next stop. In 1895 the route included 131 stands in 190 days.

That year Nate Salsbury was desperately ill, nearly died, and survived for another half dozen years as a semi-invalid unable to assume the full administrative burden of keeping the show on the road. His role as mainspring was assumed by James A. Bailey, a circus man one year younger than Cody and Salsbury. It was his circus background that impelled Bailey, who became a junior partner in the enterprise, to book so many one-day stands. The Wild West Show was getting bigger every year, and now there were 700 people on the payroll who had to be transported, along with the animals and equipment, in two long trains.

Cody's home on wheels was Car No. 50, which was rather lavishly appointed for an old plainsman who once regarded a saddle blanket, a cook fire, and a frying pan full of sizzling bacon as epicurean luxury. He was attended from 1895 on by a valet named Alfred Heimer, a German immigrant, who seemed to possess all the best qualities of a manservant. Heimer was loyal, close-mouthed, self-effacing, and shrewd enough to anticipate the needs of an often moody, sometimes difficult employer. The moment Cody wearily came in from the arena and the final chore of galloping to the rescue of a settlers' wagon train, Heimer was ready with Cody's dressing gown, slippers, whiskey, and cigar. In his middle years, ensconced in mobile comfort, Cody was indistinguishable from any touring theatrical star or railroad magnate. Car No. 50 was originally called the Mayflower and had carried Adelina Patti on her concert tours. It had four staterooms, a living room, a dining room, a kitchen, and plenty of storage space for the cases of whiskey that traveled everywhere with its proprietor.

Despite such comforts, despite the rewards of a career unmatched by anyone else in show business, he was already thinking of retiring, with the year 1900 as his target date. He would have quit before that, he averred, if only the money didn't seep away, through a dozen channels, as fast or faster than it came in. In 1895 he was forced to write Salsbury asking for his co-signature on a $5,000 loan, pleading that he was in "a tight place . . . this is to keep my credit good. And if I fail to make money next summer I will sell everything and pay you and others I owe. And start in fresh. This being pushed to the wall I will not stand. . . ." At the end of the season, bankroll replenished, he was grandly informing reporters, "We calculate on making $500,000 every season. There has not been a week since I began the business, twenty-five years ago, that I have not made money. We have 52 cars, ten more than Barnum and fourteen more than Ringling. I would not take a million dollars for my holdings."

Those holdings, which caused an additional and incessant drain on his income, now included the Shoshone Land & Irrigation Company, which had acquired the 400,000 acres of land in the Big Horn Basin that he had first glimpsed as a guide for the Yale fossil hunters and always dreamed of possessing. A day's ride from Yellowstone National Park he established the TE Ranch. Nearby he started building the town of Cody, Wyoming, with a log-walled hotel for starters. Despite strenuous publicity efforts, the town attracted less than 1,000 thousand settlers by 1901. He was also pouring money into construction of the Cody Canal, which was to irrigate that vast parched hacienda. Much too optimistically he proclaimed that the irrigation canal would make crops "a sure thing." In the surrounding mountains, he was also convinced, were vast deposits of gold, silver, and coal, which would make the area "the next Eldorado of the West." Mining ventures began to exercise a magnetic effect on all his spare cash.

Nowadays it is apparent that there was more than wishful thinking in Cody's fling at town building. A mini-empire, largely based on tourism, exists today in that northwest corner of the Big Horn Basin. The town's population doubles in the summertime; even in the winter, according to the 1970 census, it stands at 5,186. There is an oil refinery in the town and considerable mining activity in the mountains above. A meter maid patrols Sheridan Avenue, named for Cody's first patron, where Cody himself once hitched his horses. Oil drillers have replaced the cowboys in the town's bars.

As Cody foresaw, however, it is the tourists' dollars which have brought latterday prosperity to his town. A finely-meshed net catches many of the 1,000,000 tourists who annually come its way en route to Yellowstone National Park. The Cody brand is stamped all over the place, promising authentic experience of what the West was really like. Thirty-eight motels in the town and dude ranches dotting the basin around it capitalize on that unfading luster of the Buffalo Bill legend. In Cody it is impossible to take more than a few steps without being reminded of its founding father. There is the Buffalo Bill Historical Center, a complex which includes memorabilia of the Cody career and Indian artifacts as well as the notable Whitney Gallery of Western Art displaying the works of Frederic Remington, Charles Russell, and others of that genre. The heroic Buffalo Bill statue looms over the town; it was executed by Gertrude Vanderbilt Whitney and is silhouetted against the mountain skyline. July 3 and 4 are Cody Stampede Days, a big event on the rodeo circuit, and the Cody Nite Rodeo enlivens every summer evening. There is also the Buffalo Bill Frontier Town to provide a Disneyland approach to commercialized history.

During his lifetime, however, the "real Eldorado" was his show-business career and not the enterprises it sustained. He had turned fifty, but the legend was only fraying slightly around the edges. Occasionally a journalistic critic would give him the peeled-eye treatment. Like the one in Chicago: "Cody's nonsensical posings grow more enticing every year. A trifle more obese, he bowed, pranced and cavorted, a charming bundle of airs and nonsense. Meanwhile a little man who couldn't break a glass ball with an ax will maintain his watchful patrol around the ticket offices and main entrances, and nobody will know that the big amusement doings inside are of his creating and planning more than anyone else. . . ." The "little man" the columnist referred to was, of course, Nate Salsbury, who had returned to the show slow-moving and deathly pale but determined to bring it back to its 1893 peak of showmanly perfection.

It was rejuvenated during the Spanish-American War period when the most publicized of voluntary regiments was the Rough Riders—the name probably lifted from Buffalo Bill's aggregation—whose part-time commander was the future President Theodore Roosevelt. Cody and his associates patriotically added more military features to the show: a "battery of light artillery," as it was advertised, but actually it was only one fieldpiece with gun team and caisson, a color guard of Cuban insurgents, and eventually an action-filled recap of the Battle of San Juan Hill.

When the War broke out, it was widely heralded that Brigadier General William F. Cody would rush to the colors and strike terror in all Spanish hearts. Six days after war was declared, the New York *World* reported the glorious news under banner headlines: BRIG. GEN. WILLIAM F. CODY WILL COMMAND A REGIMENT. READY TO START IMMEDIATELY. The Wild West Show was then playing to capacity audiences in Madison Square Garden. Goatee bristling, he roared at a delegation of newspaper reporters, "I could drive the Spaniards from Cuba with 30,000 Indians," but no one thought to ask him where he could raise a bronze-skinned levy of that proportion. To reassure the millions of his fans, Burke added to his bellicose announcement that "Buffalo Bill will come back again, but he will leave a record behind him that neither Cuba nor America will be apt to forget, while Spain will remember him with a groan."

The nation waited breathlessly for Cody to ride off to war. In mid-May he was telling newspapermen, "I am ready to leave at any time," and Burke was still boasting that as far as the enemy was concerned it would take Cody "about two months to catch 'em all, and when caught, about five minutes to lick 'em."

Then came a deflation of the Buffalo Bill legend which all of Burke's efforts could never quite overcome. On May 26, through Burke, Cody announced that he "felt dutybound to remain with the Wild West as long as General Miles does not need my presence in camp; but my heart is with the troops." Amid wartime fervors his explanation that it would cost $100,000 to close down the show and throw hundreds out of work seemed to lack the bravura that his admirers had been encouraged to expect of Buffalo Bill.

Afterward when reporters asked Burke why Cody's patriotism seemed to have evaporated so suddenly, the chief icon-maker would froth with indignation. The nation needed Buffalo Bill on the homefront as inspiration, as keeper of the martial flame, as the symbol of former conquests. "Damn it all," Burke would bellow at nonbelievers, "what we are doing is educating you people! I am not afraid to say, sir, that the Wild West symposium of equestrian ability has done more for this country than the Declaration of Independence, the Constitution of the United States, or the life of General George Washington. Its mission is to teach manhood and common sense. We are not traveling to make money, sir, but only to do good." Burke's way of delivering these multisyllabled diatribes, with the relish of a Shakespearean actor, accomplished much in convincing the public that Buffalo Bill had not let the nation down, at the age of fifty-two, by neglecting to help destroy the Spanish forces in Cuba.

Opening again at the Madison Square Garden in the spring of 1899, the show sounded the imperialistic theme that had become so infatuating to many Americans, with the war against Spain somehow leaping a continent and an ocean to break out in the Philippines, first for the Filipinos, then against the Filipinos when they indicated they could do without American domination. The United States was being conditioned to reach for an overseas empire, with Manila merely a stepping stone to eastern Asia. With such imperialists as General Miles, Admiral "Fighting Bob" Evans, Colonel Theodore Roosevelt, Mrs. Elizabeth Custer, and Chauncey Depew in the boxes opening night at the Garden, Buffalo Bill and his associates were, as they proclaimed in the show's advertising, dramatizing "the conquering march of civilization under Old Glory's protecting folds."

Other superpatriotic demonstrations were soon added to the program. One spectacular was titled "The Storming of Tientsin" after the climactic episode of the Boxer Rebellion. American and other Allied soldiers charged up the Chinese wall and slaughtered its Chinese defenders to a clamor of bugle calls. The Chinese were actually Indians who had been coaxed and bullied into putting on pigtails, padded tunics, conical straw hats, and sandals. An old fan of Buffalo Bill's, whose written praise was still used as part of the show's advertising, came to the opening at Madison Square Garden. Mark Twain had become a leading figure in the Anti-Imperialist League, however, and in a recent issue of the *North American Review* had defended the cause of the Boxers and their efforts to drive out the foreign devils. Snorting with disgust, he left his box at Madison Square Garden before the end of the Tientsin spectacular.

Mark Twain's disapproval was the least of Cody's worries at the moment. His troubles with Mrs. Cody were reaching their emotional peak. Through intermediaries she informed Cody that she knew all about his extramarital capers, especially the young woman who traveled with the show, supposedly as one of Burke's press agents. She knew that during appearances at Madison Square Garden his private box was always occupied by chorus girls and actresses. The report had also reached her that at New York dinner parties the debutantes could be pacified only by working out a rota, each girl taking her turn sitting next to him at the table.

He had been surrounded by designing women since the

earliest years of their marriage, and Louisa could understand that wasn't entirely her husband's fault. But that female press agent was another matter. Her name, it was revealed in subsequent court proceedings, was Bessie Isbell. Cody admitted that he presented her with a silver-mounted saddle but denied there was anything improper in his relations with her. Louisa wasn't about to believe that, not after what happened when she arrived in New York in the autumn of 1898. She checked into the Waldorf-Astoria, as she later testified, and called her husband's suite at the Hoffman House. A young woman, whom Louisa identified as Bessie Isbell, answered the phone. Thereupon Louisa flew into a tantrum, smashed mirrors and vases, and otherwise wrecked her room at the Waldorf. Cody, of course, paid the damages.

Such incidents only strengthened Cody's conviction that he would never be happy until Louisa gave him his freedom and provided him with the opportunity to marry another woman who could supply him with a son and heir. Regarding his hopes for a divorce, he wrote his sister Julia: "I have tried & tried to think that it was right for me to go on through all my life, living a false lie—Just because I was too much of a Morral coward to do otherwise. But I have decided that if the Law of man can legally join together the same law can unjoin. And that it's more honorable to be honest than to live a life of deceit [*sic*].

"There is no use of my telling you of my Married life—more than that it grows more unbearable each year—Divorces are not looked down upon now as they used to be—people are getting more enlightened. Some of the very best people in the world are getting divorced every day. They say it's better than going on living a life of misery for both. God did not intend joining two persons together for both to go through life miserable. When such a mistake was made—A law was created to undo the mistake. As it is I have no future to look forward to—no happiness or even contentment. Lulu will be better contented. She will be her absolute master—I will give her every bit of the North Platte property. And an

annual income. If she will give me a quiet legal separation—
if she won't do this then it's war and publicity. I hope for all
concerned it may be done quietly."

They were definitely estranged at Christmastime, 1900,
but Cody had always arranged to appear at the Welcome
Wigwam on Christmas no matter how things stood between
him and Louisa. Louisa served him a late supper when he
presented himself, somewhat the worse for a long drinking
session in North Platte. Cody collapsed at the table. When he
came to, he bellowed accusations that Louisa had tried to
poison him. Other persons present at that unfestive occasion
believed he had been overcome by food poisoning, since
Louisa rather hastily and carelessly served him salmon from
a tin opened some time before.*

That episode only reinforced his determination to obtain
a divorce. He had a candidate for the role of Mrs. Cody No.
2, a statuesque blond English actress named Katherine Clemmons, who was beautiful but not greatly talented, with
whom he had maintained a liaison for several years. He had
met her on one of his English tours and told friends that he
considered her "the finest looking woman in the world." And
he paid dearly for that opinion.

Miss Clemmons, who was not terribly discreet, later revealed to newspaper interviewers that Cody had spent almost
$80,000 on promoting her career. Shortly after they met in
London, he had put up $30,000 for Katherine to tour the
English provinces in a play titled *Theodore*. Perhaps the
English didn't appreciate her sufficiently. Subsequently he
brought her to the United States and installed her in a New
York theater. A play titled *A Lady of Venice* was bought to
serve as her showcase. Neither that nor several subsequent
vehicles tended to enhance her reputation or her draw at the

---

* The physician summoned to treat Cody concurred in the opinion that
ptomaine caused his collapse. Mrs. Cody had given her husband an emetic of
hot water and mustard. "Good thing for you, Colonel, that Mrs. Cody acted
so prompt. She did the best thing possible. If it weren't for her you'd be a
dead man." To which Cody ungallantly replied, "That's what she wanted
me to be."

box office; they only proved the New York critics' verdict that she had a beautiful profile and a lissome figure but was devoid of acting ability. Such setbacks she met with the insouciance of the born adventuress. After her second theatrical disaster, she telegraphed Cody: PLAY ROASTED. COMPANY ROASTED. I MORE THAN ROASTED. WHAT WILL YOU TAKE FOR YOUR INTEREST? By way of answer, Cody disappeared on a bear hunt.

"I would rather manage a million Indians," he was heard to groan, "than one soubrette."

Mrs. Cody may or may not have learned of his relationship with and patronage of Katherine Clemmons during its initial stages. She could not have ignored it, however, after certain insinuations appeared in the newspapers.

There was a rash of journalistic interest, for instance, when Cody knocked down a man in Chamberlin's restaurant in Washington during an off-season. The news stories suggested that they were fighting over the somewhat fickle affections of Katherine Clemmons. John Burke quickly came forward with the explanation that they were fighting over a bottle of wine. Since Cody was a notoriously free spender, nobody could imagine him quarreling over a mere bottle of the bubbly unless it was the last one left in Washington.

Cody had walloped a fairly dangerous citizen. His victim was Fred May, the violence of whose temper could be attested by Cody's old friend and patron James Gordon Bennett, Jr., who had been engaged to May's sister Caroline. On New Year's Day, 1877, Bennett had attended a party at Caroline May's home and brought it to a scandalous end when he drunkenly urinated in the fireplace (some reports indicated it was the grand piano, but this seems physiologically improbable). A few days later, to remedy the affront to the family honor, not to mention its hearth, Fred May horsewhipped young Bennett on the steps of the Union Club. May and Bennett subsequently faced each other over dueling pistols at Slaughter's Gap on the Delaware-Maryland border. Both fired and missed, but the proprieties had been observed.

May was not about to duel with a marksman of Cody's caliber, and in any case Cody took his bruised knuckles back to North Platte and the Scout's Rest Ranch. A worried Nate Salsbury hurried out to consult with him. Buffalo Bill was a family institution, and scandal, worse yet a divorce, would have been disastrous to the Wild West Show. He found Cody in a penitent mood and later quoted him as saying, "I have quit my nonsense for good. The past winter has taught me a lesson that I should have learned a long time ago."

Although he realized that Katherine Clemmons was not likely to offer any permanent sort of happiness, and despite his promise to Salsbury, Cody went ahead with his plans for a divorce. Pretrial depositions were taken before Judge Charles Scott in Cheyenne early in 1905. His friends and associates pleaded with him to drop the suit, which could only harm him and had little chance of success. Louisa, from the standpoint of outsiders, was the aggrieved and injured party. Some of those close to the family circle agreed that much of the fault was Cody's, even while conceding that Louisa was extremely jealous and often bad-tempered. Dan Muller, the orphaned son of an old friend of Cody's, was brought to the Welcome Wigwam by him and given a foster home. He had every reason to be grateful to Cody, yet in later life he recalled in a memoir that when Cody came home he could spare barely a word for his wife but bustled around overseeing the refreshment and entertainment of the guests he brought with him. Cody would preside over the baronial dining-room table while Louisa and young Muller ate in the kitchen. Nevertheless Cody, at sixty, was determined to start a new matrimonial career.

Book III: Legend

13

A Very Tired Trouper

LATE on the night of October 28, 1901, the Buffalo Bill show train, now traveling in three sections, began moving out of Charlotte, North Carolina, bound for the last stand of the season at Danville, Virginia. It had been a fairly profitable year; a spring stand at Madison Square Garden, then a Western tour, a return to Buffalo for an engagement at the Pan-American Exposition, followed by a Southern tour in the autumn. In Charlotte they had drawn 12,000 customers. In a few days, as John Burke had trumpeted to the press recently, Cody would be able to return to Cody, Wyoming, and get busy on plans for the projected Cody Military College— surely a future rival of West Point and the Virginia Military Institute—and the International Academy of Rough Riders.

The show, particularly in its personnel, was showing signs of age. Cody's hair had turned almost completely white and his voice had lost its resonance. Johnny Baker, his "adopted" son, was a heavy-set widower given to wearing derby hats and chewing on fat cigars; no longer a marksman, he carried the title of "arena director." Even the ageless Annie Oakley was showing lines around her eyes from squinting into the sunlight at her targets. Nate Salsbury was confined to a wheelchair. John Burke was as energetic and stentorous as always but with his white Dundrearys looked more than ever like a banker whose books didn't quite balance. Even the Indians were beginning to look a trifle paunchy, slower afoot and less daring on horseback.

When the three sections of the show train pulled out that late October midnight, their several departures well-spaced to prevent any rear-end collisions on the winding Piedmont grades, most of their occupants were looking forward to going home and settling down for a few months.

Annie Oakley was retiring for the night with her husband, Frank Butler, in a stateroom in the second section; Cody was traveling ahead with the first section. Just as the second section left Charlotte, a freight train was traveling south from Greensboro on the same tracks and somehow did not receive a telegraphic order to pull into a siding and let the second section of the Buffalo Bill train pass. The freight crashed head on into the locomotive of the show train. The night was filled with the hissing of steam from ruptured boilers, the cries of passengers, and the screams of dying animals.

Annie Oakley was trapped in her shattered stateroom but was finally rescued by her husband and some of the train crew. No humans were killed, but 100 horses were crushed to death in the wooden stock cars and had to be buried in a huge pit in a nearby cornfield.

It was Annie Oakley's condition that greatly worried Cody that winter. She was taken to her home in Nutley, New Jersey, with internal injuries and a paralysis of her left side. Her hair had turned white overnight. Later that winter she began to hobble around with the aid of a brace and a cane. There were serious doubts over whether she would be able to resume her career. Eventually she recovered the ability to walk and move without any artificial aids and appeared with Cody off and on until 1912, the most valued and trusted of his fellow performers and certainly the most dignified member of a harum-scarum outfit. She and her husband wound up their careers presiding over the skeet range of a resort hotel at Pinehurst, North Carolina.

Cody would gladly have retired after the train crash, or believed he would, though he may have underestimated the narcotic effect of constant adoration and would have suffered unbearable withdrawal symptoms. In any case, he could not quit. He was caught in the works of a money machine he had fabricated himself, the design of which should have earned the admiration of the late Rube Goldberg. So many projects magnetizing his money. So many hands confidently reaching. The Cody Canal seemed to flow with Cody's greenbacks instead of water. A copper mine near Oracle, Arizona, turned out to be a bad investment. Exploratory efforts to find gold in the hills above his ranchlands were costly but unproductive. He had persuaded the Burlington railroad to extend its tracks to Cody, Wyoming, and paid for a lavish barbecue and beer bust to celebrate the occasion, but settlers weren't flocking in. Salsbury was a junior partner in some of his Cody enterprises and wrote him a letter warning against sinking everything he had or mortgaging his future to turn the town of Cody into some sort of utopia. "You are carrying a lot of 'little' things," Salsbury wrote in one of his last communications with his longtime partner, "and a lot of little people in the Big Horn Basin that will eat up every dollar you can get for the rest of your life if you don't get rid of them. When I was at the Big Horn Basin I saw your affairs conducted in a way that made me sick to my stomach, and from what I hear they are in no better condition now."

But Cody, Wyoming, and the basin in which his TE Ranch was located was the capital of his dreamworld. They would be the enduring monument to his life. "When I die," he told a reporter in the winter of 1901-02, "I want the people of Wyoming who are living on the land that has been made fertile by my work and expenditure to remember me. I would like people to say, 'This is the man who opened up Wyoming to the best of civilization.' Why, all I have been running that Wild West show for is to get money to put into the Wyoming land. I have 205,000 acres watered by irrigation from the Shoshone River in the Rockies. I have 150 miles of sluices. The loam is 21 feet deep."

Cody was on to something, but it would be more than half a century before his visionary projects would come to fruition. He was certain that tourists would come by the hundreds of thousands to visit Yellowstone Park, and he established a stagecoach line to take visitors into the park and two wayside inns to accommodate them. But Western travel was still something for the wealthy, traveling to Cody in their private Pullmans, and the multitudes would not come until much later in the century. Spend-a-Million Gates, the son of Bet-a-Million Gates, descended on the town one summer and gave $300 raccoon coats to every lady who said good morning to him on the street. But what Cody, Wyoming, needed was volume, not the stray eccentric millionaire.

He was confident the tourists, attracted by his fame, would come in droves as soon as the place was built up, and meanwhile he devoted himself during the off-season months to unique methods of civic betterment. The Episcopal church, the first in town, was built through donations from the poker table over which Cody daily presided. It had come to his attention that the town had a dozen saloons but not one church. One afternoon he and Tom Purcell and George T. Beck were playing poker in Purcell's saloon. There was a $500 pot in front of them when Cody suggested that the winner should contribute it to building an Episcopal church. Beck raked in the pot when it reached $550, kept the pledge, and not only built the church with that and other donations but took over the pulpit when no regular clergyman could be lured to Cody, delivered the sermons, and directed the choir. Rarely has one man been so sanctified by winning a poker hand.

When Cody found it impossible to raise enough money by himself to finance the irrigation of the countryside, he persuaded the federal government and the admiring Presi-

dent Roosevelt to undertake the Shoshone Reclamation Project in 1904. The Buffalo Bill Dam, 328 feet high, was built
in Shoshone Canyon four years later and the parched land
around Cody began receiving water from its reservoir.

A perceptive view of Cody in his role as guiding spirit of
the town he named for himself was provided more than a
half century later by Charles Wayland Towne, a young Boston newspaperman who attracted Cody's attention with an
article he wrote about the show in the spring of 1902. Cody
fastened the sobriquet "Baked Beans" on the proper young
Bostonian and invited him to come out to Cody, Wyoming,
for a visit that summer.

Towne arrived in Cody before his host came off the road
to preside over the opening of the Hotel Irma and found it
a rather grubby place except for the new splendors of the
hotel, a village of about 1,000 residents who had their water
hauled at twenty-five cents a barrel from the Shoshone River,
formerly and more accurately known as the Stinkingwater.
"Yet even then," he wrote several years ago, "in that struggling panorama of stovepipe-punctured tents, one-room log
huts and pine-clad shacks, I could sense Progress. I saw it in
its lavishly littered Emporium, cloaking with a false front an
honest effort to 'supply everything.' I felt it in the air, where
everybody and everything hustled—including the wind. I
heard it in the organized discord of pick and shovel, hammer
and saw, anvil and trowel. I smelled it in the aroma of fresh
paint and the barleycorn fumes of its teeming saloons. Boom-
town could already point with pride to a town hall, postoffice,
railroad station, livery stable, blacksmith shop, two water
wagons, two churches, three newspapers, four hotels, six
saloons, a dozen stores and shops, 44 broncos, half a hundred
dwellings, one brothel, three chained bears, one corralled
elk, and a caged eagle. . . . I learned that every Sunday,
summer and winter, for lack of bathtubs, half the town
moved five miles up the river where men, women and children got salubriously stewed—in the benign waters of
DeMaris hot springs."

The Hotel Irma opened November 18, 1902, with the estranged Louisa notably absent from the festivities, but with Cody, his daughters Irma and Arta, and his three sisters, Mrs. Julia Goodman, Mrs. Helen Wetmore, and Mrs. May Decker of Denver, on hand. There were 1,000 guests, many of them coming for hundreds of miles, to gape in wonder at the velvet draperies, the polished floors, the imitation Oriental rugs, the genuine oil paintings, and the chandeliers illuminated with acetylene gas.

It was, as everyone later agreed, the greatest hoedown in the pioneer history of Wyoming. "In the lobby and on the verandas," to music furnished by a cowboy band and the Rocky Mountain Fiddlers, as Towne recalled, "resolute waddies in chaps and spurs paired off with buxom waitresses wearing long, dark skirts and high-collared shirtwaists, the popular Gibson Girl getup of the day. A clerk from the Big Store, self-conscious in a dress suit, bashfully offered to step the light fantastic with a plump dowager, armored in black taffeta; a lean forest ranger in highlaced boots partnered with a worn little ranch wife, radiant in homemade tight velvet bodice and flaring cashmere skirt. . . .

"The climax came when the Colonel, pointing to a radiant couple standing by the lobby entrance, boomed forth the announcement of 'My daughter Irma's engagement to Lieutenant Scott of the United States Army.' The jubilation which followed grew even noisier when Mike Russell, a specialist in such business, invited all hands to free drinks at the bar. Old Dad Pierce, the sheepman, sprained his ankle in the stampede."

After the grand opening, Towne accompanied Cody and some of his old friends on a hunt for big game. The young journalist was somewhat disappointed because instead of stalking game "Cody and the other old scouts were content to laze around camp, playing poker and swapping yarns of bygone days. . . . Every kind of prairie and mountain game, furred and feathered, had been hunted with zest and enthusiasm by this mighty nimrod. Yet here he was, still in

prime physical condition at 56, his sporting instinct satisfied
with a deck of cards and a stack of chips, oblivious to the
bark of the coyote and the mating call of the moose." It
wasn't until the last day that Cody suddenly displayed his
prowess. Just after breaking camp, they spotted five mountain sheep on the rimrock. The range was 500 yards, yet
Cody fired twice and dropped two of the sheep. Splendidly
horned rams, their heads later decorated the barroom of the
Hotel Irma.

Towne lingered on at Cody after his host left for the East
and soon was enmeshed in the absentee owner's business
affairs. First he took over the hotel's management for a
time, a task made all but impossible by Cody's return to the
hotel-keeping methods that had bankrupted the Salt Creek
Hotel just after his marriage. "Too many relatives, pen-
sioners and employes were permanently bedded down in
twelve of the Irma's twenty rooms. . . . Profits, if any, had
to be sought elsewhere. . . . The only possible locale for
the more abundant life was the barroom. But here again I
was stymied. Cody's sisters had insisted that no gambling be
permitted, and the Colonel had good naturedly consented."
Towne began turning a profit for the hotel by furnishing
music and an enormous free lunch in the barroom. A thousand handbills were distributed to proclaim "Food by Al-
phonse, late of Paris, now Creator of Colossal Comestibles
for Cody Connoisseurs." Within four weeks black ink was
being used on the hotel's ledgers.

Then Towne was rushed into the breach when Colonel
J. K. Peake, editor of the Cody *Enterprise,* another family
institution, fell ill. Buffalo Bill was then touring England
and when he heard the news of Peake's illness cabled in reply, "Put in Baked Beans, he's a newspaperman."

As Towne recalled in his memoir of Cody during its
infancy, "This vote of confidence I welcomed with something less than ecstasy. Here was another money loser—a
seemingly incurable ailment, since there were two other
weeklies competing for business in this town of less than

1,000." The weekly receipts, he found, barely covered the payroll, while bills for ink, paper, and other requirements were piling up. Towne's solution was to issue a special twenty-four-page edition, fat with advertising, proclaiming the future prosperity of the Big Horn Basin. Payment in various commodities was accepted for both advertising and "blurbs" singing the praises of various residents. "Olesen, the granger, offered ten bushels of potatoes; Farmer Snodgrass, a dozen chickens. . . . Even Bronco Bill, suspected of cattle rustling, wanted in and promised to deliver a wagonload of dried cowhides. . . ." Financially the special edition was a success, and temporarily the Cody *Enterprise* was put back on its feet. Later transfusions of Cody's cash were required—the weekly is very much alive today—but by then young Mr. Towne had gone on to a more profitable career as publicist for Anaconda Copper.

All his projects, constantly demanding more financial support, sent Buffalo Bill back on the road year after year. Not one of his ranches, hotels, gold or copper mines, or any other enterprise ever reached the profit-making stage despite Cody's investment of a roughly estimated million-plus dollars. Some of his projects were too visionary, others were badly managed. His only real asset was his manufactured personality and the showcase in which it was presented. The road-show business got tougher all the time. There was competition from a dozen imitators, other outdoor attractions, and circuses. Every year the motion pictures, advancing from Edison's peepshow to the theatrical form, took a bigger bite out of Cody's potential audience. As film-making techniques improved and more money was spent on production, the movies were able to present a version of the Western frontier more compelling and realistic than could be produced in an arena.

Artistically the show began falling apart after the death of Nate Salsbury on Christmas Eve, 1902, when the company had gone over to play the English circuit again. Joint efforts had developed the Buffalo Bill Wild West Show and kept it going. It could not have prospered without Cody's fame and magnetism, but it surely would have foundered without Salsbury's showmanship, his firm management, and his ability to handle Cody and other diverse temperaments. Cody and Salsbury complemented each other perfectly. With the latter's death it could never be the same.

With James Bailey as the chief administrator, the show toured England throughout 1903, then played engagements on the Continent for two years. The foreign tour began promisingly enough when the show played to large crowds in London and his old friend, now King Edward VII, not only bestowed the royal patronage but presented Cody with a well-publicized diamond pin.

Bad luck kept haunting him, however. He was thrown from a horse and was unable to appear in the arena for three weeks. That, along with a cold, wet summer, was bad for business. And when the show crossed over to France it was still dogged by bad luck and poor business at the box office. An epidemic of glanders broke out and more than 300 of the show's horses had to be killed.

A career rivaling Buffalo Bill's for showmanship and commercial success began when the show was touring France. Somehow a stranded Arab acrobatic troupe attached itself to the show, though at first it did not appear in the arena. The top mounter of the Hamid family's tumbling act was a ten-year-old boy born in Lebanon, and many years later he recalled in his autobiography how Annie Oakley saved him, his uncles, and his cousins from starvation and the powerful impression Buffalo Bill could make on ordinary mortals. Cody was aging, but when mounted on his white charger, as he was when young Hamid first saw him, he looked to the Lebanese Christian boy like some Biblical warrior.

Half a century later Hamid would remember how Annie Oakley befriended him. "That night, and a hundred times later, she fed me bits saved from her own meal. And that first night, she noticed us when no one else paid any attention or had any sympathy. . . .

"That first time, after she had fed us in her tent, she took our hands and led us across the lot. The crisp black night, the overpowering smell of the circus, and the sight we were about to see fixed it all indelibly in my mind. We approached a special tent, set somewhat apart, wondering what this kind lady was leading us to now. Yellow lamplight seeped through the cracks, and through the entrance. We walked in quietly, and Annie spoke to a man sitting in a chair, with his back to us. He turned around and I recognized the wonderful man on the beautiful horse, the man who had just stepped out of the Bible. Now I was looking for the first time into the face of Buffalo Bill. He was magnificent. Knowing none of the great legends that had grown up about the man, I was nevertheless caught by his power, awed by his stature and poise, and warmed by the depth of his bluish-gray eyes. . . ."

Cody employed the Lebanese tumblers, and later the boy doubled as one of the Arab horsemen. Still later George A. Hamid, Sr., greatly prospered as the proprietor of the Steel Pier at Atlantic City.

Cody had to interrupt his touring abroad when his divorce case came up for trial in the spring of 1905. The attendant publicity was almost totally adverse. His reckless charges against Louisa made people wonder if his mind had slipped its moorings. And Louisa sounded all the right notes to win public sympathy, as when her testimony at the deposition hearings was read: "I suppose Will wants a young wife, one who will bear him an heir, as our own son is dead."

She gathered still more sympathy when it was testified that their daughter Arta died suddenly (on January 30, 1905, in Spokane, Washington, shortly after her second marriage) and Mrs. Cody claimed that her death could only be attributed to a broken heart because her father refused to drop his divorce suit. The sob sisters made the most of it in the nation's press when Mrs. Cody tremulously declared from the witness stand in Judge Scott's Cheyenne courtroom: "Will is one of the kindest and most generous men I ever knew. When he was sober he was gentle and considerate. If I had him to myself now, there would be no trouble. His environments have caused him to put this upon me."

Louisa was also successful in refuting her husband's charge that she had tried to poison him during that ill-fated Christmas reunion a half dozen years before. It wasn't tainted salmon, she insisted. She had slipped into his coffee a drug guaranteed to cure him of his addiction to alcohol. Perhaps she had given him too strong a dose, or the chemical had tangled with the alcohol already in his system and thus rendered him unconscious. Mrs. Cody added that she had always hated liquor and that the first quarrel of their married life had been over his insistence on keeping a bar in the hotel at Salt Creek.

She denied a charge that she had told someone, regarding her husband, "I wouldn't go anywhere with that old reprobate!" On the contrary, she testified, she had asked to go along on the European tours but Cody had demurred on the grounds that it would cost too much money. Yet, she added, he had been able to spend thousands of dollars on financing the career of Katherine Clemmons.

More titillating testimony was offered by other witnesses. Mrs. John Boyer, the wife of the superintendent of the Scout's Rest Ranch, told the court that it wasn't an anti-alcohol drug Mrs. Cody slipped into her husband's coffee. "She gave him Dragon's Blood," Mrs. Boyer testified. Under questioning it developed that Dragon's Blood was a love potion Mrs. Cody had bought from a gypsy. Another witness, Mrs. H. S. Parker, testified that Mrs. Cody was violently jealous of English royalty, up to and including Queen Victoria, suspecting them of a more than friendly interest in her husband. Judge Scott immediately ordered the testimony concerning the late queen stricken from the record.

It was a messy trial which resulted only in tarnishing Buffalo Bill's commercially priceless image. Was the Great Scout (the public could only wonder) merely another unhappy husband, another common drunkard, and worse yet, a sucker for an English actress?

The judge threw the case out of court, holding that Louisa was blameless and that "all the allegations in the plaintiff's petition and amended petition and supplemental petition are disproved." Judge Scott also ruled that Mrs. Cody's countercharges involving her husband and other women were "disproved."

Will and Louisa Cody, a classic mismatch, stayed married until parted by death. Neither could forgive the past. It always particularly rankled him that his famous friendship with Queen Victoria had been stained by the testimony of one of his wife's friends; he was outraged by the suggestion that there could have been anything but the most formal relations with the Widow of Windsor, who was in her late sixties when he was first presented to her.

His playboy days seemed to be over. Katherine Clemmons had married another even wealthier man after it became apparent that he would never be able to divorce his wife. Several years later the old, expensive, and debilitating affair with Katherine cropped up again in another messy divorce trial.

He was rich, famous, and miserable in his early sixties, always a troubling period in a man's life. His legend had become burdensome, his career a grind, his hopes largely closed out. He would never be able to pass on all he had won to a male heir.

The changes in the West, the overrunning of the prairies, which he had helped to bring about, sickened him. Even the Scout's Rest Ranch was no solace anymore because, as he explained, "There's nothing now but farms and damned barbed-wire fences." The only peace he could find was in the blessed emptiness, the complete solitude of his thousands of acres on the TE Ranch in Wyoming. The man who had

basked in the adoration of crowds now found contentment
only in the face of a wild animal.

One blow after another fell. James Bailey died in 1906,
and the general management of the show was entrusted to
John Burke and Johnny Baker. At sixty-odd, Cody found it
harder and harder to climb into his buckskins, gallop out
into the arena, and maintain his old characterization of the
Great Scout galloping through history for all time. One-day
stands in Europe or America, essential to the commercial via-
bility of the enterprise, became a form of systematized torture. Without Salsbury or Bailey around, more and more of
the administrative responsibilities fell on his sagging shoulders; every time a horse got sick and a section of the show
train was sidetracked, it seemed, they had to send for him,
and he did not realize until then how many burdensome details had been handled by his late partners. Incredibly, he
had become an old man. His hair had whitened, then
thinned out to such an extent that he had to have a toupee
made. He tried to cut his drinking down to four drinks a day
but soon found himself backsliding.

Then the old affair with Katherine Clemmons came back
to haunt him, not privately over his whiskey bottle late in
the night as the show train roared across the landscape, but
publicly, nastily, and in court. Katherine had married How-
ard Gould, one of the playboy sons of the late menace of
Wall Street, Jay Gould. The marriage lasted only a few
years. She filed suit for a separation; Gould counterfiled for a
divorce on charges that Katherine had secretly been meeting
Cody. His wife's relations with Cody, in the language of his
lawyers, were "criminal and meretricious." There seemed to
be no truth in Gould's allegations. Cody had broken off with
Katherine when she married the heir to the Gould millions.
Summoned to testify against Katherine, Cody instead
charged that Gould had offered him $50,000 to make damag-
ing admissions regarding his conduct with Mrs. Gould. Cody
added that he not only refused the bribe but threatened to

sue Gould for all the money he had spent on Katherine's abortive acting career.

In 1907 he had returned to make a long and profitable stand at the Madison Square Garden, though one newspaper critic observed that in his shooting act he missed more glass balls than he hit. All the profits of that season, and several of the preceding ones, went to James Bailey's estate because of money Bailey had advanced to the show.

He had been making big money for almost a quarter of a century, yet none of it had stuck to his fingers. Whatever he didn't spend or give away was drained by his various sideline enterprises. He simply loved the status of being a company president. At the moment he was involved in eleven different enterprises—in all of which he seemed to be the sole or major support—and was president of five of them.

The tap root nourishing all those outside interests, the Wild West Show and Congress of Rough Riders, was beginning to wither. The season of 1907 there were nine *new* Wild West shows taking the road, most of them sketchy affairs out to trim the rubes behind extravagant advertising, but if one of them got into a town ahead of Cody's troupe it tended to skim off the profits. Some sort of coup would have to be pulled off, and soon, or Cody's enterprise would founder.

About that time, at the end of the 1907 season, Gordon Lillie, whose Great Far East Show was his most successful competitor in the outdoor exhibition field, came up with an intriguing proposition. Lillie—or Pawnee Bill, as he advertised himself—had started out in show business as the interpreter of the Pawnee group that had traveled with Cody in his first season. He had made money in more modest amounts than Cody but, being as conservative and frugal as Cody was spendthrift, he had managed to save most of it. Probably the most reckless act of his career was to agree to a proposition from the Bailey estate to buy out its interest in the Cody show. Then Cody's version of the Wild West would be melded with Lillie's lantern-slide views of the Far East. You couldn't get much more educational than that; or, as

John Burke's fervent prose conveyed the sense of the occasion: "The Occident meets the Orient in Gorgeous Pageantry, Pomp and Procession. The Red Men of two hemispheres ride side by side and many nations contribute Man and Beast to a Triumphal March of the Ethnological Congress." What Burke meant was that Cody's cowboys and Indians would be augmented by Hindu fakirs, snake charmers, Australian boomerang throwers, performing elephants, and Singhalese dancers.

According to Lillie, Cody himself welcomed the merger but most of his associates bitterly resented the idea of Pawnee Bill becoming a full partner, knowing that with fresh money to pump into the enterprise he would assume the right to make the important decisions. The two shows traveled separately during the 1908 season, at the end of which Lillie went down to New Orleans to confer with Cody on how the merger could be effected. Later Pawnee Bill recorded his impressions of that meeting, at which Cody was friendly but some of his associates cold and hostile. "Since the death of Mr. Bailey, there had been several clashes between Cody and the assistant manager [Louis Cooke]. In one of these, Cody had knocked down the manager. Orders had come from headquarters in New York: 'Unless Cody apologizes and begs Cooke's pardon, close the show at once and ship it back to winter quarters at Bridgeport, Connecticut.' Cody held out to the last moment, refusing to humble himself. But when he saw them making actual preparation to close the show, he apologized. This had so wrought up the Colonel that there was no friendly sentiment left in him. It was a cold dollar-and-cent proposition, and a change in management was welcome." Cooke, of course, was the watchdog of the Bailey interests. It would be a pleasure to have him replaced by Gordon Lillie, who had worshiped Cody as a youth and no doubt used him as model for fashioning himself into a symbol of Western adventure. Lillie wrote that he knew that Cody was temperamental and difficult to handle at times but that he was determined to get along with him. He also realized it might be even more difficult to manage some of the more obstreperous elements in the show that were loyal to Cody and likely to make life miserable for anyone they considered an outsider.

Lillie recalled that one of the Ringling brothers, who had considered buying the Bailey estate's interest in the Cody show, warned him that Cody and company were tough customers, that Cody "had that Wild West bunch lined up against the Bailey end of the show. Those cowboys, Indians, Mexicans, with all those guns, tomahawks and war clubs kept the Bailey end of the show in dread all the time. Wait till you open and are out on the road. You'll have trouble. They'll about scalp you."

During their three-year partnership, however, Lillie found Cody to be as genial, easygoing, and immature as when Lillie first met him. Where money was concerned, Cody was downright infantile. As a case in point, there was the Campo Bonito Mine seven miles northeast of Oracle, Arizona, into which Cody had been literally sinking money for a half dozen years. It produced almost as little profit over the years as another Cody investment, White Beaver Cough Cream, a nostrum produced by another of Cody's friends.

His mining partner, Lillie learned, had bilked Cody by charging him double on purchases of equipment and had also bought neighboring claims for $250 each but told Cody they cost ten times that much. It wasn't that Cody was stupid but because he had an extremely trusting nature. "If he was for you at all," Lillie noted, "nothing ever excited his suspicion against you. In his business dealings, he was like a child. He apparently cared nothing for money, except when he wanted or needed to spend it. Then, if he did not have, or could not borrow it, it made him sick—actually sick, so that he would have to go to bed."

The Campo Bonito mine had formerly produced copper, but an ex-Indian agent, Colonel D. B. Dyer, convinced Cody that although the copper veins might be played out there was gold, tungsten, and lead in quantity on the property. The

Cody-Dyer Mining and Milling Company was formed in 1903; roads for the ore wagons were built and a smelter planned. Legend, if not geological surveys, encouraged belief that there was a bonanza in the Catalina Mountains, which served as the background for Harold Bell Wright's best-selling novel about the "mine with the iron door." According to legend, Spanish adventurers had discovered a vein of gold so productive that they built an iron door to protect the mine shaft and guarded it night and day. Then they were all killed by an Apache war party and the location of the mine was one of the unlocked secrets of the Catalinas.

Naturally Cody was excited by the possibility of locating a fabled treasure, keyed up by the prospect of striking another vein of copper through the dozen tunnels he and his partner drove into the Catalina slopes, and if the more precious metals weren't found in quantity they could always recoup on the baser ones. The mine was producing scheelite, a high-grade tungsten ore. Since tungsten had replaced carbon as a filament in electric light bulbs, there seemed to be a booming market for that ore and a justification for building a stamping mill to extract it. But the venture wasn't as lucrative as it seemed.

During the last dozen years of his life, the mine near Oracle would drain away a half million dollars of his earnings.

In his new show-business venture, however, Cody was fortunate to have acquired an honest, hardheaded, but often sympathetic partner. Like Salsbury, Lillie understood the necessity of protecting Cody from himself and his importunate friends. Lillie was brisk and businesslike and had their combined companies incorporated in New Jersey, like Standard Oil, with Cody as president and himself as vice-president and general manager. Naturally, and rightly, Lillie kept the purse strings attached to his own pudgy fingers.

But he trusted Cody's superior instincts in matters of showmanship. It was Cody's idea to advertise their tours of the United States during the next three years as their joint farewell appearances. Three years might be a little long to stretch out saying good-bye, but the tours would be carefully routed to cover every section of the country. At the end of their lengthy bow-out, Cody was convinced, the potential of the Wild West Show as an enterprise capable of carrying hundreds of people on the payroll would be exhausted. Now it was not only the rival entertainment being offered the public but the thousands of inexpensive cars being manufactured in Detroit that threatened such attractions. In a tin Lizzie, a man could find his own adventures instead of experiencing them vicariously.

At each appearance Cody was to deliver a valedictory throbbing with emotion. The words were probably John Burke's, but Buffalo Bill's baritone furnished the music.

"The time has come," he would declaim to a hushed audience, "for parting words to the friends of my lifetime and my best patron, the American public. Time beats us all at last. [Dramatic pause.] Few remain of the great leaders in war and peace, many of whom came out of the west—the west of the old pioneer days—the Wild West, with which all my life has been so closely interwoven. Now, as I am nearing the three-score-and-ten limit, the warning comes that the years are lurking in ambush for Buffalo Bill, who must prepare to retire in good order from the arena, or take the chances of being left to 'lag superfluous on the stage.' "

Later in the farewell tour which rivaled for longevity those of certain opera singers and classic actors, he would add —almost as though neither his audience nor himself was convinced that they could part from each other—"On my honor as Buffalo Bill, my present visit will positively be my last hail and farewell in the saddle to you all."

At the outset the joint venture of Buffalo Bill and Pawnee Bill prospered. Most Americans, it seemed, were willing to spend one more dollar to watch them fade into the sunset and, incidentally, shed themselves of a few last romantic illusions about the Old West. America was changing rapidly since the turn of the century; progress and ever-beneficial change keynoted the national mood, and the modern hero was the hustling entrepreneur rather than the gun-toting adventurer. Buffalo Bill, in a word, was old hat. But it was still worthwhile to take the kids out to the arena so they could tell their grandchildren they saw Buffalo Bill make his last appearance.

Combining the two shows, with their disparate elements, caused a lot of grief when they prepared for the opening in Madison Square Garden early in the spring of 1909. Pawnee Bill's outfit was cumbersome with scenic effects and a veritable zoo including elephants, camels, and water buffalos. Cody's horses were frightened by the exotic beasts of the Orient and were calmed down only after all the animals were stabled together and got to trust each other. The biggest technical problem was bringing all those animals up from the Garden's basement and into the arena through a passageway only ten feet wide and with a steep incline. In rehearsal after rehearsal, with Johnny Baker superintending as arena director, there were traffic jams and near panic in the passageway. The dress rehearsal was a disaster, but that is regarded as a good omen in show business. On opening night, by some miracle possibly connected with Saint Jude, the patron of all performers in distress, the performance ran smoothly before a full house.

The combined shows were a hit in New York, trouped through various Eastern cities, and were making money, not like the old days but solidly in the black.

Cody's personal finances were another matter, though his share of the take must have run into the thousands of dollars weekly. After four weeks of lavish entertaining in a suite at the Waldorf-Astoria, however, his drawing account on the show's treasury was bled white. Everything he owned was in hock. There were mortgages on his big ranches at North Platte, Nebraska, and in Wyoming and on the Hotel Irma in Cody. Thus he was badgered by what formerly would have been minor creditors to be dismissed after payment from petty cash.

One creditor was a prominent actor who held Cody's IOU for $5,000 and demanded immediate settlement. Cody referred him to Lillie as the show's moneybags. Lillie told the actor that the show was not responsible for Cody's personal obligations, upon which the actor threatened to attach the show: the old bugaboo of all outdoor showmen. The worried Pawnee Bill investigated the contents of the "treasure wagon" and found only $12,000 in cash on hand, plus the bill from the Waldorf for Cody's stay, which came to $1,442. It wasn't much of a cushion against possible adversity; a few days of rainy weather would wipe it out.

Lillie brought up the threatened attachment with Cody, who had taken to his bed like a prairie dog running for his hole in time of danger. "It's my nerves," Cody told his partner. "They always go back on me when anyone threatens to attach the show. Something must be done to get it off my mind or I'll never be able to give a performance tonight."

Pawnee Bill finally agreed to pay off the IOU, upon which Cody sprang out of bed and began capering around the room as springy as a lamb let out to pasture.

The fifty-car show train rolled on through the 1909 and 1910 seasons, and during those first two years they skimmed the cream off the Buffalo Bill/Pawnee Bill enterprise. In 1910 the show grossed more than $1,000,000 and netted $400,000. It was Cody's chance to get back on his feet, pay off the mortgages on his more worthwhile properties. Instead he sank his share of the profits into the Arizona copper mine and the Big Horn Basin development.

Next year, 1911, the profits dropped off to half of what they were in the bonanza year, 1910. One reason was that the show was routed through some cities and towns where he had already made a "farewell appearance," and people were getting a little cynical about that "last hail and farewell in the saddle."

He was sixty-five years old and often weary to the point of illness by the constant travel, the incessant demands of public display, the feeling that he could not escape the spotlight.

"For twenty-eight years," he wrote a friend at the end of the 1911 season, "I have hammered one spot daily until the spot has grown too sore to stand it any longer. I am nervous and oh so tired. Every cloud in the sky, every time the wind flaps my tent or shakes the big top, it gets on my nerves. At night every hard stop or start of the cars I think it's a wreck. . . . I have just got to break away from this strain or die. . . . This season has told on me more than ever before. Just the thought that I have got to be at every performance, sick or well, has gotten onto my nerves. I have put in many hard years at it, and I don't care, neither do my friends want to see me die in the arena."

That copper mine in Arizona kept eating him alive. He sent Johnny Baker to Oracle to investigate just why its exploratory costs were so high. One reason, Baker learned, was that Colonel Dyer, Cody's partner and manager of the mine, had thirty-six names on the payroll but there were only four men actually working around the shaft. Even so, Colonel Dyer, hurrying to explain matters to Cody, managed to sell him another slice of pie in the sky. Sign another note, Dyer urged, and he would be able to install a gravity railway and new machinery. Deeper penetration, Dyer assured Cody, would reach copper deposits estimated by a geologist to be worth $3,000,000. Cody had an inexhaustible supply of optimism and looked forward to the day, as he told Johnny Baker, when the mine was producing thousands of tons of copper and "we take our money from nature's treasury vaults."

Meanwhile, he could only yield to Lillie's suggestion that they go out on the road for a fourth season. By now even the tank towns were becoming downright leery of Cody's apparently endless "hail and farewell." By hitting the smaller towns for the exhausting routine of one-day stands, they managed to eke out a total profit of $123,000 that season and agreed to make one more assault on the public's goodwill the following year.

Cody knew he was like a punch-drunk ex-champion who

insisted on going into the ring and laying himself open to
scorn. "Those farewells acted as a boomerang," he remarked
later. "If I went on like an old played-out mule, the public
would soon drop me."

During the off-season, early in January, 1913, he was suddenly confronted with a demand for $20,000 to cover his
share of the costs of keeping the show in winter quarters.

Cody was then staying at the home of his sister May in
Denver. Earlier in the winter he had met Harry H. Tammen, a florid, glad-handing ex-bartender who had scrambled
his way up in the world through a native ability to squeeze
money out of apparently hopeless businesses. With a partner
named Fred G. Bonfils, whose business background was even
more dubious, he had acquired ownership of the moribund
Denver *Post*. Bonfils and Tammen knew nothing about journalism but they understood something about public tastes.
In a few years they turned the *Post* into the most sensation-
mongering newspaper in the country, with a circus makeup
featuring headlines in red and black traveling most of the
way down the front page and the launching of one meretricious but clamorously pursued crusade after another.

Tammen posed as an openhanded prince of good fellows,
which was what attracted Cody to him in the first place, but
beneath the bonhomie was a bedrock acquisitiveness. He
offered Cody the loan of $20,000 but cannily insisted on the
physical properties of the Wild West Show as collateral
against a six-month note.

What Harry Tammen really had in mind was acquiring
Buffalo Bill, legend, buckskins, boots and all, as his personal
property. Recently Tammen had bought the Sells Circus,
which he renamed the Sells-Floto, after Otto Floto, the sports
editor of the Denver *Post*. His scheme was to make Cody a
headliner with the circus. To that effect, he insisted as a codicil to the $20,000 loan that Cody appear under the Sells-
Floto big top in 1914. Thus, as Cody would learn to the
regret that embittered him to his last day on earth, he had

made himself Tammen's bondservant, a bondage from which he never entirely managed to release himself.

Still unaware that he had sold himself down the river for a measly $20,000, Cody wearily went out on the road again in the spring of 1913, with his partner Pawnee Bill so disgusted at the arrangement Cody had made with Tammen—giving him a lien on the show, in effect—that the two men spoke only when they had to.

Cody was a pathetic sight, a ghost of the Great Scout, worn and haggard. The kids in his audience, who had been weaned from the dime novels that nourished their fathers' imaginations, must have wondered how that frail old codger could claim to be the scourge of the whole Indian race. A graphic picture of how diminished by age and illness Buffalo Bill was on that last tour with Pawnee Bill was provided by Raymond Thorp, who watched the preshow parade in Kansas City. "As the parade moved up Walnut Street, it was stopped by a traffic mishap, and Buffalo Bill sat his white horse at the junction of Sixth. I was with a crowd of other steamboat men, watching the parade, when an incident took place that I have never forgotten. A trio of bums at the curb were baiting the old showman by holding up bottles of gin and offering drinks. One of them bolder than the rest, stepped into the street and reaching up, placed his bottle right beneath the rider's nose.

"One of the steamboat men was a Cherokee Indian from Oklahoma whom I knew quite well, whose name was John (Highpockets) DeHaas. Highpockets stepped into the street, seized the bum by the coat collar, and threw him among his fellows. He then drew a sheath knife and exclaimed, 'You leave that old man alone, or I'll take off your ears and give them to him.' "

A mounted policeman rode up and ordered DeHaas to put his knife away on the grounds that "We don't want our bums killed just because they ask a man to have a drink with them."

It was a brutally ironic reversal—Buffalo Bill rescued by an Indian from white molesters—which further signified how times had changed, how Cody was now viewed by his contemporaries as just another boob-catching showman, and how depleted his legend had become.

14

On Location at Wounded Knee

ONE day in July, 1913, the show train of the Buffalo Bill's Wild West and Pawnee Bill's Far East extravaganza pulled into the marshaling yards in Denver after several disastrous months on the road. At one stand the company's box office took in a total of $7.15, and on a sunny day at that. The show had lost money on 100 successive appearances.

To the shrewd Harry Tammen it was apparent that the enterprise was staggering toward involuntary bankruptcy and would soon be picked clean by its creditors. Pawnee Bill had plenty of money salted away but wasn't about to sink more into the combined shows. An Eastern lithographer was known to be pressing for settlement of his account. And the courts usually favored the creditors in such cases, because outdoor showmen were known to be slippery operators artful at dodging writs of attachment and bankruptcy petitions, quick to head across state lines when such actions threatened.

What Tammen particularly wanted to retrieve from the wreckage was the title "Buffalo Bill's Wild West Show," which he believed still had drawing power at the ticket wagon. On February 5 he had proudly published the announcement in the Denver *Post*: "The most important deal ever consummated in American amusement enterprises was closed in Denver a few days ago, when Colonel William F. Cody (Buffalo Bill) put his name to a contract with the proprietors of the Sells-Floto Circus, the gist of which is that these two big shows consolidate for the season of 1914 and thereafter.

"The Pawnee Bill interests now associated with Colonel Cody's Wild West Show are not included in this arrangement—the idea being that the Sells-Floto Circus shall continue in its entirety, and the Buffalo Bill Exposition of Frontier Days and the Passing of the West, with the historic incidents associated with them, shall also be preserved, added to and given with the circus performance.

"This means, not only from a showman's, but a layman's standpoint, the strongest combination ever formed in the history of American amusements, if not the world. . . . The present combination would seem to make the Sells-Floto shows the monarchs of the amusement field."

The Buffalo Bill-Pawnee Bill outfit had no sooner pitched its camp on July 21 than the legal eagles descended. Attorneys for the United States Printing and Lithographing Company filed suit for a writ of attachment. Two small creditors, one with a claim for $36 worth of hay and grain, filed a petition in involuntary bankruptcy in the federal court. But the lawyers for Harry Tammen were even quicker to pounce, and six deputy sheriffs appeared on the show grounds with a writ allowing them to sequester $6,000 in the treasure wagon as well as all of the show's records.

The upshot of all the litigation was that Tammen and Sells-Floto acquired Buffalo Bill and the title to his show because of the $20,000 note Cody had signed the past winter. And on August 21, to help satisfy the lithographers' claim against the show, its equipment went on the auction block. Under the hammer went a vivid assortment of the properties that comprised the Wild West Show in its last struggling months: mirrored wagons, broncos, trick horses, steel cages, stagecoaches, travel-stained backdrops; all the livestock, all the trumpery that provided a background for Cody's re-creation of the winning of the West.

Cody was especially heartsick when his old white horse, Isham, the charger on which he had galloped into arenas for many years, went up for bids. Fortunately an old friend of Cody's, Colonel C. J. Bills, of Lincoln, Nebraska, was on hand to salvage something of sentimental value to Cody. Bills bought Isham for $150 and sent him to Cody's TE Ranch, where he went into retirement.

There would be no retirement for his old master. Cody could only look forward to more endless trouping as a chattel of the Sells-Floto Circus, climbing into his sweat-stained buckskins and going on with the Buffalo Bill charade.

"I have to start life all over again, and with no capital," he told a friend shortly after the auction. All he owned was mortgaged to the hilt. His only income would be what Sells-Floto chose to pay him. This was Cody's finest hour—and Buffalo Bill's, too, for that matter, for the man and his persona had become indistinguishable—when he faced up to his situation, at age sixty-seven, and did not simply shoot himself.

Instead he went up to the TE Ranch in Wyoming. In the past few years a tentative sort of reconciliation had been arranged between Cody and his long-suffering wife, and occasionally they were reunited. If they lived long enough, they might even become friends; it had been a long journey since he courted the properly reared French girl in St. Louis as a private in the Union Army. Now she joined him at the TE Ranch, and he wrote their daughter Irma, "Yesterday Mother and I went out and gathered two bushels of wild gooseberries. We put a table cover under the vines and then with sticks knock the vines."

The endless vistas of the Big Horn Basin, with the purplish haze of the mountains blending into the big blue sky and the absence of people around him trying to figure out how to take one more bite out of his aging carcass revived him. It was amazing how quickly he could bounce back from a series of jarring defeats. A few weeks of rest and home cooking and he was ready to tackle the world again.

Various schemes were churning around in his head. Somehow he had to scratch together enough money to buy his freedom from Harry Tammen and the Sells-Floto outfit. There were offers of quick money from cheap-jack promoters of vaudeville tours and other entrepreneurs on the fringes of show business, but he wasn't going to have Buffalo Bill emblazoned over the entrance to a flea circus. He was a star, by God, and he wouldn't cheapen himself. When the manager of a London theater cabled him an offer of $2,500 a week to appear with a shooting act, he sternly replied that Buffalo Bill never appeared anywhere for less than $5,000 a week.

For the first time in several years, he had leisure that summer to think over what had happened to him. Obviously he had let his talents be used by other men for their profit but seldom, since Nate Salsbury's careful guardianship, for his. And he hadn't moved briskly enough with the times. Western movies had superseded the Wild West shows because they could be made cheaply and shown to millions of people who were willing to part with a dime for an hour's entertainment. Names like Bronco Billy Anderson were bigger now than Buffalo Bill. He had let himself be outmoded, shuffled into the discard by a mere technological development.

Most horse operas, he knew, were faked-up things filmed in barns called studios or in warehouses. Why not give the film-going public a taste of the real thing? Why not make a Western movie in a Western setting, where it belonged?

The more he thought about it, the better he liked the title: William F. Cody, Film Producer.

No more riding into dusty arenas, no more sleeper jumps, no more one-day stands or fretting every time the rain clouds grew blacker or waking up in the middle of the night dreaming of a head-on train crash.

His idea, conceived at the lowest point in his fortunes, was to produce films based more or less on historic fact in their original setting. He would use the participants, portraying themselves, in actual events. Envisioning a whole series of films which would form a panorama of Western history, he would restage his own duel with Yellow Hand, the death of Custer, the Ghost Dance uprisings, the slaughter at Wounded Knee, and other happenings.

Cody, in fact, would seem to have invented the film documentary. A search of the Hollywood archives produces no other person who ventured into that field so early. As in anticipating the flood of Western tourism, he was way ahead of his time.

The first problem was financing. Who could he turn to? The banks already held too much of his paper. His wealthy Eastern friends were either dead, or had been tapped already, or were scattered (like James Gordon Bennett in Paris) beyond his immediate reach. His only hope of seed money for the enterprise was Bonfils and Tammen, much as he hated to get in any deeper with that tightfisted pair.

He hurried down to Denver and laid out his plans before the publishers of the Denver *Post,* and they were impressed.

"Cody," said Harry Tammen admiringly, "you are a wonder!"

Tammen and his partner quickly proceeded to make the necessary financing and releasing arrangements with the Essanay company of Chicago and Hollywood. Essanay was the MGM of the pre-World War I era and produced its own films in a Chicago warehouse and a studio in California and also backed independent producers. It was part of a motion-picture trust which dictated, among other things, that no feature run longer than two reels.

The deal with Essanay provided that Cody would produce and direct a film based on the "battle" of Wounded Knee through the W. F. Cody Historical Pictures Company. Cody would receive a one-third interest without putting up any capital, Essanay a third, and Bonfils and Tammen a third. Using their clout in Washington, Bonfils and Tammen would persuade the War Department to provide cavalry troops and equipment for the filming.

Essanay was talked into the venture largely because one of its two founding partners, Gilbert M. Anderson, was a Western buff and uncritical admirer of Buffalo Bill. Anderson was none other than Bronco Billy Anderson, who would make 375 two-reel Westerns between 1908 and 1915—the John Wayne of his day. Born Max Aronson in Little Rock, Arkansas, Bronco Billy had started out as a traveling salesman, stumbled into an acting career, and appeared in Edwin S. Porter's landmark film *The Great Train Robbery*. In 1906 he and George K. Spoor founded Essanay, the name of their company deriving from their initials, with an Indian head as their trademark.

The bulk of the Essanay product was Westerns starring Bronco Billy, but Anderson and Spoor also branched out into comedy and recruited cross-eyed Ben Turpin for a series of one-reelers and later Charlie Chaplin. Their California studio was in Niles, a town of 400 in an alfalfa-raising section near San Francisco. This was where Bronco Billy films were turned out on an $800 budget and usually brought in a gross of $50,000.

Bronco Billy and Buffalo Bill got along swimmingly, both men having an artist's contempt for nickel-nursing. The striking difference between them was that Anderson was a millionaire, Cody an ex-millionaire. Charlie Chaplin later wrote of Anderson that he was an eccentric among the early-day film moguls. "Although a millionaire, he cared little for graceful living; his indulgences were flamboyantly painted cars, promoting prize fighters, owning a theater and producing musical shows. When he was not working in Niles, he spent most of his time in San Francisco, where he stayed in small moderate-priced hotels. He was an odd fellow, vague, erratic and restless, who sought a solitary life of pleasure, and although he had a charming wife and daughter in Chicago, he rarely saw them."

Just the partner for Cody. If he had not been chained to Bonfils and Tammen, Cody might well have pursued a career in California and ended his days as one of those early

Hollywood pharaohs surrounded by starlets and yes-men. The life would have suited him rather well.

"Now that I have financial backing I'll do something," he told his friends. "It does look like my luck has turned."

As usual he thought in large terms, planned for spectacular effects. This would be no studio film with cardboard scenery and a few Broadway hams putting on Stetsons and pretending to be cowboys. He bustled around taking care of the endless preproduction details. When the Secretary of War visited Denver, Cody buttonholed him and got permission to use three troops of U.S. Cavalry in his picture. He journeyed to Colorado Springs to visit the Secretary of the Interior and obtain the right to shoot his film on the Pine Ridge agency and employ Indians on that reservation to re-create the battle of twenty-three years before with as many of the original participants as possible.

Single-handed, Cody planned for the film as though movie making had been his lifelong occupation. He had several Indian villages built on the bank of Wounded Knee Creek and hired a merry-go-round to keep the Indians, adults and children alike, in good spirits. Johnny Baker returned to Denver and agreed to act as assistant producer, with the Indians as his responsibility.

Lieutenant General Nelson A. Miles, who had commanded at Wounded Knee, had retired recently from the Army as commanding general but did not think it beneath his dignity to appear in the film as himself. Several other generals were also enlisted. Among the Indian leaders who agreed to participate were Short Bull and Iron Tail, who had traveled with the Wild West Show, and No Neck.

The technology of the silent film was so uncomplicated that Cody, Baker, and their whole production crew could be crowded into a compartment on the train bound for South Dakota. All that Producer Cody needed for his epic was a cameraman and his assistant, a camera, and a supply of raw film stock.

Once arrived at the Pine Ridge agency, Cody was to experience many of the difficulties of shooting a film on location. Available lighting was fine, cinematically speaking, but its availability depended on the weather. The human element was a variable, too. Putting people before a camera and registering their images on moving film caused a certain giddiness, marked by a touch of megalomania, in human behavior; feelings of self-importance ballooned, and ordinary folk developed a swagger worthy of Richard Mansfield.

"Making a film," Cody groaned one night in his tent, "is harder to organize and run than three circuses."

The first actor to make a fuss was General Miles, whose vanity and sense of self-importance had not diminished with retirement. If one of his military achievements was to be recorded for posterity, he insisted, there must be accuracy in every detail, and damn the expense. At Wounded Knee and in the subsequent campaign to round up the hostiles he had commanded 11,000 troops. So there must be 11,000 troops available to parade before the camera, though there was no lens big enough to capture that many people in one scene. The general brushed aside such minor technical details. He also insisted that the pursuit of the fleeing Ghost Dancers across the badlands must be filmed exactly where it took place, not near the location site.

Cody craftily solved the troop problem by making the most of the 300 troopers he had on hand. Each troop was paraded past the camera 40 times. After the first few marchpasts, the cameraman cranked away without any film in the camera, but that was a secret between him and Cody.

Worse yet, General Miles insisted that the climactic battle scene be filmed exactly where it took place, over the mass grave in which the Indian dead had been buried.

This caused an uproar, justifiably enough, among the Indians. They believed it amounted to a desecration of their fathers' and grandfathers' graves. Johnny Baker tried to pacify them by making one of the spokesmen a colonel and another a captain. He also made a convincing case for the film itself from the Sioux's viewpoint: It would show that Wounded

Knee was not the culmination of an Indian conspiracy to start a war, as many white men believed.

Cody was assured that the Indians would behave themselves when it came time to reenact the battle, would fall down and die on cue. The night before the climactic battle scenes were to be filmed, however, Chief Iron Tail slipped into Cody's tent and warned him that the younger braves present were bent on making "big trouble." They were going to use real bullets instead of blank cartridges and thus would have avenged the deaths of their forefathers. The Second Battle of Wounded Knee would be an Indian victory, and white people could see for themselves, on film, what a massacre looked like.

Producer Cody wasn't looking for that much reality to capture on film. He summoned a midnight council of the Indians and told them that what they were plotting would only result in a Third Battle of Wounded Knee; the whole U.S. Army would take the field and run them down. And he managed to convince them that they must act like actors, not warriors.

The sham battle took place the next day as planned, though more than one brave, sighting down his rifle at General Miles posturing on horseback, waving his sword, and shouting orders, must have been tempted to slip in a live cartridge.

The filming was completed without further trouble. Cody's first and only film turned a decent profit, in which he shared in driblets, not enough to buy his way out of bondage to Bonfils and Tammen. He evidently hoped to continue making films in his projected historical series and told reporters, "I had yet a great life work ahead of me before I hit the last trail."

He was soon to learn that while his creative soul might belong to Hollywood, his body belonged to Bonfils, Tammen, and the Sells-Floto Circus.

15

◆—◄◉►—◆

Buffalo Bill Makes Another Final Bow

THE late and much lamented Gene Fowler, the biographer of such diverse figures as John Barrymore, Jimmy Walker, and Mack Sennett and a journalistic legend to match Buffalo Bill's, got to know Cody very well in his declining years. Fowler was then a reporter on the Denver *Post* and thus a fellow employee. He and Cody eventually became drinking companions, but the relationship got off to a shaky start.

It wasn't that young Fowler didn't admire Cody; he simply refused to worship at the shrine of Buffalo Bill. Later he would remember Cody as "perhaps the handsomest American of all time" who "sat his white stallion like a dream prince" but who was visibly flawed by a wayward disposition. "Indiscreet, prodigal, as temperamental as a diva, pompous yet somehow naïve, vain but generous, bigger than big today and littler than little tomorrow, Cody lived with the world at his feet and died with it on his shoulders. He was subject to suspicious whims and distorted perspectives, yet the sharpers who swindled him the oftenest he trusted the most. And sometimes he repaid quiet devotion with thundercloud doubts and ruthless attack."

No doubt Cody in his late sixties was a more difficult man,

more testy of temper, than in the genial days of his greatest success. His health had begun to fail him. He suffered from neuritis, rheumatism, and prostate trouble. The latter indisposition could have been relieved by an operation, but he kept postponing the date for surgery. With his fatal optimism, he believed that any sort of ailment, like a run of bad luck, would go away if you outwaited it.

With the utmost reluctance, he went out on the road in the spring of 1914 with the Sells-Floto Circus, as he would the following year. Tammen had him nailed to a contract, which precisely stated what Cody was to do as a performer. He would ride into the arena and introduce the show, but in a subsequent appearance during the performance he would ride in a phaeton behind two white horses. Whenever possible, he would journey to the circus' next stand ahead of the show to give interviews to the newspapers and appear at lodge meetings and businessmen's club luncheons to make a pitch for Sells-Floto; thus he was serving both as a performer and an advanceman.

He also had to sign a pledge stating that he would take no more than three drinks a day. By that, of course, his employers meant three shots of whiskey, in a day when a shot was a respectable two ounces. Cody got around that proviso by having his three drinks served in beer steins. He could not have survived on a mere six ounces of whiskey a day. He was having trouble with his kidneys—premonitory indications of uremic poisoning—and as a self-qualified medical expert had always prescribed large doses of whiskey for any trouble with the plumbing.

On its part, the Sells-Floto managemant was to pay Cody $100 a day, plus 40 percent of the daily gross above $3,000. Since it was a 25-cent admission show, it was highly unlikely that any day's receipts would reach that mark, and besides he had to trust the circus treasurer—traditionally a post filled by a man as crooked as a ram's horn—for a fair count of the proceeds. His wages were enough for him to buy his way out of bondage to Sells-Floto if he had been able to save a fair portion of them, but money and Buffalo Bill had a tendency toward disaffinity: They parted like hostile molecules. He still liked to walk into a strange barroom and slap the money down for a drink all around, old creditors still haunted him, and there were always relatives to be supported. That meant instead of paying Tammen back on that original $20,000 loan, he was always requesting a salary advance.

That summer was one dusty, windblown circus lot after another, many times blurred by the pain incurred by climbing into the saddle with his inflamed prostate and his rheumatic legs. It took more courage for the old man to mount up for his entrance than to fight a dozen Yellow Hands in his youth.

Somehow he stuck it out until the last performance in Texas during mid-October, when he collapsed. He was helped into the drawing room of a Pullman and did not leave it until it reached Denver and his brother-in-law, L. E. Decker, the husband of his sister May, took charge of him. Tammen would not let him leave town until he signed a contract for the next season, and the revised document was a masterpiece of thimblerigging. It provided that his percentage of the gross would be based on daily receipts above $3,100, instead of $3,000 as during the 1914 season, which would reduce his daily take by $40 on most stands. Later he claimed he was so sick when Tammen and his lawyers shoved the contract in front of him that he didn't know what he was signing.

Once again, that autumn, the ranch in Wyoming was his salvation. In a few weeks his health improved and his hopes rebounded. His resilience was still something to marvel at. He went out hunting and found that his marksman's eye was still keen enough for shooting game, if not little glass balls in an arena. One night he went out and shot the deer that were feeding on his alfalfa.

Once his health was restored he began scheming, trying to find a way out of his financial dilemma. Dude ranching had already become a profitable occupation out West, and he considered turning the TE Ranch into a tourists' paradise, but perhaps the thought of sharing his spread with strangers was too much for him. Besides it would take more financing to build guest houses.

He told his friends that he "must be doing something to keep from thinking and worrying." Personal appearances with the film he had made the previous year, which so far had brought him only a few thousand dollars, were one venture he considered. Johnny Baker had gone over to London to appear at the Anglo-American Exhibition and was arranging for British exhibition of the film. A vaudeville circuit offered him $800 a week to appear in person with the film, but he turned it down with a lordly disdain. The World War had broken out and people, he believed, were more interested in military subjects. Why couldn't a New York theater be engaged, with Short Bull or some other Indian chief and himself delivering lectures or debating on the stage, with a museum of Indian artifacts in the lobby? He hunted up the dessicated scalp of Yellow Hand and the bowie knife he had plunged into Yellow Hand's breast to be photographed for publicity purposes. But the Broadway theatrical engagement never got off the ground. The public was more interested in Krupp cannon and the titanic battles involving millions of infantry than in the homely memories of subduing a few woebegone Indians. Then, too, a new generation, while profiting from that conquest, wasn't all that proud of it. A great separation in time was required for the reglamorization of the West, for the reestablishment of the myths that provided soft lighting for harsh realities.

Cody spent the winter months down in Denver, where he could find reassurance that he was still a great man. John Burke was there, still his personal press agent, even when Cody couldn't pay him, and they were joined by Johnny Baker when he finished his London engagement. Burke's loyalty to the legend he helped to create was all but incredible.

Courtney Ryley Cooper, the circus press agent, provided a

touching reminiscence of Burke's dedication to the cause of Buffalo Bill. "One wintry morning in Denver I watched him, whiskers flying, threadbare coat pulled tight around his rotund form, set forth to what I knew by experience would be a meager breakfast. But in ten minutes he was back in the circus [Sells-Floto] offices, a copy of the New York *Times* tucked under his arm. 'You didn't take long for breakfast, Major,' I said. He grew red-faced. 'Well, I just decided I didn't want any,' came at last. 'I noticed this New York *Times* and I just thought I'd see whether it had anything to say about the Colonel. . . .' I bought the Major's breakfast that morning. The ten cents with which he had started for his coffee and rolls had gone upon the altar of his devotion."

Cody's home away from home that winter was the Windsor Hotel's barroom, a temple to the art of quaffing, the likes of which would never be seen after Prohibition. There the drinker could meditate in stately surroundings of black walnut paneling, hand-painted china cuspidors, a mahogany bar behind which twelve bartenders labored, and a Chinese boy in pigtails and native costume sweeping the marble floor clean of cigar butts. Here Cody talked business, spun grandiose schemes into the smoky air. Here he allowed listeners to buy him drinks while he told them, in his booming baritone, how it was out there in the West when it was hairy.

That winter, too, he had to make himself available as part of the Sells-Floto publicity apparatus and a prize exhibit of the Denver *Post*.

For whiskey money—and perhaps, too, the satisfaction of his exhibitionist tendency—he held court every Saturday at the Denver *Post* offices, somewhat in the style of a department store Santa Claus. Mothers brought their children to him as he sat in a massive oaken chair at the top of the stairs outside the editorial department, and he told them tall tales as they sat on his lap.

Once young Gene Fowler was assigned to interview him, and having an impudent attitude toward legendary figures, his first confrontation with Cody was not a success. Young

Mr. Fowler, in fact, believed most old frontiersmen were full of lies and gasconade.

He hunkered down at Cody's feet and began the interview by inquiring, "Well, Colonel, how are all the girls?"

Cody reprimanded him for asking such an insolent question of a man of his years.

Fowler then recalled John Burke's telling him about Cody's womanizing in England, of a liaison with a lady whom Burke delicately referred to as "the Duchess of B——."

"Colonel," he asked, "what did the Duke really say when he caught you in the lady's bathroom?"

Cody rose from his chair, sputtering with indignation. "Young man," he roared, "my hair is hoary—"

"Yes," Fowler cut in, "but not with the years."

The two later became well acquainted in various bars and over various poker tables. When they got on friendly terms, Fowler recalled, Cody would occasionally speak frankly of his greener years and the sexual opportunities open to a young plainsman; romping with Indian maidens was a more dangerous pastime, he indicated, than dalliance with duchesses. "Seducing an unwed Indian wench in my younger days was child's play. But the practice was not advisable for a white man unless he had the hearing of a coyote and the quick take-off of a jack rabbit. Those young braves were most possessive, son."

In the spring of 1915 came the dreaded summons to go on the road with Sells-Floto. His relations with the circus management and its owners could hardly have been worse. In the first place, he objected to the Sells-Floto doctrine of regarding every paying customer as an unshorn sheep. The circus had reduced its program and personnel by one-third, yet had doubled the admission price without advertising the fact. What particularly outraged Cody was that people came out to the lot and didn't know they were going to have to pay 50 cents until they got to the window of the ticket wagon. Cody himself had always tried to deal fairly with the public. When he and Salsbury ran the Wild West Show, they would

not permit games of chance, shell-game operators, pickpock-
ets, flimflam artists, or any of the other parasites who habitually attached themselves to such an enterprise.

Worse yet, surveying the operation with an expert's eye
convinced him that the Sells-Floto outfit was being
mishandled, that many of its work crew were inexperienced,
that it was hiring slave labor instead of seasoned roustabouts
capable of quickly setting up and dismantling the tents. Experience was necessary, too, in confronting any of the disasters to which outdoor shows were prone. His premonitions
were justified by a near disaster which occurred at Madison,
Iowa, shortly after the tour began. The circus had taken up
its stand near a swamp. Heavy rains fell and caused an
overflow of water from the swamp. Suddenly the circus lot
was awash in two feet of water. Worse yet, when the cook-
house was flooded during the performance, the crew was
seized by panic, and Cody had to calm them down before
they would cause a stampede in the big top. All but 6 of the
400-man crew, Cody said, ran away. Meanwhile the big tent
was threatening to cave in because its gear, the ropes and
tackle, were rotten. Cody and the half dozen who stuck it out
helped the women and children to safety.

"We came within five minutes of drowning a thousand
women and children," he wrote a friend from the show's
next stand, explaining his concern that a disaster sooner or
later would result because Bonfils and Tammen were too
tightfisted to take the proper precautions and hire responsible, experienced men for the crew. "There was no one in
charge. I don't want to be arrested for it. The court will say I
was and am an experienced showman and should have reported it. I want to go on record as swearing that this big
show tent is not safe. I don't wish to be held by law to fulfill
my contract, to help draw people into a death trap." He
added that he was "sick and nearly crazy" with apprehension.

His subsequent attempts to free himself from Sells-Floto
were almost frenzied. First he appealed to, then demanded of
Harry Tammen that he be released from his contract. Tam-

men's response was a counterdemand that Cody repay the balance of the loan and the salary advances made from the show's treasure wagon. Instead of freeing himself, Cody was confronted by the circus' treasurer deducting $50 a day, on Tammen's orders, for repayment of his alleged indebtedness.

Frantically he wrote friends back in Denver, in North Platte, in New York, and elsewhere for assistance in disengaging himself from Sells-Floto and its owners. He begged them to get him a "good sagebrush lawyer" to take Tammen and Bonfils into court. One friend was asked, "Do you think we could scare him [Tammen]? By that storm and flood at Fort Madison? He had no one in charge of at least 3,000 women and children. [It had been 1,000 women and children in a previous letter.] And he is still using an unsafe top. If your lawyer thinks so I'll throw it into him."

Another letter to a friend was almost incoherent with rage and despair. "There must be some law to protect me from him [Tammen] robbing me. Ask some good lawyer to stop this. I have stood between savagery and civilization most all my early days. Won't someone who knows the law come to my rescue. God bless you. I am old and tired. . . . This man is driving me crazy. I can easily kill him but as I avoided killing in the bad days I don't want to kill him. But if there is no justice left I will."

Late in the season, after months of exchanging angry letters and threats of legal action, Tammen and Cody got together in Lawrence, Kansas. There was no meeting of the minds. Cody told his employer he would never go out with the Sells-Floto Circus again. Tammen replied that he would sue and keep Cody tied up by legal actions until the day he died. He did agree, however, to order the circus treasurer to pay Cody his $100 a day until the show went into winter quarters. The latter concession no doubt was wrung from Tammen because Cody's trembling hand occasionally strayed toward the loaded guns resting on a table nearby.

That was the end of his association with Bonfils, Tammen and company, though he was dogged to the end of his trail

by their lawsuits, writs of attachment, and other bedevil-
ments.

Cody went into winter quarters himself, up at the TE
Ranch, and again, in the reviving atmosphere of the high
plains, mulled over schemes to get himself back on the road
to prosperity. How often he must have groaned over the fact
that he hadn't appreciated money, the freedom and independence it could buy, when it was rolling in too fast to
count anything less than hundred-dollar bills. Now his
friends were urging him to go into personal bankruptcy to
buy time enough to get back on his feet, but he indignantly
refused to consider the suggestion. With Cody, his debts were
a matter of personal honor, and pride went after the fall, if
ever.

Instead he brooded over plans to develop the Big Horn
Basin, to build tourist facilities into and around Yellowstone
Park. He would surface the Cody Road from the town of
Cody to the eastern approaches of Yellowstone Park; the
tourist lodges Wapita and Pahaska could be renovated and
expanded, and the Irma Hotel in Cody would be booked
solid all summer. (But it was years before that road was
finished and later became the spectacularly scenic Buffalo
Bill Highway—much too late to do Cody any good.) His
schemes at least had the backing of that all-time Western
buff, ex-President Theodore Roosevelt, who said, "My old
friend Buffalo Bill has hit the trail up there, and if he was
good enough to guide such men as Sherman, Sheridan, Carr,
Custer and Miles with their armies through uncivilized regions, I would take chances on building a road into the middle of eternity on his statement, and Bill says it is all right, as
he has been over it on horseback." A heartwarming enco-
mium, but Roosevelt was then residing in Oyster Bay, not
1600 Pennsylvania Avenue, whose present occupant had a
professorial distaste for Western heroics.

Cody also had hopes that a new refining process for low-
grade ores developed by Thomas Edison might retrieve the
fortune he had sunk into the Arizona copper mine.

Somehow, to further his interest in those enterprises, foundering as they were under mortgage payments, he had to whip together a new show and take to the road again.

The Miller Brothers 101 Ranch was up for sale, having cleared a hefty profit during the 1915 season with the current heavyweight champion Jess Willard as its star attraction. Willard had quit the show, however, and the Miller brothers could not find a suitable replacement. It was a pseudo-Western show patterned on Buffalo Bill's original model and might serve his purposes if he could raise $65,000 to buy out the Millers.

The winter of 1915-1916 was spent in a desperate search for well-heeled sponsors, and failing that, for enough cash to buy a majority interest in the 101 Ranch. Johnny Baker was given a power of attorney and told to sell the Arizona mine if possible. Cody himself labored with a ghost-writer over a new version of his autobiography. He disposed of his one-third interest in the Wounded Knee film. He dickered with William Randolph Hearst, whose mother had invested money in the Big Horn Basin development, over a monthly column to appear in Hearst's *Cosmopolitan* magazine.

Meanwhile, eternally optimistic, certain that he would be able to buy out the Miller brothers, he planned a revamping of the 101 Ranch show to provide more topical interest. If nobody was fascinated by the Buffalo Bill legend anymore, he would give them something else to keep the turnstiles spinning. In early 1916, with many Americans believing that the United States would inevitably enter the war, there was a considerable clamor for preparedness in the pro-Allied press and among politicians, military men, and munitions makers eager for armed adventure overseas. So Cody designed a "Pageant of Preparedness" as the centerpiece of his projected new show and hired twenty-four soldiers to appear in it. Old Glory would be whipped to a frazzle as trumpets blared and signal guns fired blanks. Cody's showmanly instincts were still sound, but if he hoped to attract the financial sponsorship of a Du Pont or a Morgan for his patriotic exercises, he was disappointed. For all his exertions he couldn't raise enough money to buy out the Miller brothers and take over the 101 Ranch himself. Furthermore, Harry Tammen claimed ownership of the title "Buffalo Bill's Wild West" and demanded a royalty of $5,000 per season if Cody appeared with another attraction.

He must have reflected with all due bitterness that if the gunslingers and Indian killers and distillers of bad whiskey conquered the West, the lawyers had somehow acquired a quit-claim deed to it.

16

The Prisoner on Lookout Mountain

EARLY in 1916, while still conceiving large schemes and hoping to die a millionaire, Cody learned that all men who had been awarded the Congressional Medal of Honor were entitled to receive a pension of $10 a month. Well, he had just passed his seventieth birthday, which ought to be age enough for a pensioner's status, so he wrote the Adjutant General of the Army in Washington: "I am a Congressional Medal of Honor man and I need that ten dollars a month in my business. As it rains all the time. How do I go about to get it? Will you please send me a blank application?"

What he didn't know was that there was a move afoot in Congress to weed out many awards of the highest military decoration. During and after the Civil War a large number of Medals of Honor had been awarded quite carelessly; there had been a scandal some years back, and regulations covering the award of the medal had been tightened. On June 3, 1916, an act of Congress was passed that ordered that all previous awards be examined, and those not entitled to the medal were to be stripped of the honor.

Cody never did get his pension, and he died shortly before a War Department review board decided that he and 910 other recipients had been wrongly rewarded. It was not that there was any question about the quality of Cody's heroism during the 1872 action on the Platte. As a statement from the Adjutant General explained for the benefit of Buffalo Bill's remaining idolators: "The board of officers which cancelled the award to Mr. Cody and certain others mentioned in its report, found that the medals in question were not issued for the cause specified in the law, viz: 'Distinguished conduct by an officer or enlisted man in action involving actual conflict with an enemy by such officer or enlisted man or by troops with which he was serving at the time of such action.' He was employed in the capacity of a civilian scout and guide at the time when he performed the act for which the medal was awarded and was not an officer or enlisted man."

Ten dollars a month wouldn't have paid his cigar bills, in any case, and the ungrateful nation took back its Medal of Honor shortly after his death.

He went out on the road the spring of 1916 with Miller Brothers' 101 Ranch, but as an employee, not the owner and manager. Since he hadn't been able to raise the purchase price, the Miller brothers decided that rather than fold the show they would send it out again with Buffalo Bill as the star attraction. At least the Miller brothers were more considerate employers than Tammen and Bonfils. They allowed him to take Johnny Baker along as arena director and John Burke as his personal press agent. They also provided him with a private car on the show train, a valet, a private tent, and a groom to tend his three horses. This was more like it. On the other hand, his duties with the new show were more strenuous than they had been in the past two seasons with Sells-Floto. His contract required that he drive his phaeton in the street parades advertising the show, that he open the show by appearing on horseback, that he shoot glass balls, and that he direct the Pageant of Preparedness in the arena.

Although he was much happier with the 101 Ranch, it was soon apparent that his health was deteriorating as the show proceeded across the country through an unusually rainy spring and a searingly hot summer. His heart was beginning to fail, his kidneys were played out, and sometimes it seemed that he would never finish the tour alive. Sheer guts kept him going when a lesser man would have said, "To hell with it, let me die in peace."

Instead he told well-wishers, illness and fatigue deeply etched on his face, that he felt strong enough to "fight a buzz-saw." And to a friend back home he wrote cheerfully:

"These people seemingly can't do enough to make it pleasant for me. If I suggest anything for the betterment of the show it's acted upon at once. I get $100 handed me every morning. I get one-third from all sources after $2,750 (gross) daily and settle every week, don't wait until the end of the season and then get beat out of it. Last week my portion was $4,161.35. Do you think Tammen would ever have stood for that? . . . I have an oil boom on my Wyoming lands. Everything is booming at Cody. My health and spirits haven't been so good for years. I am climbing for another fortune. . . ."

Not long after he wrote that, the show began struggling through bad weather and poor attendance. His optimism during its first weeks turned out to be entirely unwarranted. There was no oil on his Wyoming property. Meanwhile, he had to keep tapping the 101 Ranch till for advances that ate up all his earnings that season. Partly the money went to keep up mortgage payments, the rest to lawyers who were engaged in defending him against Sells-Floto and Pawnee Bill lawsuits, involved cases complicated by overstated claims and counterclaims, idiotic wrangles that merely enriched the lawyers and prodded Cody along toward his grave a little faster.

Toward the end of the tour, as it reached the East Coast, every performance was an agonizing trial. The Great Scout no longer was a picture of magnificent manhood when he rode into the arena, wraithlike, death in his eyes, a ghastly caricature. He was never more admirable than in those last days of the 1916 season when he insisted on making every appearance and living up to the letter of his contract.

Later Johnny Baker provided a touching account of the

ordeal Cody faced every time he entered the arena. Above all, Baker recalled, Cody dreaded "dying in the arena before all those people." Behind the drawn curtains of the runway, Baker would help him mount his horse. Then, awaiting his cue, he would sit in the saddle with his head sagging against his chest, as though gathering every last ounce of his strength. The curtains parted to reveal a blur of faces. "Ready, Colonel!" Baker told him. Cody straightened himself with an effort, trying to achieve the casual grace of his greener years, and rode out with a sweep of his big white Stetson. With agonizing effort he held that pose, riding around the ring, popping a few glass balls, then backing his horse into the runway and bowing to the cheering crowd. Groaning, he would slide from the saddle into Johnny Baker's arms and be helped to his tent.

Yet at night, in his private car, with a glass of watered whiskey in front of him, he gathered Baker and Burke around him and plotted for a real comeback the next season. Like any born Westerner, he always kept his eye on the horizon, certain there was a greener land just over the rise. Next year he would take the road with his own show. Agreeing with Baker and Burke that his wealthy former friends in the East would never answer his appeals for backing, he decided to turn to a professional fund raiser. The money would be raised through stock sold to the public; the little people still believed in Buffalo Bill even if the big ones were faithless.

He stuck it out until the last performance in Portsmouth, Virginia, on November 11, 1916. He was fighting a bad cold, but instead of going home immediately he journeyed to Chicago to confer with the fund raiser. His health continued to fail and he was forced to head back home. On his way to Cody, Wyoming, he stopped off at the home of his sister May, who urged him to stay there and submit to medical treatment. No, he had to get back to Cody because there was going to be a dinner given in his honor at the Irma Hotel and he was determined not to let his friends down. His friends were dismayed by his appearance and begged him to go to the hospital, but he shook his head. He had to hurry back to Denver to "talk business."

Instead, on the verge of collapse, with uremic poisoning spreading through his system, he was taken to the mineral baths at Glenwood Springs, where Dr. W. W. Crook was said to perform miracles with patients suffering from kidney disorders.

Only his incredible vitality, which had carried him through so many adversities, was keeping him alive. But one more foreclosure was inevitable, and coming soon. There was nothing the magicians at Glenwood Springs could do for him; the uremia, which might have been successfully treated earlier, was too far advanced, and his heart was failing rapidly.

On January 5, 1917, the Denver newspapers broadcast the fact that the sole surviving totem of the Old Wild West, except for such lesser figures as Bat Masterson and Wyatt Earp, who had settled for more tranquil pursuits when the frontier disappeared, was dying. A statement from Dr. Crook read: "Colonel Cody is slowly but surely nearing the end. There is no hope whatever for him. He suffered a nervous collapse yesterday and his mental faculties are seriously threatened. . . . We will leave with him this evening for Denver, where his wife and daughter will meet him. If possible they will take him home to Wyoming."

But Cody's last wish, to gaze again on the summit of Cedar Mountain overlooking the town he had named for himself, was not to be granted. In Denver it was decided that he was too weak to make the journey to Cody, and instead he was taken to the home of his sister May Decker, at 2932 Lafayette Street.

The family gathered there: Louisa and their daughter Mrs. Irma Garlow and another of Cody's sisters, Mrs. Julia Goodman.

A new doctor, named East, took over from Dr. Crook. It would seem that Dr. East was a somewhat unorthodox practitioner. Immediately after assuming charge of the patient, he gave the Denver *Post* a statement which must have puzzled his more conventional colleagues. Cody, he said, was being weakened by an eclipse of the moon. "It has been known for ages," Dr. East explained, "that eclipses of the sun and moon influence all life on earth and especially one in ill health. I consider Colonel Cody's condition very serious as metabolism has ceased. By metabolism I mean the change of organic or life forces."

According to Dr. East, in an interview later published in the Cody *Enterprise,* Cody faced the imminence of death as gallantly, with all the insouciance with which legend had credited him, as any of his admirers could have expected.

Shortly after he was settled in bed at his sister's home, he sent for Dr. East and said, "Sit down, Doctor, there is something I want to ask you. I want you to answer me honestly. What are my chances?"

"There is a time," Dr. East replied, "when every honest physician must commend his patient to a higher power."

"How long?" Cody demanded.

"I can only answer that by telling you your life is like an hourglass. The sand is slipping gradually, slowly, but soon the sand will be gone. The end is not far away."

A trifle impatient with the physician's fondness for imagery, Cody reiterated, "How long, Doctor?"

"About thirty-six hours, sir."

Cody hauled himself up on the pillows and called for Lew Decker, his brother-in-law. "The doc says I've got thirty-six hours," he told Decker. "Let's forget about it and play some cards."

Mrs. Cody would have preferred that he consult with a spiritual adviser, no doubt convinced that his passage into the next world would be difficult enough with all his earthly transgressions to account for, but he insisted on passing the time, a heathen to the end, with what many good people called "the devil's picture cards."

For the next few days the whole city waited for the last bulletin from the house in Lafayette Street. In the publishers' office at the Denver *Post,* which was called the Red Room, and sometimes the Bucket of Blood, Harry Tammen was laying plans for a spectacular funeral. Oddly enough, the roly-poly Tammen considered that Cody still belonged to him; dead or alive, Buffalo Bill was the property of the Denver *Post* and the Sells-Floto Circus. The publisher summoned his most imaginative reporter, Gene Fowler, and told him to start planning to give the Cody funeral the works, not forgetting to find a role for Sells-Floto.

On his penultimate day on earth, a newspaper friend named Chauncey Thomas visited Cody's bedside and later supplied an affecting portrait of Cody in his last hours. "The old scout was in pyjamas and slippers, and over them was drawn a housecoat. . . . Just the man himself standing there, waxen pale, his silver hair flowing down over his straight, square shoulders, his hand out in the last farewell. . . . It was the last time. I knew it; he knew it; we all knew it. But on the surface not a sign."

Next day, January 10, he died in bed with his wife and daughter beside him. COLONEL CODY DIES AT NOON blared the Denver *Post* in tall red headlines.

There was a footnote about six weeks later, which attracted much less attention. Arizona John Burke, co-creator of Buffalo Bill, died in Washington. Some people said—they still said things like that in 1917—that he died of a broken heart. And perhaps he did.

A gruesome farce ensued, one which Cody, even with his uproarious sense of humor, would not have enjoyed. He had made it clear that he wanted to be buried on Cedar Mountain overlooking Cody, Wyoming. Certainly he would have been outraged if it had ever been hinted to him that his mortal remains would pass under the control of Harry Tammen, whom he probably hated more than any man he had ever met, the man who had bedeviled his last few years.

His body, enclosed in a bronze casket, lay in state in the rotunda of the Capitol building for two days. On January 15, funeral services were held at the Elks' Lodge in Denver, with the rector of St. Barnabas Episcopal Church officiating. Eighteen thousand persons marched in the funeral parade. Then the body was placed in a vault until the matter of final burial could be decided.

The Denver *Post* was beating its editorial tom-toms for burial under a monument on Lookout Mountain above the city. It had started a nationwide campaign to raise the necessary funds through pennies donated by schoolchildren. Editorial broadsides thundered indignation at the rival claims of North Platte and the town of Cody.

The *Post*'s campaign was viewed with contempt by its journalistic rivals and by many ordinary citizens who could not quite swallow the *Post*'s assertion that Cody had often been heard to say he wanted to be buried on Lookout Mountain; on the contrary, he had often declared he wanted to be buried in Wyoming, which had offered the only peaceful interludes of a harried later life. The Boulder (Colorado) *Camera* was especially acerbic in its comment: "Why not let the Denver *Post* proprietors determine the kind of shaft to erect over Buffalo Bill? He was their meat. It was they who brought him down after a gallant career, by breaking his proud heart. Why should not the shaft be crowned with a miniature 'Red Room' bearing the device: 'Abandon hope, all ye who enter here.' "

There was no doubt of Cody's own wishes. A decade earlier, in New York, he had drawn a will in which one clause read: "It is my wish and I hereby direct that my body shall be buried in some suitable plot of ground on Cedar Mountain, overlooking the town of Cody, Wyoming, in order that my mortal remains shall lie in close proximity to that fair section of my native country which bears my name and in the growth and development of which I have taken so deep and loving an interest, and to which wheresoever and to whatever parts of the earth I have wandered I have always longed to return. . . .

"I further direct that there shall be erected over my grave, to mark the spot where my body lies, a monument wrought from native red stone in the form of a mammoth buffalo, and placed in such a position as to be visible from the town, in order that it may be a constant reminder to my fellow citizens that it was the great wish of its founder that Cody should not only grow in prosperity and become a populous and influential metropolis, but that it should be distinguished for the purity of its government and the loyalty of its citizens to the institutions of our beloved country. I give to my said executors the sum of ten thousand dollars for the cost of the monument and its erection and to carefully keep the ground about it in proper order."

That seemed plain enough, except that there wasn't $10,000 left to his name for the monument. His wishes were circumvented by Louisa Cody and Harry Tammen. The widow produced a later will, a brief document signed in North Platte and leaving his entire estate to her. It didn't mention a burial place. After conferring with Tammen, Louisa announced that he would be buried in a place and manner of the Denver *Post*'s choosing. The report circulated that she was paid $10,000 by Tammen for the privilege of selecting the burial site; it was disbelieved only by those who could not imagine the tightfisted Tammen paying that much for anything.

Months later, under the auspices of the Denver *Post*, Cody's casket was carried up the mountain road for burial. Thousands of vehicles were in the procession as it moved up to Lookout Mountain. Naturally part of the Sells-Floto Circus, its garishly painted wagons, took its place in line. Many years later Gene Fowler, in *Timberline*, recalled the occasion without undue solemnity. "There was a circus atmosphere about the whole thing. A lot of us drank straight rye from bottles while speeches were being made by expert liars."

That unprogrammed wake was the one feature of the ceremony that probably would have pleased the subject of the funeral oratory. It did not please Mrs. Cody. Another unplanned aspect to the occasion was even less pleasing to the widow, who hardly needed reminding that the figure behind the glass pane in the bronze coffin had been anything but a model husband. Across the grave was ranged a delegation of the colonel's surviving inamoratas claiming the privilege of unofficial widowhood. As Gene Fowler recalled the rather bizarre scene: "Six of the Colonel's old sweethearts— now obese and sagging with memories—sat on camp chairs beside the grave of hewed-out granite. The bronze casket lay in the bright western sun. The glass over the Colonel's amazingly handsome face began to steam on the inside. You could not see the face after a while, on account of the frosted pane. . . . One of the old Camilles rose from her camp chair, with a manner so gracious as to command respect. Then, as though she were utterly alone with *her* dead, this grand old lady walked to the casket and held her antique but dainty black parasol over the glass. She stood there throughout the service, a fantastic, superb figure. It was the gesture of a queen." With such fellow players on the funeral stage, the widow undoubtedly felt that her own role was degraded.

An overly imaginative person might have fancied that he heard a mocking laugh from the Great Scout, rising from the grave and reverberating through the mountains and over the plains he once rode in successful pursuit of legendary fame.

Notes on Sources

The complete listing of many sources indicated below under their author's surname may be found in the Selected Bibliography, which follows.

1. The Descendant of Irish Royalty

Cody's meeting with Buntline is described in Monaghan, *The Great Rascal*, 3-6, and *The Autobiography of Buffalo Bill*, 193-194.

His childhood is sketched in his *Autobiography*, 3-17, not always the most reliable source; Walsh, *The Making of Buffalo Bill*, 20-25, and the ghostwritten memoir of his sister, Helen Cody Wetmore, *Last of the Great Scouts, passim*.

Proslavery newspaper quoted, Platte *Argus*, July 14, 1854.

Cody told of witnessing the subsequently fatal knifing of his father in *Autobiography*, 11-12.

Alexander Majors' recollection of Cody as a boy is quoted in Walsh, 42.

Cody describes the killing of his first Indian in his *Autobiography*, 19-20, and his *Great Salt Trail, passim*.

His stay at Fort Laramie is recalled in *Autobiography*, 28-31.

His edgy relations with Alf Slade and their collaboration in Indian-fighting, *Ibid.*, 52-54.

His recollection of the "grand spree" at Sweetwater Bridge is quoted by Walsh, 72-73.

2. "Under the Influence of Bad Whiskey . . ."

Cody's military activities before and during the Civil War are sketched in *Autobiography, passim,* and Walsh, 79-80.

His courtship of Louisa Frederici is described in her *Memories of Buffalo Bill,* 2-15.

Cody's ineptitude as a hotel proprietor is indicated in Wetmore, *passim.*

His activities as a cavalry scout are recounted in *Autobiography,* 97-110, and Lieutenant General Philip H. Sheridan's *Memoirs,* Vol. II, *passim.*

Cody's recollection of how his town of Rome literally vanished overnight is contained in *Autobiography,* 108.

General Dodge's report on the value of the buffalo to the Indians is quoted in Walsh, 109.

General Sheridan's cynicism on the same subject is conveyed in the remarks quoted in O'Connor, *Sheridan the Inevitable,* 325-26.

Newspaper identification of Cody as a "noted guide" from the St. Louis *Democrat,* February 17, 1868.

General Sheridan's description of Cody's epic three-day ride is contained in his *Memoirs,* Vol. II, 300-1.

General Carr quoted on Cody's capabilities, Price, *Across the Continent with the Fifth Cavalry,* 104-5.

3. Idylls of the Border King

Cody's claim to having killed Chief Tall Bull is recorded in *Autobiography,* 191.

Lute North quoted on the same subject, Walsh, 151.

Cody's assistance to Bat Masterson in sheltering a fugitive from justice is included in O'Connor, *Bat Masterson,* 88-89.

Journalist quoted on the contemporary sport of shooting buffalo from train windows, Walsh, 165.

General Davies' sardonic remarks on New York society gentlemen taking the hunting fields are quoted in O'Connor, *Sheridan the Inevitable,* 320-21.

The Bennett buffalo hunt is described in *Autobiography*, 166-67.

Journalist quoted on Hays City night life, O'Connor, *Wild Bill Hickok*, 132-33.

Mrs. Cody described her hectic experience as hostess to Lord and Lady Dunraven in her memoir, 182-84.

Cody related his experiences as hunting guide of Grand Duke Alexis in *Autobiography*, 230-37.

4. A Social Lion in New York

Cody's trip to New York is recaptured in *Autobiography*, 240-43, and Louisa Cody's *Memories*, 218-19, as well as the Chicago *Tribune* and the New York *Herald* during the months of March and April, 1872.

The New York *Herald's* review of the play *Buffalo Bill* was published March 10, 1872.

Cody's appearance at the Liederkranz Masked Ball was covered by the New York *Tribune*, March 22, 1872.

Cody recounted his participation in the Dismal River skirmish in *Autobiography*, 250-56.

The citation for Cody's Congressional Medal of Honor is from the Adjutant General's Records, National Archives.

5. A Living God Behind the Footlights

The Mari Sandoz quotation is from her *The Cattlemen*, 77.

Mrs. Cody's account of her husband's attack of stage fright, *Memories*, 229-31.

Scouts of the Plains was reviewed by the Chicago *Tribune*, *Times*, and *Inter-Ocean* on December 17, 1872.

Death of W. J. Halpin from injuries sustained during a performance was reported by the New York *Herald*, January 8, 1873.

John Burke wrote his recollections of first meeting Cody for *Billboard*, which were quoted by Sell and Weybright in *Buffalo Bill and the Wild West*, 105.

David Curtis' estimate of Burke's character was quoted by Walsh, 183-84.

Wild Bill Hickok's misadventures with the Cody troupe were recounted by O'Connor, *Wild Bill Hickok*, 207-16.

Hickok's reckless ad-libbing was described by Buel, *Life and Marvelous Adventures of Wild Bill Hickok,* 122.

6. Buffalo Bill Lifts a Scalp

The death of Kit Carson Cody is related by Mrs. Cody, *Memories,* 260-65.

Cody's dispatch to the New York *Herald* on the "damnedest Indian war" was published June 10, 1876.

Cody's comments on the Custer massacre, *Autobiography,* 261.

His own account of the duel with Yellow Hand, *Ibid.,* 263-66.

Mrs. Cody's reaction to receiving Yellow Hand's scalp was contained in her *Memories,* 268-69.

Lieutenant King's dispatch to the New York *Herald* was published on July 28, 1876. After leaving the Army, King became a well-known writer on Western and military subjects.

The glucose content of Captain Jack Crawford's style was conveyed in an interview published by the Chicago *Inter-Ocean,* May 12, 1875.

Advertising copy for *The Red Right Hand* quoted by Walsh, 197.

Cody's apology for "lying so outrageously" was contained in a letter to his publisher quoted by Sell and Weybright, 127.

Cody's disgust at the necessities of maintaining a character off and on stage was quoted by his sister Helen Wetmore in her *Last of the Great Scouts,* 147.

The North Platte paper's comment on Cody as the town's first citizen is quoted by Walsh, 211-12.

7. Buffalo Bill Goes Outdoors

Cody's recollection of Sheridan's discouraging a Wild West show was quoted by Walsh, 216.

The history of Hickok's pioneering efforts with a Wild West show is detailed in O'Connor, *Wild Bill Hickok,* 199-202.

Nate Salsbury's memorandum on the conception of a Wild West show is quoted by Walsh, 221-22.

Doc Carver's background was gleaned from Raymond Thorp's biography, *Spirit Gun of the West,* and his articles titled "Doc

Carver vs. Buffalo Bill," published by *Real West,* March and April, 1967. *Real West* is the trade paper for Western buffs, whose number may be indicated by the magazine's circulation of about 200,000.

Courtney Ryley Cooper's comment on the first Wild West show's alcoholic vicissitudes was contained in his *Annie Oakley,* 25-26.

The Hartford *Courant's* praise of the show was published June 24, 1883.

Cody's renunciation of the Doc Carver partnership was quoted in Walsh, 230.

Carver's story of the breakup with Cody was related by Thorp, *Real West,* March, 1967.

Carver's warning to the public against Cody's appearance in St. Louis, *Ibid.*

Salsbury's recollection of Cody as "boiling drunk" in St. Louis was contained in a memorandum quoted by Walsh, 233.

Account of the party given for the New York press published by the New York *Herald,* June 16, 1884.

The legal battle between Cody and Carver is described by Thorp, *op. cit.*

Cody's telegram to Salsbury on show's disaster, and Salsbury's reply, quoted by Walsh, 242-45.

8. Little Annie and Sitting Bull

Annie Oakley's career is recited in detail by Cooper, *Annie Oakley,* and Havighurst, *Annie Oakley of the Wild West.*

The "misty-eyed" reminiscence of Annie Oakley in the arena is Walsh's in his *The Making of Buffalo Bill.* In later years Walsh was a prominent book publisher (The John Day Company) and the husband of novelist Pearl Buck.

Annie Oakley's virtuosity as a markswoman was discussed in loving detail by Holbrook, *Little Annie Oakley and Other Rugged People,* 3-4.

John Burke recalled the reason for Annie Oakley's placement in the show's program in his *Buffalo Bill from Prairie to Palace,* 112.

Annie Oakley's recollection of Sitting Bull is quoted in O'Connor, *Sitting Bull,* 117-18.

The menu at the Indian rib roasts was published in the *Dramatic News,* July 2, 1885.

A long account of Cody's presentation of the "Drama of Civilization" was published in the New York *Herald,* November 25, 1886. The negative review was published by the *World,* same date.

9. A Sea Change or Two

Cody's style of living in London was described by Havighurst, 120-21.

Cody's firing of Burke was related by Mrs. Cody in her memoir, 293-94.

The journalistic ode to Cody's London appearance was published in the London *Globe,* April 20, 1887.

The "delightful sensations of youth" quote is from the London *Daily News,* April 16, 1887.

Mr. Gladstone's conversation with Red Shirt was reported in the London *Daily Telegraph,* April 28, 1887.

The interview with Red Shirt was published in the Sheffield *Leader,* May 5, 1887.

Cody's account of the "four kings" riding the Deadwood stage was quoted by Mrs. Cody in her *Memories,* 296-97.

Ralph Blumenfeld's reminiscence of Cody as a social lion in London are from his autobiography, *Procession, passim.*

Adverse comment on aristocracy's truckling to Cody was published by *Vanity Fair,* August, 1887.

The *Times* of London's claim that the Wild West Show brought England and America closer together was included in an editorial published September 20, 1887.

Description of Cody and his company returning to America, New York *World,* April 28, 1887.

10. The Further Adventures of Buffalo Williamus

Newspaper ode to "Buffalo Williamus" quoted by Walsh, 275.

Annie Oakley's estimate of Cody's character was published by the Cody (Wyoming) *Enterprise* shortly after his death. Undated clipping in Denver Public Library's Western history room.

Salsbury's recollection of Shah of Persia's visit to the show quoted by Walsh, 277.

Account of how Cody's cowboys "broke" the Prince of Sermonetta's wild horses is from a Rome dispatch to the New York *Herald*, May 4, 1890.

Annie Oakley's account of how German intelligence spied on the Wild West Show is from her journal, quoted by Havighurst, 144.

Threatened hostilities between Cody and Doc Carver shows in Hamburg were covered by the New York *World*'s Berlin correspondent in a dispatch published August 26, 1890.

Chief Red Fox's defense of Cody's treatment of the Indians with his show was included in his article "I Was with Buffalo Bill," *Real West*, April, 1969.

11. To Sitting Bull's Rescue

How Cody arranged a peace treaty between the Sioux and the Chippewas was recounted by Le Seur, *North Star Country, passim*.

Sitting Bull's interest in the Ghost Dancers and his relationship with Mrs. Weldon from O'Connor, *Sitting Bull*, 124-32.

Buffalo Bill's thwarted peace mission and its aftermath is reconstructed by Johnson, *The Unregimented General: A Biography of Nelson A. Miles*, 276-80.

Sitting Bull's death and its consequences are related in O'Connor, *Sitting Bull*, 136-42.

Cody's dispatch to the New York *Herald* on Miles' campaign quoted by Walsh, 290-91.

Cody's letter to Annie Oakley quoted by Havighurst, 152.

12. Adventures with an Expensive Soubrette

Quotations from Annie Oakley's diary on the German Army's adaptation of Cody's logistical arrangements, quoted by Cooper, 182.

Frederic Remington's observations from his article in *Harper's Weekly*, September, 1892.

Amy Leslie's comparison of the various riders in the Wild West Show, Chicago *Daily News*, April 2, 1893.

A full account of the Chadron-to-Chicago cowboy race may be found in Sandoz's *The Cattlemen,* 416-18.

Amy Leslie's character sketch of Cody, Chicago *Daily News,* April 10, 1893.

Her interview with Annie Oakley, *Ibid.,* April 20, 1893.

Stewart Holbrook's estimate of her unique celebrity from *Little Annie Oakley and Other Rugged People,* 1-2.

Dexter Fellows' recollections of Cody were quoted by Sell and Weybright, 226.

Cody's appearance before the Edison kinetograph, Havighurst, 188-89.

His letter to Salsbury complaining of being in a "tight place" was quoted by Walsh, 309.

Chicago critic on Cody's "posings" quoted, *Ibid.,* 311.

Cody's bellicose statements on the Spanish-American War, New York *World,* April 25, 1898.

Account of Cody's marital troubles derived from Russell's *The Lives and Legends of Buffalo Bill,* 430-33; Denver *Post,* March 11 and 12, 1904, and Croft-Cooke and Meadmore, *Buffalo Bill,* 204-5.

Dan Muller's testimonial to Mrs. Cody was contained in his memoir, *My Life with Buffalo Bill,* 48-50, 75-80.

Cody's letter to his sister Julia, *Letters from Buffalo Bill,* 49.

13. A Very Tired Trouper

Injuries suffered by Annie Oakley in the train wreck from Havighurst, 206-9.

Cody's optimism over his Wyoming Land company, Sell and Weybright, 233.

Salsbury's warnings to Cody on how money was being wasted in the Big Horn Basin development, quoted by Walsh, 327.

Charles Towne's recollections, "Preacher's Son on the Loose with Buffalo Bill," *Montana,* Autumn, 1968.

George Hamid's recollection of joining the Wild West Show and meeting Cody and Annie Oakley from his autobiography, *Circus,* 34-35.

Account of the Cody divorce trial from the Denver *Post,* March 31, April 1 and 2, 1905.

Details of the partnership with Pawnee Bill from Shirley's *Pawnee Bill, A Biography of Gordon W. Lillie,* 177-81.

Pawnee Bill's recollection of Cody's show's difficulties, *Ibid.*, 179.

His disposition of Cody's personal indebtedness, *Ibid.*, 193-94.

Cody's partnership in the Oracle mine and its financial consequences, Russell, 434-35.

Cody's letter to a friend complaining of his weariness was quoted by Walsh, 338.

Rescue of Cody from harassment in Kansas City by an Indian was recounted by Thorp, "Buffalo Bill vs. Doc Carver," *Real West*, May, 1967.

14. On Location at Wounded Knee

Seizure of Cody's assets was reported in the *Rocky Mountain News*, July 22-23, 1913.

Denver *Post*'s announcement that its publishers had signed up Cody was published February 5, 1913.

Background of Essanay and career of Bronco Billy Anderson was gleaned from Goodman's *The Fifty-Year Decline and Fall of Hollywood*, 340-42, and Crowther's *The Lion's Share*, 27, 34.

Charlie Chaplin's thumbnail sketch of Bronco Billy is from his *Autobiography*, 160-65.

15. Buffalo Bill Makes Another Final Bow

Gene Fowler's relations with Cody from his lively and informal history, *Timberline*, 42, 371-72, and Will Fowler's biography of his father, *Young Man from Denver*, 51-53.

Details of Cody's 1915 contract with Sells-Floto from Walsh, 348.

Cooper's recollection of Burke as a down-and-outer, *Annie Oakley*, 278.

Cody's letter on the Fort Madison disaster quoted by Walsh, 351.

His diatribe against Harry Tammen, *Ibid.*, 352.

16. The Prisoner on Lookout Mountain

Correspondence regarding Cody's pension claim, Adjutant General's Records (1917), National Archives.

Cody's letter to friend on his satisfaction with the Miller Brothers 101 Ranch show, quoted by Walsh, 356.

Dr. Crook's statement on Cody's condition was published by the Denver *Post*, January 5, 1917.

Dr. East's "moon eclipse" statement, *Ibid.*, January 8, 1917.

Gene Fowler's recollections of the Cody funeral are from *Timberline*, 43.

Selected Bibliography

Selected Bibliography

Blumenfeld, Ralph D., *Procession*. London, 1935.

Buel, J. W., *Life and Marvelous Adventures of Wild Bill Hickok*, Chicago, 1880.

Burke, John M., *Buffalo Bill from Prairie to Palace*. Chicago, 1893.

Cody, Louisa Frederici, with Courtney Ryley Cooper, *Memories of Buffalo Bill*. New York, 1919.

Cody, William F., *The Autobiography of Buffalo Bill*. New York, 1920.

———, *Letters from Buffalo Bill*. New York, 1923.

Cooper, Courtney Ryley, *Annie Oakley*. New York, 1927.

Croft-Cooke, Rupert, and Meadmore, W. S., *Buffalo Bill*. London, 1952.

Crowther, Bosley, *The Lion's Share*. New York, 1957.

Fowler, Gene, *Timberline*. New York, 1933.

Fowler, Will, *The Young Man from Denver*. New York, 1962.

Goodman, Ezra, *The Fifty-Year Decline and Fall of Hollywood*. New York, 1961.

Hamid, George A., Sr., as told to George A. Hamid, Jr., *Circus*. New York, 1950.

Havighurst, Walter, *Annie Oakley of the Wild West*. New York, 1954.

Holbrook, Stewart H., *Little Annie Oakley and Other Rugged People*. New York, 1948.

Johnson, Virginia W., *The Unregimented General: A Biography of Nelson A. Miles*. Boston, 1962.

King, Charles, *Campaigning with Crook*. New York, 1890.

Le Seur, Meridel, *North Star Country*. New York, 1945.

Majors, Alexander, *Seventy Years on the Frontier*. Chicago, 1893.

Monaghan, Jay, *The Great Rascal, The Life and Adventures of Ned Buntline*. Boston, 1952.

O'Connor, Richard, *Bat Masterson*. New York, 1957.

———, *Sheridan the Inevitable*. Indianapolis, 1953.

———, *Sitting Bull*. New York, 1968.

———, *Wild Bill Hickok*. New York, 1959.

Pearson, Edmund, *Dime Novels: or, Following an Old Trail in Popular Literature*. Boston, 1929.

Price, George F., *Across the Continent with the Fifth Cavalry*. New York, 1886.

Russell, Don, *The Lives and Legends of Buffalo Bill*. Norman, Oklahoma, 1960.

Sandoz, Mari, *The Cattlemen*. New York, 1958.

Sell, Henry Blackman, and Weybright, Victor, *Buffalo Bill and the Wild West*. New York, 1955.

Shirley, Glenn, *Pawnee Bill, A Biography of Gordon W. Lillie*. Albuquerque, 1958.

Smith, Henry Nash, *Virgin Land*. Cambridge, 1950.

Walsh, Richard, *The Making of Buffalo Bill*. Indianapolis, 1928.

Wetmore, Helen Cody, *Last of the Great Scouts*. New York, 1899.

Index